DOING THE BUSINESS OF GROUP RELATIONS CONFERENCES

Group Relations conferences offer opportunities to learn about group, organisational and social dynamics; the exercise of authority and power; the interplay between tradition, innovation and change; and the relationship of organisations to their social, political and economic environments.

This book, the fifth in a series of Tavistock Group Relations Conferences, contains a collection of papers presented at the fifth Belgirate conference, plus three additional papers reflecting on and making sense of several participants' conference experiences. Taken together, these chapters study the discourse of Group Relations conferences as well as reflecting on the changing nature and shifting patterns of this discourse. In *Doing the Business of Group Relations Conferences*, authors reflect on the vicissitudes of meanings this expression generates.

Eliat Aram has been CEO of the Tavistock Institute of Human Relations (TIHR) for 10 years. She has directed the Institute's Leicester Conference for almost a decade 2007–2015 and contributes her experience in directing and staffing GRCs internationally.

Coreene Archer, Consultant, executive coach and senior manager at the Tavistock Institute of Human Relations (TIHR) since 2007. Co-Director of the Coaching for Leadership and Professional Development course and Director of the Launching Young Leaders group relations conference.

Rachel Kelly, BA, MSTAT, is the Professional Development Manager at the Tavistock Institute of Human Relations and a Teacher of the Alexander Technique. She manages/promotes the institute's courses and conferences, including the annual group relations Leicester Conference: Task Authority Organisation.

Gordon Strauss represents the A.K. Rice Institute for the Study of Social Systems (AKRI) on the Management and Administrative Team for the Belgirate conferences. He is a former AKRI Board member and has attended all of the Belgirate conferences since they began in 2003.

Joseph Triest (PhD), Training Psychoanalyst (IPS; IPA), Clinical Psychologist. Past president of the Israel Psychoanalytic Society, Lecturer at Tel Aviv University and founder of 'Triest-Sarig Clinic'; Co-Director of the Program in Organizational Consultation and Development – A Psychoanalytic-Systemic Approach; Member of OFEK, Israel.

THE GROUP RELATIONS CONFERENCES SERIES

Group Relations conferences offer opportunities to learn about group, organisational and social dynamics; the exercise of authority and power; the interplay between tradition, innovation and change; and the relationship of organisations to their social, political and economic environments This series of books on the Tavistock Group Relations Conferences provides edited collections of papers presented at the Belgirate conferences, plus additional chapters which examine the respective conference as a whole.

Titles in the series:

For further information about this series please visit:
https://www.routledge.com/The-Group-Relations-Conferences-Series/book-series/KARNGRC

DOING THE BUSINESS OF GROUP RELATIONS CONFERENCES

Exploring the Discourse

Volume V

Edited by Eliat Aram, Coreene Archer, Rachel Kelly, Gordon Strauss and Joseph Triest

Routledge
Taylor & Francis Group

LONDON AND NEW YORK

First published 2019
by Routledge
2 Park Square, Milton Park, Abingdon, Oxon OX14 4RN

and by Routledge
52 Vanderbilt Avenue, New York, NY 10017

Routledge is an imprint of the Taylor & Francis Group, an informa business

British Library Cataloguing-in-Publication Data
A catalogue record for this book is available from the British Library

Library of Congress Cataloging-in-Publication Data
Names: Aram, Eliat, editor.
Title: Doing the business of group relations conferences / [edited by] Eliat Aram [and four others].
Description: Abingdon, Oxon ; New York, NY : Routledge, 2019.
Identifiers: LCCN 2018031590 (print) | LCCN 2018033865 (ebook) | ISBN 9780429444258 (Master eBook) | ISBN 9780367001490 (hardback) | ISBN 9780367001520 (pbk.)
Subjects: LCSH: Group relations training. | Group relations training--Congresses.
Classification: LCC HM1086 (ebook) | LCC HM1086 .D65 2019 (print) | DDC 302/.14--dc23
LC record available at https://lccn.loc.gov/2018031590

ISBN: 978-0-367-00149-0 (hbk)
ISBN: 978-0-367-00152-0 (pbk)
ISBN: 978-0-429-44425-8 (ebk)

Typeset in Palatino
by Integra Software Services Pvt. Ltd.

CONTENTS

EDITORS

Eliat Aram, PhD, has been the CEO of the Tavistock Institute of Human Relations (TIHR) for 10 years. The TIHR, a not-for-profit outfit operating in the UK and abroad for over 70 years, is a world-leading research, evaluation, consultancy and professional development organisation. Believing in the abundant potential of human relationships and love for people are the drivers in the way she shapes the direction of the institute and the multitude of its activities. She has directed the Institute's flagship GRC, The Leicester conference, for almost a decade since 2007 and has directed the AK Rice Institute annual GRC in the USA for 3 years 2016–18. She has made a number of fundamental changes and innovations in both these conference, all aimed to ensure the conference deals with current socio-political dynamics in embodied and contemporary ways.

Coreene Archer MA, Consultant, executive coach and senior manager at the Tavistock Institute of Human Relations (TIHR) since 2007. She is Co-Director of the Coaching for Leadership and Professional Development course and Director of the Launching Young Leaders group relations conference. Coreene's passion is in initiating new ways of working with and developing leadership for young people, informed by her belief that we are not defined by where we start but by how we finish.

Rachel Kelly, BA, MSTAT, is the Professional Development Manager at The Tavistock Institute of Human Relations and a Teacher of the Alexander Technique. She is interested in further integrating the psychophysical at work: embodying role; wellbeing at work; how we perform (both moment-by-moment and when presenting); self-care; ways of being; movement and play, all towards a deeper learning organisation. She manages/promotes the Institute's courses and conferences, including the annual group relations Leicester Conference: Task Authority Organisation.

Gordon Strauss MD, is Professor of Psychiatry at the University of Louisville School of Medicine where he directs student psychiatric services for the university's student health service. He is a member and fellow of the AK Rice Institute for the Study of Social Systems (AKRI). He is also President of the Midwest Group Relations Center and a member of GREX, both affiliate centers of AKRI. He received advance training in organizational consultation from the Cincinnati Psychoanalytic Institute.

Joseph Triest PhD, is a clinical psychologist and supervisor, training analyst of the Israel Psychoanalytic Institute (IPS), and organizational consultant. He is a lecturer at Tel-Aviv University and Co-owner of the Triest-Sarig private clinic. Since October 2014, he serves as the President of The Israel Psychoanalytical Society. He is a Member of OFEK, the Israel Association for the Study of Group and Organisational Processes, and Co-director of the Program in Organisational Consultation and Development: a Psychoanalytic-Systemic Approach (POCD). He has taken up a variety of roles in GR conferences, including the director's role in some of them, and is the author of several papers in the field of Group Relations.

CONTRIBUTORS

Eduardo Acuña, Professor, Department of Administration, Faculty of Economic and Business Administration (FEN), University of Chile. His work activities, teaching at under- and post-graduate courses. Consultancies and researches are focused on using mainly the socio-analytic approach. He was the creator and first Director of the Master in Human Resources Management and Organizational Dynamics, Postgraduate School at the FEN. He lives in Santiago, Chile.

Daphna Bahat, MA, is a senior clinical psychologist, supervisor and organisational consultant. She works with groups and individuals for the empowerment of women through belly dancing. She is a member and former board member of OFEK, the Israeli Association for the Study of Group and Organisational Processes, where her roles included treasurer of the organisation and head of the marketing committee.

Louisa Diana Brunner PhD, lives in Milan, Italy, and works as a leadership consultant, executive coach, family business advisor and mentor. She has served on Group Relations Conference staffs in Cyprus, England, Israel, Italy, Poland, USA and the Netherlands. She is a founding member of PCCA, an honorary member of Il Nodo Group, and a Fellow of the Family Firm Institute. She is a member of ISPSO, OFEK and OPUS.

Jinette de Gooijer, PhD, MappSci, GradDipBA, BVA, BSocSci is former Director of Innovative Practice Pty Ltd providing role analysis, supervision and organisational consultancy services. She has worked on staff of group relations conferences in Australia and internationally, and published several articles, book chapters and a book in the field of systems psychodynamics. Jinette is also an exhibiting artist who integrates socioanalysis into her studio practice. She is a founding member and Past President of Group Relations Australia, Member ISPSO, and Associate OPUS.

Franca Fubini, Psychoanalytic psychotherapist, group analyst, organisational consultant. Founder member, Socialdreaming.it. Trustee, Gordon Lawrence Foundation. Senior consultant within mental health institutions, Italy and UK. She has lectured at Rome, Perugia, L'Aquila University in Psychology/HR. Senior Fellow, University College of London (UCL). Consultant and director of the Italian Group Relations conferences (ALI and ECW). Member, IL NODO group (Italy), OPUS (UK), ISPSO. Convener, Listening Post, Rome. Contributor, 'Blossoming in Europe', connecting European countries through cultural events.

Zahid Hoosein Gangjee BSc (Psychology Honours), MSc (Applied Psychology); Fellow (IIM, Ahmadabad); Chief Executive, "Zahid Gangjee & Associates: Organisation and HR Consultancy", Kolkata; Honorary Fellow, Coaching Foundation of India; Associate Member, Group Relations India Forum. Directed and been a staff member at GRCs since 1977 mainly in India but also in Israel, France, South Africa & UK. Involved with Yoga (Bihar School, Munger) since 1993.

Bernard Gertler, PhD, is an organization consultant, psychotherapist, and psychoanalyst in private practice. Dr Gertler received his PhD degree in clinical psychology from the City University of New York, is certified as a psychoanalyst by the William Alanson White Institute and holds a Qualification in Organizational Consultation from the Tavistock Institute.

He is faculty and a supervisor at the White Institute and was faculty and co-director of the White Institute's Organization Program. He is a Fellow of the AK Rice Institute for the Study of Social Systems.

Seth Harkins, EdD, is chief executive officer of the Philip J. Rock Center and School in Glen Ellyn, Illinois. He is a career educational administrator, having served in a variety of leadership roles in public and private education. He has been adjunct professor and assistant professor of education at National Louis University, Chicago, for thirty years. He has been active in Group Relations conference work since 1985. He is a member of AKRI and is the past president of the Chicago Center for the Study of Groups and Organizations.

Xiaochang (Jasmine) Huang, MEd, is international PhD student in Clinical Psychology at Palo Alto University, USA. As a certified psychological counselor with 4 years psychodynamic psychotherapy training from CAPA (China American Psychoanalytic Alliance), she has worked as a clinician over 10 years in China. Her professional interests include applying psychodynamic approach in mental health service, group dynamic and cross-cultural trauma research.

Suma Jacob MD, PhD is an Associate Professor of Psychiatry at the University of Minnesota. Her doctoral work was in Social Neuroscience, studying how modulator pheromones influence another's biology and unconscious behaviors. Her clinical research has focused on biomarkers and treatments for autism. She uses data-driven approaches in early development to predict outcomes. Dr Jacob has been involved with group relations since 2002 and is a member of the AK Rice Institute and Group Relations International.

Saliem Khliefi, BA Social Worker; Organisational Consultant; Group Therapist; Member of OFEK; Israel.

Dannielle Kennedy, PhD, LICSW is an organization consultant. A principal at Worklab, she works with individuals and teams providing role consultation, leadership coaching, strategy implementation/team alignment. Her approach addresses the practical level and deeper psychological aspects of high performance. She holds a PhD from Simmons College School of Social Work and is a graduate of the Advanced Studies in Organizational Development Program, Boston Institute. Currently a candidate at the Boston Graduate School of Psychoanalysis.

Julian Lousada, Psychoanalyst, Former Clinical Director Adult Department, Tavistock NHS Foundation Trust: Former Chair of the BPC. Julian has been on the staff and directed Group Relations conferences both nationally and internationally. Founding Member of People-in-systems and is in private practice.

Ugo Merlone, PhD, is Associate Professor, Psychology Department, University of Torino, Italy, teaching Conflict Management/Negotiation and Strategic Decision Economics. Previously, Visiting Scholar and Professor at Harvard University, London School of Economics, University of Arizona and Universidad de Chile. Main area of interest: the modeling of human behavior / organisations. A licensed psychologist in Italy and an AK Rice certified consultant/associate. Provides consultancy/training to organisations, companies and police forces on Conflict Management, and both Business and Crisis Negotiation.

Victoria Te You Moore, LCPC, is a Chicago-based psychotherapist and organizational/leadership consultant. She is also a clinical supervisor for the China American Psychoanalytic Alliance, a board member of the Illinois Group Psychotherapy Society, and a member of the Workshop Committee of the American Group Psychotherapy Association. She has lived in China, France, Japan, and the US and has previously worked in public policy, management consulting, nonprofit development, and the arts.

Neil Neidhardt was president of the A. K. Rice Institute until October 1, and he continues to serve on the Board as past president. Neil has been involved with AKRI since 1993, and has been a member of both the Central States Center and the Midwest Group Relations Center, serving on conference staff with both those Affiliate Centers, as well as on conferences sponsored by the Washington-Baltimore Center and AKRI's Training and Certification Committee. Neil's GRC work as a Conference Administrator directly informed the structural and functional emphasis of his role as AKRI president.

Barbara Lagler Özdemir MA, is Co-founder and Co-Director of oezpa GmbH Academy & Consulting, Bornheim (Cologne-Bonn), Germany. Senior Lecturer in "Methods and concepts of organizational consulting", Fresenius University, Bachelorclass in Business Psychology, Cologne. Founder of "Digital Change GmbH (DCG)", Lucerne/Switzerland. Executive Consultant, Trainer and Moderator. Member and Cooperating Partner of the International Coach Federation, ICF. Senior Coach of DBVC (German Association of Coaching).

Hüseyin Özdemir, PhD, Dipl Oec, is a member and cooperating partner of International Coach Federation and of SIETAR; Senior Coach of the Germany Coaching Association DBVC. He is a senior organisational consultant, management trainer, executive coach and Director of oezpa GmbH, Academy & International Management Consulting for Strategic Organizational Development. Program Director of oezpa Leadership – OD, Coaching Programs and Group Relations conferences. He has published numerous books/articles and is Senior Lecturer on Leadership and Organisational Development at: Fresenius University Cologne; European School of Management & Technology and Lorange Institute of Business. Cooperating partner, Tavistock Institute of Human Relations, President of International Leadership Academy – Cooperation of Business Schools and Academics.

Anuradha Prasad PhD is a human process and institutional development consultant engaged with social development. She is a founder trustee of Group Relations India (GRI) and a professional member of the Indian Society for Applied Behavioural Science (ISABS). She is certified in Depth Psychology from the Jung Center, India. She is a life coach, certified by Leadership that Works, USA. She is a practicing Yoga teacher trained at Atmadarshan Yogashram, affiliated to the Bihar School of Yoga.

John B. Robertson, Jr, MD, is the co-owner of Center for Family Psychiatry P.C. and Attention Deficit Center in Knoxville, Tennessee. He is certified by the American Board of Psychiatry and Neurology in three areas: general psychiatry, child and adolescent psychiatry, and addiction psychiatry; his medical practice is quite diverse. Awards include selection by peers multiple years for Top Doctors of Knoxville. Group Relations work includes serving as staff consultant for many AKRI-sponsored Group Relations conferences since 1993, conducting workshops and presenting at AKRI national symposia and presenting at Belgirate IV.

Jeffrey D. Roth, MD, is an addictions psychiatrist and group psychotherapist. He has directed ten Group Relations conferences on recovery from addiction. He is the past-president of the Chicago Center for the Study of Groups and Organizations, a Fellow of the American Society of Addictions Medicine and a Fellow of the American Group Psychotherapy Association. He is the author of the book *Group Psychotherapy and Recovery from Addiction: Carrying the Message* and the editor of the Journal of Groups in Addiction and Recovery.

Rune Rønning, DMan, CandPsych is a senior consultant and head of research at AFF, The Administrative Research Institute at the Norwegian School of Economics. He is a licensed clinical psychologist, with a degree from the University of Bergen. He completed the Tavistock Institute's AOC Programme in 1999, and has a doctorate in management (DMan) from the

University of Hertfordshire. He has worked as an organizational psychologist and as a researcher in leadership and organization for the last 30 years.

Matías Sanfuentes, PhD, is Doctor in Psychoanalytic Studies, University of Essex; Assistant Professor, Faculty of Economics and Business and Director of Master Programme in Human Resources Management and Organizational Dynamics, University of Chile; Associate Researcher, Centre for Social Conflict and Cohesion Studies (COES); Clinical Psychologist and Organizational Consultant. He has directed group relations conferences in Chile and has been on staff at the Leicester Conference and in Australia and Argentina.

Evangeline Sarda, JD, is an Associate Clinical Law Professor at Boston College Law School where she is the inaugural Faculty Director of Leaders Entering and Advancing Public Service Program, and Co-Director of the Criminal Justice/Prosecution Clinic. She teaches group relations courses, organizes and develops GR trainings, and is focused on developing a diverse group of GR-minded individuals. She developed the annual *Authority, Power and Justice: Leadership for Change* Boston College Group Relations Conference Series. She has held most roles in GRCs and continues to take up the role of member spanning USA, Asia, South America and Europe.

Mannie Sher, PhD, is Principal Social Scientist and former Director of the GR Programme at the Tavistock Institute of Human Relations, London. A Fellow of the British Association of Psychotherapists, he is a psychoanalytical psychotherapist. He has published on consultancy, leadership, organisational development, ethics and corruption. His latest book is *The Dynamics of Change: Tavistock Approaches to Improving Social Systems*. He is a former member of ISPSO and a member of the Israel Association for the Study of Group and Organisational Processes.

Miri Tsadok, MA, is a clinical psychologist and organizational consultant; she practices psychoanalytic psychotherapy as well as teaches in the area of organizational and group psychodynamics. She is currently on the faculty in the Management and Business Psychology Program at the College of Management, Rishon Le'Tzion, and faculty in the Program in Organizational Consultation and Development: a Psychoanalytic-Systemic approach. She is a Board Member of OFEK, the Israel Association for the Study of Group and Organizational Processes.

John Wilkes MA, Cert.Ed, discovered Psychoanalytic Approaches to Organisations at Leicester GRC in 1996, then studied at the Institute of Group Analysis and the Tavistock Centre in London, subsequently ending 30 year

Civil Service career in 2001, final 10 years working on change management in Whitehall, now works as Leadership Coach and Consultant, was on staff at Leicester and Vilnius GRCs, exited to now work with Barbara Williams and Fabio D'Apice, on Exploring Differences Workshops.

Jeanne M.S.T. Woon, PhD, is a Psychologist and interim director of the counseling center, University of Central Missouri; trainer and consultant on group and organizational process. She was introduced to group relations work while pursuing her doctorate at Teachers College, Columbia University. Member of AKRI and its New York and Midwest affiliates. Past chair of AKRI's training & certification committee; currently serving on its affiliate relations and research & publications committees.

FOREWORD

It seems that the Group Relations Conference community is asking the questions, "how do we work together to provide maximum opportunities to new people and sectors?", "how do we work together to collaborate and co-ordinate what we offer?" and "how do we go beyond our defences and embody in our behaviour what we invite members to study?". In this context writing the foreword for this book is both unnerving and a privilege. These questions resonate with those that are occupying my mind as I find my way into the role of Director of the Group Relations Programme at the Tavistock Institute of Human Relations. In particular, from our various satellite positions in this global Group Relations constellation, what is the nature and form of the Followership that is required to keep up with and support the ambitions of the Leadership and innovation enacted by the Group Relations Community.

This is a finely edited and collated collection of the papers from the presenters and participants at the Belgirate V conference in Italy, exploring Un/conscious Dynamics, Systems and Ethics of the Business of Group Relations Conferences. It can be felt as a resounding clarion call to the community of practitioners and organisers of Group Relations Conferences to hold themselves to a higher standard, to work with and through the ambivalence and defences of the human condition and strive to do what we provide space for members to explore in the conferences in our gathering and dealing with each other.

The papers are challenging to those experienced in Group Relations Conferences. It asks questions and posits hypotheses that also resonate with those in the world of leadership of organisations; whether in the private, corporate, family, non-profit and public sectors, and those in public political leadership. If our collective wish is to provide many opportunities to Learn for Leadership, how do we connect with that purpose and mould and craft the way in which our primary task is constructed? How do we work together and co-ordinate our activities so that we can maximise the numbers of possible participants to Group Relations Conferences, and allow those organising conferences to build on each other rather than get lost or killed in wild competition? These are tough business questions and the community is grappling courageously with them.

One of the questions put to me at my first ever group relations conference was "how did you get here, I've not seen you before?". Like Alice meeting the caterpillar in Lewis Carrol's *Through the Looking Glass*, who asked her "who are you?", I was puzzled and curious about the question. Why would this question be asked in the context of a learning about how we function in systems in relation to authority and role taking? Essentially existential in nature, the question emerges from a nexus of belonging, the mystery of choosing staff and the impact of friendships and special relationships, not to mention the revelation of the unspoken and hidden defence against learning, competition, rivalry and the ambivalence toward innovation and adaptation that are hall-marks of the human condition.

This book holds no punches in it's thoughtful exploration of some difficult issues and is bold in offering some solutions but above all, invites the critical reflection into the capacity of Group Relations Conferences to provide meaningful learning opportunities for leaders and followers facing our post-modern manifestations of complexity.

Leslie Brissett
Director of the Group Relations Programme
May 2018

Introduction

Why are we having these Belgirate conferences, still, after 13 years?

There are actually three main reasons for having the Belgirate conferences:

First, it is a wonderful opportunity to meet friends and colleagues, who we sometimes call 'Leicester Mates'. By that, we usually mean a particular kind of unique relationship which is based on intense, intimate encounters, followed by long periods of disconnectedness between our separated worlds. Surprisingly enough these friendships are often very real, deep and steady.

This time round, the conference attracted 70 people: 51% women, 49% men, from 15 countries, a range of ages (between 20+ and 80+ with an average age of 59) and from a variety of organisational and professional backgrounds. All participants had had roles in GRCs: 34 people had administrated; 36 people had directed conferences; 31 had been Associate Director; and 59 had consulted.

The second reason to have these conferences every three years is that it is an opportunity to share our work experiences, by creating a market-place where one can present some of the 'business' we are doing all around the world.

The first time the idea of introducing the word 'business' came to us was in the planning of the conference.

Belgirate V was led by a changed management team, with two representatives of the three partners succeeding the previous MAT members and one remaining. The process of succession was difficult and at least one key aspect of this difficulty was something about the relationship between success and succession. The discourse of psychoanalysis, open systems thinking and organisation was not enough, we felt, in understanding all of what that process meant for us. Succession triggered other feelings and concepts: business competition versus collaboration; success of GR organisations around the world versus the threat of survival to others; providing the merchandise – what it is in the context of Group Relations; who has the authority to deliver it how and where and so on. Bringing in the notion of business has enriched our preconference discourse in a way that both excited us and left us fraught with debates and arguments amongst ourselves to do with values and ethics.

Experiencing the provocation of the 'business' within ourselves, we anticipated the provocation to the Group Relations community and judged it timely to do so.

The third reason to have these conferences is it is a rare opportunity to look at our discourse and try to explore some of the conscious and unconscious forces which shape it and are shaped by it.

Using the term 'discourse' may call for some explanation. By discourse, we mean the *language* we use, our *terms*, our *ethical values* (explicit or implicit), the nature of the *concepts* we use in our theoretical writings; our *metaphors* and their hidden meanings, the tools and methods we use in our *practice*, the nature of our *work* – in short, our professional *culture*.

However, exploring our discourse at the same time as we are doing our business, is no easy task. We have felt it then, whilst 'in' the experience, and are feeling it now in the writing about it. In order to review our discourse we have to look afresh at it and at the way we structure our work. For example, we may find it useful to explore the titles we use for our conferences, the events we design, and what may be most important – the ways in which our paradigms and structures are influencing and being influenced by each other.

The discourse we create may not only represent the way we understand reality – it may actually create the reality we understand – and at the same time, leave outside our consciousness all what we don't understand – and more than that - even don't want to understand. This may be relevant not only for our profession but for all scientific disciplines. To mention just one association – when Hawkins talks about 'Baby-Planets' it is not just a metaphor; it is a metaphor which shapes our physical concepts and the way we understand our universe.

The title of the fifth conference upon which this book is based was:

Doing the Business of Group Relations Conferences: Un/conscious Dynamics, Systems and Ethics.

Introducing the word 'business" into the title of the conference might represent a shift in our discourse. It has certainly been a provocation, not an entirely unconscious one, we may add. It may indicate that another vocabulary, which possibly introduces different values, has been brought in, or, perhaps, has been there all the time but is now surfacing and possibly shaping our ethical attitudes as much as our theory and practice.

We ask ourselves, what is the relationship between what business means – marketing, advertising, selling, earning and the work we call Group Relations. Over the years it has been called an educational event, an experiential learning that cannot be replicated and hence cannot be sold as training; a socio-political movement, a vocation, a not-for-profit activism; and so on.

What hasn't changed is that we earn very little when we work on a GRC and we often run conferences at a loss.

So how do we think and explain these ways of thinking about this business of Group Relations? How do we narrate our identities and roles as GRC practitioners? What are the political agendas driving and shaping our thoughts and practice?

These were the management team's questions working on the planning and executing of the conference, and in our editorial roles, are hoping to present the discussions in some coherent fashion that will be interesting to more than just those who attended the conference itself. Most chapters in this book contain presentations of aspects of the title that the writers were mobilised to address. In the process of converting the presentations into book chapters, some writers have updated their writing by referring to current affairs (notably, Lousada). In addition, some chapters contain reflections on the conference learnings.

In terms of the conference design, we had a structure of three keynote addresses, one on each day of the conference, a series of parallel presentations, an exploratory event, a dreams, reflections and associations session each morning of the conference, ample free time and spaces to meander in between and during meals.

True to our organisational discourse, we have articulated the primary task of the conference as follows:

'To provide opportunities to study the discourse of Group Relations conferences hence doing its business both as dynamic systems with conscious and unconscious processes and as organisations within an ethical context.'

We have done our best to structure the rich and diverse chapters offered for the book into sections that, at least broadly, address aspects of the Group Relations discourse.

Section I includes chapters which explore the discourse of Psychoanalysis, one of the pillars of Group Relations thought. Section II includes chapters which explore issues and practices in the business of the organisation of Group Relations, known by some as B-A-R-T (Boundaries – Authority – Role – Task). Section III contains chapters exploring doing the business of Group Relations across boundaries including questions of collaborating and competing, selling, marketing, commercializing and so on. Section IV, true to the book series' tradition, contains post-conference reflections of participants at the conference.

Eliat, Coreene, Gordon and Yossi
September 2016

INTRODUCTION TO SECTION I

Exploring the discourse of psychoanalysis in Group Relations

This section explores the discourse of our 'GR Business' from a psychoanalytic perspective.

Julian Lousada's rich and thoughtful chapter describes a new defence mechanism – *complacency* – illustrating his proposition with clinical as well as organizational and current political materials. He calls for awareness of the 'life threatening' quality of complacency to every 'business' – ours included.

Daphna Bahat's chapter is a sharp, painful critique of our community. Her main contention is that the GR community tends to abuse the psychoanalytic tools designed for exploring the unconscious as a defence against that self-same task – especially when working among ourselves, as we do in Belgirate.

Bernard Gertler's chapter focuses on the changes and developments that occurred in psychoanalysis during the last postmodern decades and their influence on GR theory and practice. His critical review rejects the image of the 'all-knowing classical consultant' as well as the 'educational-psychotherapy-help-oriented' trends (associated with the United States) – and calls for a new balance between changes, adaptations and tradition in GR.

These three chapters offer altogether a rich and fascinating kaleidoscope – keenly demonstrating the importance of ongoing exploration of our developing discourse.

Complacency

The defence of the privileged

Julian Lousada

> Success breeds complacency. Complacency breeds failure. Only the paranoid survive.
>
> Attributed to Andrew Grove (1936–2016)

I t was said with some authority that the evidence that the 'don't-knows', some 10–15%, were most likely to vote for the status quo. How reassuring. But as it turned out how decisively wrong it turned out to be. Trying to digest the enormity of the UK's decision to leave the EU, I am left wondering how it was that the danger that exit posed was not taken seriously enough. It was as if metropolitan England was so out of touch with the reality that it observed the campaign like a spectator sport which had no serious implications for itself. There are multiple reasons that informed the 'out' decision, but I want to suggest the presence of complacency, a turning away from the threat of the emerging reality and a reliance on the status quo, was one of the contributing factors.

This chapter seeks to explore the notion that organisations and individuals can, and do use, complacency as a defence against the recognition of the need for change. Complacency can occur in circumstances where there is a threat to the powerful identification with and belief in the 'product', or the service delivered. The strength of identification seems to militate against confronting and engaging with the possibility that future sustainability cannot be taken for granted. Organisational complacency occurs in circumstances where the conditions which gave rise to profit or influence change dramatically. It might be argued that the psychoanalytic project, in the UK at least, has been undergoing something akin to this experience, one in which there is a continuing identification with its thinking and activity at the expense of engaging with the systemic weaknesses that the changes in its environment and market has exposed. As Harvey Taylor (2013) writes, 'There has been a lack of attention paid to institutional development and the building of a professional infrastructure ... which has had disastrous effects when the cold economic and cultural winds began to blow in 1979.'

The issue is not the continued quality in psychoanalytic thinking nor is it in the quality of its clinical practice but rather in capacity of its organisations to engage with the change in its place in the market and its relatedness to its emerging competitors. It is, I would suggest narcissistically difficult, having once occupied a position of innovation and leadership to be faced with the possibility of becoming located not at the apex but on the margins of influence.

We live and work in what Hannah Arendt (1967) described as 'dark times' and perhaps we are entering a similar 'time" in which fake news distorts both public discourse and the emergence of truth.. It is impossible to be completely free of the dynamics of the market place and the received 'wisdom' that supports it. The dilemma is surely how to be 'in and against' the market. There is no place outside, but on the inside it is hard to sustain the deep necessarily different and at times critical thinking that Group Relations represents. Sustaining this capacity to both hold onto and represent complex thinking cannot be taken for granted. The implications of neoliberalism and its assessment of what is to be done requires understanding if complex thinking is not to be dragged into the shallows. Group Relations, like psychoanalysis requires the preservation of 'deep' rather than 'shallow' thinking. It has a continued commitment to the exploration of the unconscious in the context of organisational and personal life, explicitly in the context of welfare – a barometer of the national state of mind – a belief in meaning that is a product of an *evolution* of personal and social experience. This stance is in contrast to a representation of objectives that are increasingly externally *cultivated* by targets and governance responding to and informed by the instruments of efficiency-seeking and a 'cost-conscious' market.

The commitment to self-reflection is an easily stated ambition, however in difficult times it can be hard to commit to, when what may have to be reflected upon becomes too painful to contemplate. This turning away from difficult thinking is further compounded in circumstances where there is the sense that nobody 'out there' is any longer listening or interested in what is being offered for reflection. In these circumstances, complacency can become a compelling defence with the danger that the distinct voice that is the mark of both psychoanalysis and Group Relations gets lost, diluted or at worst just shared amongst ourselves.

A contemporary characteristic is the demand for and delivery of success. Put simply, it is impossible to sell a treatment that is tentative about what can be understood and achieved, or to offer a learning opportunity that does not guarantee the realisation of the learning outcomes. In this atmosphere, it is difficult not to be drawn into a collusion. For example, I heard it said that 'conference design does not matter so much: conferences are invariably a success'. What do we mean by success? Is success a membership which leaves feeling pleased with their experience? If so, how can we be sure we are not colluding with a 'flight into health'? (a process in the lexicon of psychoanalysis to describe patients who responded 'too quickly' to therapeutic intervention whilst actually engaging in escape tactics to avoid the pain and anxiety of further exploration of conflicts and self-disclosure). Is learning axiomatic with conference success? It seems to me that the emphasis on success places GR under tremendous pressure and assumes the capacity to overcome not knowing and what can be learnt from failure. Or, to put this another way, the demand for success subtly discredits what needs to be learnt from suffering and injustice. It is not just scientific activity that demands trial and error but also psychic and political development. The demand for success might result in working in the shallows, working and exploring that which is already systemically familiar. For example, in the discussion following a particularly disturbed 'organisational event' there were repeated grateful accounts of what the members had learnt for themselves. However, it seemed as if no learning could be gained from the systemic disturbance that had been created. The urgent need was seemingly to export what could be learnt from the disturbed system in order to establish an uncontaminated site of individual learning, and in so doing banish what was reflected in the collective disturbance.

When we consider individual, group, and systemic defences we think of unconscious psychic processes that provide the 'ego' with relief from the state of psychic conflict. Defence mechanisms come into play to enable the ego to reach compromise solutions to problems that it is unable to solve, by letting some component of the unwelcome mental contents emerge into consciousness in a *disguised* form. (Freud 1923) Klein, makes an important contribution when she describes how children adopt various psychic defences to protect their ego against anxiety aroused by their own destructive fantasies.

Perhaps complacency as a defence has been somewhat overlooked in that the psychic conflict that informs it is the experience of the anticipation of success and the anxiety associated with the its loss. It seems that complacency is one response in situations where success is threatened. Another way of thinking is that complacency might be deployed as a defence against the loss of privilege and the sense of superiority that accompanies it. It creates a situation of satisfaction with the believed-in status quo. What is lost sight of is the knowledge that better conditions in the future will never be achieved if there is systemic satisfaction with the conditions that exist at present. Complacency does not I think present itself boldly. Rather it disguises itself within a superior costume of well-rehearsed roles and practices.

In what follows, I want to argue that complacency is insidious. It is an infection of thinking which can only be defended against by healthy self-criticism. I will illustrate this with reference to a clinical and organisational intervention and will conclude by wondering whether there is any evidence of the infection creeping into Group Relations thinking.

Common to all the examples is a sense of superiority deployed as a defence against the painful experience of losing what I am describing as privilege, namely the prospect of giving up the individual or collective sense of being better than others. The ensuing resistance to change might be informed not by the requirements of change itself but by the fear of losing a perceived privileged position.

I take privilege to be a source of pleasure, an immunity against the anxiety associated with an engagement with others regarding their difference and the change that might arise from this association. My interest is in the relationship between privilege and complacency – or, more precisely, the prospect of losing privilege and the emergence of complacency. Complacency needs an audience to recruit to its project of avoiding the dangerous knowledge associated with reality.

A sense of complacency does occur following the satisfaction associated with some actual achievement. But it can be used as a defence using splitting mechanisms in order to prevent the awareness of the 'object as whole' In these circumstances, the satisfaction conveyed in complacency is used to promote wellbeing at the expense of knowing and engaging with disturbing knowledge, in other words, a reality that contains both threats and opportunities.

I had never really considered how complacency can come to be used as a possible defence until I was confronted with it in my work with a patient. I was unexpectedly, and very uncomfortably, confronted by the discovery that what I was sure was good work, was in fact not so. It was not that no 'work' was being done but rather its quality was shallow, as if there was an agreement that nothing disturbing should be approached. There is nothing particularly unfamiliar with this manifestation of resistance – indeed many conferences and clinical treatments begin in this state of mind, but what was a surprise was to discover sometime further on, was the extent to which I was contributing to and colluding with a 'shallow project' and all the while thinking I was doing good work – stuck then in the grasp of a complacent working relationship.

Complacency is then a defence against change. It is, one might say, perverse, in that it does not just turn away from reality but rather it misrepresents it, so that change is frustrated or avoided.

The definition of Complacency, as a defence, I shall be using is as follows:

> a feeling of smugness or uncritical with oneself or one's achievements.
> A feeling of quiet pleasure or security, often while unaware of some potential danger, defect, or the like . . .

> (OED)

Complacency belongs in a family together with indifference, by-standing, and turning a blind eye. These defences differ one from another in how the threatening object is psychically managed. For example, indifference not only distances the self from the object but, in the process, diminishes and de-humanises the object. Complacency on the other hand is driven by a misleading satisfaction. That is to say, what is desired is distanced from any limitations that reality might impose. Frustration or anger is avoided and, instead, what is desired is felt to be attainable and, moreover, attained.

Whatever the nuanced differences between these concepts, they share and are a response to perceived danger or threat, and are invoked as a defence at such times when there is a challenge to the relatedness between the internal and the external world.

Complacency, as a defence, has three principal characteristics. First, it misrepresents reality, and in so doing distorts relationships. Second, the special characteristics of complacency is the anxiety associated with the giving up of the privilege linked with success. Privilege is for the most part associated with wealth, status, and power. However, I want to suggest that it can also be a powerful experience, an identification with the narcissistic pleasure connected to the explicit or implicit belief that one is more fortunate or better than others. At its most entrenched, complacency is accompanied by a sense of superiority and entitlement. It is no longer related to the quality of the 'product' as such, but more to do with the lived experience of being better than, or superior to 'others'. Complacency then can protect a sense of superiority under the guise of preserving established standards and the highly-valued set of ideas, practices and relationships. Change is hard enough, but when it becomes associated with the loss or dilution of privilege it can lead to an aggressive intolerance. Third, complacency because of its self-righteous quality is difficult to spot or interrogate partly because of its plausibility and partly because it mobilises the narcissism of the clinician or group consultant and thus colludes with the resistance to change in the group or patient.

It would be wrong to suggest that no learning, or change is undertaken in the company of complacency; however it is the quality of the work that is compromised.

Complacency does not belong to what Klein described as psychotic or paranoid schizoid defences as it is not concerned with persecutory anxiety or splitting but is driven by the anxiety of losing the loved internal object.

> Under the influence of complacency the hardships of the depressive position appear to be suffered, acknowledged and worked through but the work in truth is a resting place rather than a staging post.
>
> (Britton 1998, p. 85)

Complacency produces a spurious sense of contentment, and an appearance of good work being done and it is precisely this sense of achievement that makes it so hard to notice and disrupt. It is as if the clinician or group consultant is being offered two choices – either to be persecutory, or to be seduced into an alliance predicated on an agreement not to disturb and certainly not to interrogate the nature of the 'good work' achieved.

I am in presenting the clinical vignette that follows illustrating the discussion above but also implicitly suggesting that the dynamics and defences described are also evident in group and organisational life.

The patient was referred to me by a colleague, who wrote in his referral 'I have a feeling that she is in trouble and I can't quite get to grips with it. Perhaps you can have better luck!'

I remember clearly thinking the first time I met her what an intelligent and capable woman she was. She was at some pains to describe why she wanted an analysis and her reasons seemed thoughtful. At the same time she conveyed how pleased she was with her life, marriage and work. Talking of her husband, she said with satisfaction how they seemed to 'fit so well one into the other'.

All seemed to be going well. She came regularly, talked intelligently and with feeling about various aspects of her experience. I was aware of looking forward to her sessions and had the sense that I was doing good work. Unusually I had decided to present this woman as 'an interesting but not too difficult patient'. As an example, I thought of an effective working alliance. My colleagues pointed out my evident self-satisfaction with my work as if there wasn't really so much to say about the patient. They pointed out that the patient would sort of complete my sentences with, they imagined, a smile of reassurance and in this way any difference of view between us was pre-empted and shut down. This feedback was hard indeed to receive but over the next period I noticed a competition in my mind between the thought that things were going well and the nagging thought that I was being invited to participate in some minor psychic tuning, on the condition that nothing of substance should be disturbed. In my countertransference, I was concerned that I would clumsily barge into something that was happily nuanced. I felt seduced, by my own connivance, and then trapped by this version of togetherness, love and achievement. With some difficulty I came to see that my interpretations – which I felt pleased with – had a mechanical quality. Like her, I was unable, or perhaps unwilling to find a voice for my own affect let alone legitimate aggression and challenge in the service of the analytic task.

I found myself preoccupied with doubt and the growing experience of being with a patient who gave the appearance of entering into a transferential relationship with me but in fact was working hard to avoid it. In short, I had been drawn into a collusion with the illusion of successful achievement. Describing myself as being caught up in an unconscious collusion did not quite describe the grip it had on me whereas the idea of a mutual contract between us seemed more accurate.

She brought a dream: she was standing on a stile feeding a donkey that belonged to her children. The donkey rejected the food and started eating her hand and she could feel the teeth on the back of her hand but left it there. She had been trying to train the donkey.

Her association of the dream was to her high chair and her mother playing games. She added that prior to coming to the session she had been in a coffee shop trying to write down things to say. She then pulled out a note book and read out a moving set of thoughts including a section in which she was curious about me, what to call me and who I was. She finished reading and stuffed her notebook back in her bag, as if our work was done and she was ready to go. I thought I was indeed the donkey who would not be trained and was being experienced as being cruel. I was on the verge of making some response to her material, pleased that I had, I thought, understood something of her communication when she got up to go. I was struck in her associations of the dream that there was no reference to outrage or pain at having been bitten. She triumphed over pain and in this state of mind unconsciously enjoyed her elevated position denigrating me by getting up to go early to avoid receiving anything from me. She constantly paraded and celebrated her loving relationship with her husband, not for her the struggle she saw in other relationships. It is not that she was self-satisfied but rather 'unrealistically free of discontent' (Britton 1998, p. 85) and it was this that gave her a smug quality. Her compliance and satisfaction with her treatment, was not just flattery, but an attempt to make me feel the beneficiary of the work and by so doing she maintained her covert superiority. And she protected herself from the threat, fear and disruption associated with her reality. She was in fact facing the truly distressing and protracted experience of failing to conceive and yet there was little or no evidence of distress, no evidence of the envy of fertile couples and no indignation at the unfairness of it all. It was as if her psychic equilibrium was to be preserved at the expense of the psychic change necessary to face her reality. One of the central points Britton makes is the impact that a complacent defence can have on the analyst who, like the patient, gets lulled into a state of mind in which there is neither healthy criticism nor discontent with the progress of the analysis.

Instead the analyst is enticed into a sense of wellbeing and a narcissistic pleasure in a job being well done.

> The explicit danger is that the analyst interprets the transference but does not inhabit it, and in so doing enters a contract in which there is sympathy but in the presence of a 'untroublesome child and untroublesome or untroubled parent'.
>
> (Britton 1998, p. 89)

It seems to me that we can find a similar complacent dynamic in organisations or systems. My colleague Andrew Cooper and I were invited to facilitate a conversation about how the organisation might maintain its share of influence and what factors might be influencing their apparent difficulty in doing so. Having presented some thoughts one member intervened to say: 'You know, when I was in supervision with Dr. A . . . (who was a well-known and much-admired analyst) what he often impressed upon me was this: never forget the unconscious.'

Whilst this speaker was undoubtedly reminding us of the core of psychoanalytic thinking she was simultaneously – and we thought later unconsciously – disabling any capacity to think new thoughts. The speaker evoked an image of a revered, but definitely now dead psychoanalyst, the sense of a master at whose feet she had been privileged to learn, and of his voice with the message beyond the grave 'don't forget or betray your central vows' (Cooper & Lousada 2010, pp. 32–45).

It seems to me that two observations can made here. First, there was sort of melancholic quality in as much as there seemed no ability to relinquish the loved object so that development could take place. The un-mourned object was not available as a source of internal strength but existed as a sort of memorial transfixing those present to the past or at best the status quo. Second, what was perplexing was that this meeting with such ease could avoid thinking and instead, appealing to our identity as psychoanalysts, invite us to join them in a discussion that had little to do with the task we had been asked to think with them about. The shared knowledge in this meeting was that the organisation was in considerable financial difficulties and yet this was completely impossible to discuss. The members were not hostile or confrontational, and appeared to understand our presentation whilst at the same time their agreement was not to engage with it. What was so strikingly absent was any capacity to consider what contribution individually and as a system they might have made of the situation they now found themselves in. Perhaps we had provoked a sense of shame and humiliation arising from the challenge that there might be a systemic flight from the risks their organisation was facing.

It was probably the dangerous knowledge of the reality the organisation was facing that, as with my patient, was avoided by the misrepresentation of reality. The contrast between the members' sense of confidence, a sort smug pleasure at our discomfort for having so misjudged them in thinking that behind the invitation was a concern for change that led me to think that complacency might also be described as conflict with a smile on.

I was initially inclined to understand this rather unpleasant organisational experience using John Steiner's concept of the 'Psychic Retreat' and the turning of a blind eye. Steiner (1993) writes:

> knowingly – the patient (*or organisation*) decides – not to know – and contradictory versions of reality are able to coexist, avoiding their most painful aspects ... Insight and understanding are therefore used to misrepresent reality, intentionally distorting relations.

Steiner's account of turning a blind eye is very useful, however, in the context of group life I felt some aspect was not sufficiently described. When a group adopts a state of mind in which 'insight and understanding are used for misrepresentation' we are witnessing a state of mind determined in spite of the cost to sustain the status quo. It seems to me that to identify this process as a group agreement, implying a like-mindedness, does not quite expose the level of organisation that is at work to sustain it. A better way of describing it, might be as a contract between the group members which unlike the 'like-mindedness' of an agreement has a binding quality, with the implication of enforcement, such that membership depends on loyalty to the contract not to the quality of the thinking, or to the task.

Another way of thinking about the concept of 'contract' is that it describes a process of shrinkage – to contract – making the issue that is to be considered smaller. So, a dual process of 'binding' and shrinkage might be at work here.

It seems to me that the complacent contract I am describing has both a conscious and unconscious element to it. Unconsciously, there is some connection to and a repetition of the 'betrayal' every infant must face on the discovery that they are not the centre of mother's world. This leaves a residue of doubt about whether humanity can prevail and protect. Consciously complacency is a watchful state in which the subject keeps the 'others' in mind and in view, with the aim of achieving a binding loyalty to them which obliterates difference and conflict. Within the organisation I have described, the threat was more associated with the disapproval of colleagues than the threat they faced from the market place which was lost from view.

At the heart of the defence I am trying to describe is an over valuation of the self and self-reliance. The group I was facilitating effectively turned away from our thinking and the possibility of finding value in it. The deployment of complacency as a defence in the patient and the organisation described does not mean that they were insensitive, free from anxiety or depression but there is a: 'penchant for settling for relatively little and a dynamic which can make a feast of crumbs'. Precisely what they are feasting on is at first hand hard to spot since it makes them ostensibly so undemanding actually behind this mask they are as Britton (1998) so succinctly describes: 'Greedy for virtue and covetous of innocence'.

Group Relations

I very much agree with Louisa Brunner (2019) when she described a tension in Group Relations between the retention of tradition, the openness to innovation, and the possibility of contamination by other ideas. This tension in my mind is also reflected in an uncertainty about the conference primary task. Is the primary task essentially one that is committed to an educational aim or is it an intervention predicted on what can be learnt from the socio-political laboratory the conference provides? Both are preoccupied with the study of unconscious processes but one might be more concerned with the members learning, whilst the other primally concerned with how the 'temporary institution' reflects and comments on the citizenship, social identity and political life that the conference produces. This is, to my way of thinking, the prime site of intervention.

I don't think for a moment that Brunner is suggesting that the primary task is a choice between the desire to provide 'learning' and the desire to make 'a social intervention'. There is no incompatibility between learning and intervention but to achieve this dual task there is a need for a continuous process of interrogation to illuminate how the one impacts upon and contributes to the other. Without such a process, there is the danger of either self-regarding conviction or a drag towards uniformity and the 'contamination of other ideas' (Brunnerin press).

The unique selling point of GR resides in the intention to interrogate the dialectic between the unconscious and social life on the one hand, and a capacity to face the 'dangerous knowledge' (Cooper 2015) concerning our own destructiveness and social injustice on the other. It seems to me what 'conferences' do so well is to give members 'sight' into themselves, their valences, and the systems they create. However, this sight into themselves is a product of the mediated world of the conference and should not be confused with the presence of 'insight' into the dynamics of the world beyond which is more preoccupied with instrumental objectives than reflective ones.

Eric Miller (1989), was also concerned with this tension between learning and intervention when he wrote:

> the experience (of GRCs) and the learning is almost inevitably personal and private relating to one's inner world. For some members it may remain so. But it is not the purpose of the conference: the design is intended to promote the application of experience in their roles in that temporary institution to the roles in institutions outside. [effective GRC] are inherently subversive. It involves calling into question the embedded myths that support the status quo.

> The drag of uniformity in thinking is powerful in a competitive market place. The capacity to resist the market's constant demand for innovation depends on a clarity about the primary task and on a willingness to use a 'subversive' state of mind to critically examine what enactments we find ourselves drawn into from within ourselves, from members or by our awareness of competitors who move into the territory we have occupied.

The ambition of Group Relations to make an intervention is well illustrated by the variety of conference titles for example:

- Ofek: Desire to influence: Leadership and Change in Organizations and Communities.
- Boston College: Authority, Power and Justice: Leadership for Change.
- GRC India: Transforming Systems:
- Poland PCCA: European Victims and Perpetrators: Now and Then.

The challenge is the extent to which staff and members work to the primary task of the title and what can be learnt as an intervention from so doing. The alternative is to use the title as an inanimate backdrop to the main event of membership learning for leadership avoiding the question of learning for whom and for what purpose. Once more, the ambition to make an intervention needs considerable attention. Shortly after I'd finished directing a small conference, a friend commented on how impressive it was that the conference had attracted a 25% (5/20) international membership. This comment made me consider why it might be that an international membership is considered such an achievement. Some of the answers are obvious: conference economy, its status and recognition, and the presence of difference. However, it also disguises the difficulty of 'domestic' recruitment.

Is Group Relations with its manifest commitment to the international at risk of avoiding what might be located and hard to engage in the national? The global community inevitably shares a dependent relationship with contemporary capitalism. For its members it offers not just opportunity, good income but exposure to differences of all kinds. To put this thought briefly, are we in danger of representing the lived experience of the global community at the expense of the toxicity of what gets left 'at home'? Given the difficulty of cost and recruitment it is understandable that there is pressure to avoid the controversy associated with intervention. The value of personal learning is indisputable. However, the pressure to achieve learning without it being located in group life or social context is great because it is so much more difficult to explore the extent to which as a group member or social participant we move between being part of, and discovering solutions to, the problems we encounter.

> There are characteristics in the individual whose real significance cannot be understood unless it is realised that they are part of his equipment as a herd animal and their operation cannot be seen unless it is looked for in the intelligible field of study – which in this instance is the group.

> (Bion 1961)

Psychoanalysis and Group Relations have a history of innovation and challenge to the status quo. Both developed in opposition to how things were done and explained. It is also the case that both interventions have created their niche and enjoyed, and in my view deserved, considerable success and admiration.

Both flourished in the postwar period. However, when the 'market' and the ideological narrative changed, both faced the problem of how to distinguish themselves from their 'innovative' competitors. The issue became and continues to be how to preserve their 'unique' identities in the changed and crowded marketplace of psychological therapies and experiential group learning. The dilemma is crudely between protecting identity and standards by continuing to do what has traditionally been done, or to make adjustments in practice to accommodate the contemporary period. The lived experience of this dilemma here is a real one and not to be underestimated and for which there is no simple straightforward answer. An exaggerated way of describing the states of mind at work is that on the one hand there is the danger of a self- regarding state of mind that turns away from reality, on the other an excitable entrepreneurial state of mind searching for influence and profit. The former is exposed to the risk of complacency and the latter the disinhibition associated with modernity as if the history of ideas and practices are now obsolete.

For my patient and for the organisations I have referred to there is the valency to retreat from the demands of reality, and whilst complacency appears to be self-assured it masks a profound disappointment that the dream cannot be secured and past success recovered.

References

Arendt, H. (1967). *Men in dark times.* San Diego, CA: Harcourt, Brace & Jovanovich, Preface, pp. vii–x.

Bion, W. (1961). *Experiences in Groups,* New York: Basic Books, pp. 133–134.

Britton, R. (1998). *Belief and Imagination,* London: Routledge, p. 86.

Brunner, L. (2019). Group relations conferences: Can "enterprises with passion" become businesses? In E. Aram, C. Archer, R. Kelly, G. Strauss, & J. Triest (Eds.), *Doing the Business of Group Relations Conferences: Exploring the Discourse: (Vol. V).* London: Routledge.

Cooper, A. (2015). Containing tensions: psychoanalysis and modern policy-making, *Juncture* 22(2): 157–163.

Cooper, A. and Lousada, J. (2010). The shock of the real. In A. Lemma and M. Patrick (eds), *Off the Couch,* Abingdon: Routledge, pp. 32–45.

Freud, S. (1923). The ego's dependent relations. In *The Ego and the Id. SE,* Vol. XIX (1923–1925): The Ego and the Id and Other Works, 1–66.

Miller E.J. (1989). The Leicester model. *The Tavistock Institute of Human Relations Occasional Paper,* No.10.

Steiner J. (1993). Perverse relationships in pathological organizations. In *Psychic Retreats,* pp. 103–116.

Taylor, H. (2013). *UK Psychoanalysis: mistaking the part for the whole.* British Psychoanalytic Council Discussion Paper. London: BPC. TCCR.

Fifty Ways to use (and abuse) the unconscious

An invitation to a (sincere and thorough) discussion about certain defences employed in the Group Relations community

Daphna Bahat

This chapter aims to touch upon some of the defence mechanisms and defensive dynamics that seem to impact the thinking within the Group Relations community, especially when working within the community itself, for example, at the international meetings held in Belgirate. These mechanisms tend to mobilize defensively the very ideas underlying the endeavour of the Group Relations model and psychoanalytic-systemic thinking. The same tools we use in clarifying reality may also be misused, blurring reality and overlooking certain aspects of the material explored. When this occurs, the tools designed for exploring the unconscious are applied out of context and their intended purpose – getting in touch with the truth, as painful as it may be – is betrayed. The aim of this chapter is to explore these dynamics in order to avoid these pitfalls and thus be able to use the model more creatively.

* * *

An uncorroborated historic anecdote[1] reports a conversation between the German and the British ambassadors. The German ambassador says to his British counterpart: 'You British, you fight for money. We Germans, fight for honour.' 'Quite so', replies the British ambassador, 'I suppose everyone fights for what they lack.' This chapter will try to touch upon what we, the Group Relations community, fight for – that is, what we lack. It often appears that organizations unconsciously lack the very values or psychological capacities that they have proclaimed on their banner or in their vision.

On a deeper level, as Shay Frogel (2009), an Israeli philosopher, put it: 'One always has to ask himself or herself, 'in what way am I wrong when I embrace a certain way of thinking, a certain theory?' What I am here inviting the reader to reflect on are the blind spots, both the mistakes our community makes when embracing Group Relations theory and practice and what we overlook or the ways we use our own methods as defences.

I have been preoccupied with these issues for a long time. When the management team published the title and primary task of the 2015 Belgirate V conference, it resonated strongly with my preoccupations. The title of Belgirate V was: *Doing the Business of Group Relations Conferences: Un/Conscious Dynamics, Systems and Ethics.* Its primary task was formulated thus: 'To provide opportunities to study the discourse of Group Relations conferences, hence doing its business both as dynamic systems with conscious and unconscious processes and as organizations within an ethical context.' This choice, apparently expressing the wish for a more critical self-reflective discourse, reinforced my understanding and hope that our community has reached sufficient maturity to engage in an honest, self-critical and ethical discussion.

In one of the Group Relations conferences I directed, there were conflicts between two of the women on the staff, on two occasions. One initially tends to think of such conflicts in personal terms, as involving individual personalities and so on. However, as an advocate of psychoanalytic-systemic thinking, I could not help thinking that it somehow reflected my leadership or the system I created – had I been projecting something onto them, perhaps my own issues or the system's issues? Such introspection might need some explaining; it might be regarded as the result of a narcissistic stance and indeed, in certain ways, it may be. However, the choice to direct a conference is, to some extent, inevitably narcissistic. In my view, if the projections affecting any given system have a definite vector, it is top-down rather than bottom-up. This is because, among other reasons, in fantasizing and building the temporary organization that constitutes the conference, the staff preceded the members and the director preceded the staff.

Those of us working with patients, and especially with children, find themselves dealing with the projections of the patient's parents. If left unattended, these projections preclude any progress in therapy. The patient naturally plays a prominent part in the emergence of the symptom, the reception of external projections and the selection of particular defence mechanisms to respond to these. Some aspects of this process, however, originated in the parents and thus in the parents' parents. Without infantilizing either members or conferences, I believe that conferences present us with a similar situation and staff projections onto members may equal the members' projections onto the staff. While the main preoccupation is with projections onto the staff, as both sides have an unconscious, we cannot abide by this tendency to marginalize or dismiss staff projections onto members. Directors say that directing a conference often entails seeing one's own inner drama played out in the conference; my personal experience supports this claim. Being the director entails a somewhat narcissistic perspective, which may involve the kind of manic and magical thinking by which everything that happens at the conference seems connected to everything and everything seems to be connected to 'me'. While this feeling represents a bias, a manic distortion, it also has a kernel of truth, because the organization or even, on a larger scale, 'reality' is the result of our combined inner realities, inner dramas or 'organizations in the mind'. As staff-members, it is thereby important to keep checking ourselves, both personally and as a team, and to try and see what we project or put in this giant cauldron which is the 'shared conference mind'. For the director, this responsibility or accountability is even greater.

Let us return to the conference under my directory, where several women had 'taken up arms'. I tried hard to search within myself and consider what was going on along with the staff: Which parts of myself, as director, were enacted through those women's conflicts? I contemplated my issues with women, my issues with conflicts, my experiences of female competition, even my mother. I wondered which painful parts of myself, parts that I had perhaps been avoiding, were finding their way back to me through the staff. It was only some months after the conference that I fully realized what had begun to emerge during the conference and gradually became clearer: a much firmer and more assertive stance was required on my part; perhaps I ought to have stopped that acting out which took too much of the staff's time, not by being 'soft' and 'interpretive' but by being 'managerial' and 'authoritative'. It seems that this had been the most painful part at the time and that it had been difficult for me to see my own aversion to conflict, to being 'strict', to the prospect of being 'hated' by my staff. Over the course of the conference and aided by these very conflicts, I assumed a more assertive position, though I still have a way to go in this respect.

I am sharing this personal experience because I think it was an instance in which I applied the Group Relations model, or the psychoanalytic-systemic model, in an attempt to reflect on myself and explore projections and fractals, while actually doing little more than 'looking under the lamppost'. A traditional Jewish joke relates what may be a commonly shared experience: Hershl, a comic character from the *shtetl* (small Jewish township in Eastern Europe), was seen standing under a lamppost looking for a key he had lost several feet away. When asked why he was not looking where the key was dropped, he replied: 'Because this is where the light is'. Much like the proverbial Hershl, I had been looking in the easiest, most accessible place, 'abusing' the model, in a way. I consider such application a potential abuse because I had felt a certain degree of right-eousness as I was trying to understand what was going on, and I acted as if I were containing those time-consuming quarrels rather than angered by them. Perhaps by adopting a more authentic approach, displaying my less-than-containing-aspects, I would have been able to make contact, engage in conflict and acquire a fuller understanding of some of the system's fractals much earlier. I believe that, in this instance, I had used systemic thinking as a rationalization that helped me avoid contact with certain emotional parts of myself. In a way, I resorted to a mode of reflection rather than action, offering 'as-if' observations instead of using my authority and power (which also meant potentially abusing these or being perceived as a 'strict' director).

My experiences have taught me that one must remain attuned to four distinct aspects of inquiry. As these four aspects entail different perspectives and emphases, they may partly overlap; nevertheless, each specific aspect serves as a valuable standard in and of itself. First, there is the philosophical aspect, the scientific-philosophic question presented above: 'In what way am I wrong when I embrace a certain way of thinking, a certain theory?' We must continually ask ourselves what are the underlying assumptions of our model that may be at fault: perhaps the notion that everything can be discussed, that looking at the system unconscious is always useful (though it could lead to the marginalization of personal issues). The second aspect of inquiry involves what we wish we had or what we want to believe we have – but nonetheless lack (such as the capacity to engage in an honest and sincere conversation among ourselves). The third aspect focuses on those things we leave out or marginalize, because they threaten our equilibrium (as may have occurred at the conference described above). The fourth aspect involves awareness of our tendency to use our own theories or methods as a means of defence, as attacks on thinking or attacks on linking, or even to employ them cynically, as a means to advance one's personal or political goals, as will be described.

Before addressing the following examples, which illustrate the need for these four aspects of inquiry, I would like to stress that I am not concerned with individual cases, mistakes or defences but with systemic tendencies of which we may or may not be aware. I believe the phenomena I am discussing may occur not only in conferences, but whenever we act as a community: in gatherings or activities, such as within our organizations, in international conferences etc., especially on occasions in which we do not have pre-assigned consultants and we try to apply our own methods.

One wonders whether, for example, our great emphasis on reflection leads to an idealization of reflection, at the expense of action. This may be related to a general 'malady' of psychoanalytic thinking, which can be formulated as the devaluation of the concrete or the idealization of the metaphoric at the expense of concrete, physical 'reality'. Through the psychoanalytic lens, every deed or act may be interpreted and devalued as sublimation at best and acting out at worst. However, when dealing with the world of organizations, we cannot afford to ignore the realm of action. In this context, one must also consider the tendency to confuse the need to reflect with the need to act, as well as the common difficulty in successfully combining the two and making actionable decisions that are truly informed by reflection. These tendencies have to do with the fact that, as a community – for instance, here in Belgirate or on our various boards – we often work without the assistance of assigned consultants.

Another misuse involves the fact that we have taken a model created after the Second World War in order to free individuals from blind obedience to authority and encourage self-authorization, and turned it into a practice that sometimes seems preoccupied with making people more blindly obedient to authority. It is as if our unconscious primary task is the preservation of authority. I am referring, for example, to the frequently heard phrase: 'This is an attack on (my) authority'. It sometimes feels as if the entire enterprise of Group Relations has been misunderstood, as if our ultimate goal is to delineate the boundaries of authority, so that none will cross them. When someone calls out an attack on (their) authority, they may be right; but still, in many ways, authority is there to be challenged.

Many times, when our community 'does its business' – as the fifth Belgirate conference put it – when someone is criticized, the easiest way to 'shake off' the accusation and any required responsibility or account-ability is to say something along the lines of: 'I have been pushed into this role by the group.' I doubt that this had been the original intention – for every fault to be ascribed to the group, for personal accountability to be ignored and the individual to disappear from view. This touches upon a much more essential and pivotal debate, inherent in the theory we use, regarding the relative balance between the explanatory power of group phenomena versus individual phenomena.[2]

An instance of supposedly using the model for learning and exploring the unconscious, while employing it as a defence occurred in the con-ference I directed, as mentioned above. Viewing the quarrels between several of the women on staff as merely 'their own fault' would have been defensive on my part or on the part of the staff, but so would regarding those fights as simply playing a role for the staff, especially if this claim came from the 'quarrelling' women themselves. When a person says, 'this is not my responsibility, the group projected this role into me', we must be willing to consider it also as a personal defence.

This example highlights the tendency to use certain tools or theories excessively, taking them to their extremes at the expense of the other pole. When this happens, we must be alert and seek out the hidden defence. In many ways, we sometimes lack the 'good enough' ability to sustain the dialectic tension of these poles and are thus compelled to let the pendu-lum swing from one side to the other. The resulting split, indicative of the community's difficulty in maintaining a complex view, then serves as a fault line that fosters and reinforces defensive reactions, as mould grows in dark, dank places. Action versus reflection and individual versus group responsibility, mentioned above, are only two of the key dialectics our community must strive to sustain.

Another instance of the defensive use of Group Relations theory, which may be either unconscious or cynical, is the use of metaphors. For example, a repeating phenomenon in Social Dreaming Matrices, mainly when the SDM is used inside the community rather than outside it (for instance, Belgirate or the OFEK annual gathering customarily hold SDMs), is the utilization of raw dream material as evidence supporting pre-existing hypotheses. Many times, participants voice their predetermined opinions, garnishing them with seemingly unconscious bits of 'beta-elements' to make them admissible. Such use hardly justifies holding an SDM session; one is better off just expressing one's opinion. When working with a more 'lay' audience, when consulting a community or an organization or at conferences, we have a less biased view of the material and we can refer to it 'without memory or desire' (Bion, 1970). We can truly listen and learn with our audience or consultees.

By and large, we tend to fall in love with our metaphors and apply them even when they are no longer relevant. I recall a situation where an onion was mentioned at an LSG, and it was used and abused as a metaphor for layers, spirals, tears, etc. The poor proverbial onion was squeezed out of every last drop. Such overuse of metaphor serves nothing but a display of cleverness, which has a defensive function. Similarly, we sometimes tend to stick to a metaphor of an informal role assigned to a participant or group, in a way that blocks movement and learning.[3]

The same kind of superficiality sometimes affects our discussion of social, political or historical issues. We may offer an association, a reference to a political or a social situation, only superficially and as a kind of 'lip service', without delving deeper into it and trying to uncover its true meaning. For example, if a group in a conference in Israel is 'occupying a territory', we may refer to it, but we seldom truly face what this situation means. Indeed, our role is neither to teach nor to force-feed our associations or interpretations of social or political dynamics. However, we must be more careful in making sure our discourse is not reduced to a shallow and meaningless display of cleverness and acuity.

These tendencies – to abuse metaphors, to leave raw material behind, or to prepare our interpretations and hypotheses in advance – may also stem from internal competition, as we are all competing for invitations to consult, finding ourselves compelled to 'show off' our ability as consultants. This leads us to situations in which discussions are composed entirely of interpretations and contain virtually no raw material, or where there is some raw material but no authentic work is done with it. As I stated elsewhere (Bahat, 2012), in such situations it seems that we have built a 'tower of Babel of interpretations', with no foundation of data sustaining it, like that tower made in child-play, where hands are placed one top of one another, until it is simply floating in mid-air (p. 182).

In that paper, I referred to yet another defensive phenomenon. I was referring to the exploratory event at the third Belgirate conference, describing those occasions in which there are no (formally) assigned consultants. On such occasions, the group tends to split into two main sub-groups: the 'as-if' consultants, who mainly interpret, usually made up of those with greater seniority in the Group Relations community; the other group, composed mainly of younger people, with fewer roles in the global network, are those who do not see the system, who 'do not understand' what is going on and are often allotted the roles 'the actors' or 'the ones who feel'. I stated that it is not only a matter of competence and astuteness, but rather a part of a false group thinking process. This argument relies mainly on the fact that these roles usually remain fixed throughout the entire event. The two groups are pushed into two sepa-rate poles and learning from real experience is aborted. In Bion's (1961) words, the group 'avoids the painful bringing together of the new idea and the primitive state' (p. 127). I argued that this split serves the hatred of 'learning from experience' and that the two sides of the coin of Basic Assumption: Dependency are active. These two complementary aspects may be described as the impotent and ignorant, who are thus in a position of neediness, and the omnipotent denial thereof – those who know everything and thus need no one (or BA: Fight-Flight). Both these states are manifest in this split between sub-groups, which hinders the development of the Group Relations community.

Revisiting the use of metaphors, let us consider the two following examples, one hypothetical and one real. First, a certain country has upcoming elections and there is a leading candidate. The public discourse happens to include much talk of electricity, perhaps because a renewable energy source was recently discovered and its uses are debated. A certain politician uses word-play to comment on the leading candidate, alluding to the theme of light/lightning: the candidate may be *enlightened* (a token of the politician's appreciation of this candidate) but may also *strike like lightning* (an expression of fear of the candidate's misuse of his power). We could argue about whether this is a good play on words or a bad one, a good or bad metaphor, true or untrue and so on. The politician used the content and context of the public discourse to create a metaphor and stress his opinion: this is a political act, a political statement.

In the second example, an organization is holding a Social Dreaming Matrix session. A person in that organization (Person A) has just heard from a colleague (Person B) that he is considering to apply for the role of CEO, a role that A is not really interested in at the moment. During the session, a dream is described which features 'light'. A says that perhaps the light is related to the phantasy that the future CEO is sitting among us and that they are full of light (a token of A's appreciation for B); he then adds that the light in the dream can also be related to the fear of B striking like lightning. How does one classify such speech – as a discussion of the unconscious? Did A need the dream about light in order to express his opinion regarding B? In my view, the answer to this question is 'no'. A's statement does not even evoke an un-thought known. A is using the search for unconscious content (the SDM) in order to express a pre-existing opinion: A appreciates B but is also afraid of his use of power (maybe A is also envious of B, etc.). In my view, such use is identical to the use made by the politician in the previous example: it is politics disguised as learning.

I suggested above that the phenomena discussed here stem from the unconscious fear of learning related to Basic Assumption: Dependency and its vicissitudes. I would now like to put forward a more radical hypothesis, which does not necessarily exclude the former. It is my contention that, more often than we would care to admit, we tend to use our tools, our methods of searching for the unconscious, as means for dealing with the conscious, the known, the political and the conflictual. All too often, things we dare not say plainly, clearly and openly, remain hidden under the guise of unconscious, metaphoric, associative discourse.

This goes hand in hand with other manifestation of the tendency to confuse the elements that are essential or inherent to the model and those which are merely traditional or historic developments, but are not funda-mental to the theory or practice of Group Relations. One of the latter is the taboo on asking to be invited to staff a conference. It seems that, in our community, if a person asks a director to be on their staff, it serves as evidence that this person is incapable of the task. It is as if they have exhibited an essential misunderstanding of the Group Relations model. Our conferences wish to mirror the actual organizational and social world. In this world, people ask for jobs, apply for positions and compete openly for desired roles. In my view, the tradition of having to wait passively until one is invited to be on the staff is one of our cultural aberrations. This hardly means that people should constantly offer them-selves, but rather that we should make room for ambition and competi-tion as well as the desire to be more explicit, transparent and clear. Hiding these aspects of our community and pretending they do not exist leaves us exposed to the dangers of the above-mentioned abuses.

I find this tradition to be a political method of leaving power and control over resources (i.e., consulting roles) in the hands of a selected group that in phantasy and in fantasy could continue to maintain its power quietly and without being challenged. It is also an act of turning a blind eye to the competition, envy, vulnerability and other emotions resulting from the fact that the number of people wanting to staff conferences is greater than the number of available roles. In other words, the reality of restricted resources and of human nature gives rise to many complex emotions, that this tradition allows us to ignore: if no one asks to be on my staff, I can pretend that no one is hurt or angry about not being invited.

In this context, I believe that how we deal with competition, ambition, envy and desire partly explains the difficulties we encounter in marketing our enterprise as a whole and constitutes one of the reasons that it is not more widespread. When we do not dare to 'market' ourselves directly, honestly and plainly, we find it difficult to improve the marketing of our model. For this reason, we often use phrases such as 'we are not talking about our competition' or 'we are not talking about envy', pretending that the matter has been addressed and that we have indeed talked about competition and envy. Once more, we end up with what can be termed 'emotional namedropping'.

In this chapter, I have described some of the phenomena I have encountered in our community and which I have found defensive. While I have much respect and appreciation of the Group Relations community and model, in my view, these tendencies, views and behaviours are weakening our community and are obstructive to further development. An often-quoted dictum in Israel argues that 'the best defence is offence'; in light of the many misuses and abuses explored above, one might deplorably say that for our community, 'the best defence is the unconscious'.

Notes

1. I would like to thank my friend Nitza Riklin – always a source of good stories – for sharing this story with me.
2. While this subject goes far beyond the scope of this chapter, it involves both the theory and practice of Group Relations and is relevant to both the phenomena we encounter and the decisions we have to take (such as when there are 'casualties').
3. I would like to thank Yigal Ginath for his illuminating remarks on this issue.

References

Bahat, D. (2012). A church with no followers: A split of knowledge and power in the group relations community. In E. Aram, R. Baxter & A. Nutkevitch (Eds.), *Group relations conferences (Vol. III)*. London: Karnac.

Bion, W. R. (1961). *Experiences in groups and other papers*, London: Tavistock Publications.

Bion, W. R. (1970). *Attention and interpretation: A scientific approach to insight in psycho-analysis and groups*. London: Tavistock Publications.

Frogel, S. (2009). Presentation: The man and the discourse – a philosophical view. In *Language of the Individual and Language of the Group – Between Bion and Foulks*. Haifa, personal communication.

Has the world changed? Has Group Relations changed?

Considerations of the Group Relations movement in a postmodern world

Bernard Gertler

Since the sixteenth century, the world has been largely dominated by Western powers, generally by one dominating center, the Spanish, the Dutch, the British, and the United States. This colonialist structure has given way since the 1950s and has collapsed. Connected with this is the collapse of a unified and universal culture based on Western values and ideals that everyone must aspire to (Lemert. 1997, p. 34). What has eroded is the belief in a common and core identity that is the same for everyone (as in the supposedly self-evident truth that "all men are created equal" in the American Declaration of Independence.) The world has been de-centered in power, culture, values, and identity. Prompted by technological change, the world has become enormously different since the mid-twentieth century. This de-centering signifies the change from a modern world to a postmodern one.

The collapse of power structures, of universal culture, of universal values and identity, the "decentering of contemporary life" all have implications for Group Relations. The postmodern critique places much less trust in reason, in the notion of progress (of things getting better), in the disinterested and objective scientific observer who dedicates herself to the betterment of the human condition, is skeptical of grand narratives of explanation – modern views of the world. Postmodernism challenges the claim of objectivity, saying that ultimately all perception has subjective elements and claims to "absolute truth" and certainty are suspect and subject to debate (Gertler and Izod, 2004). In a postmodern world, can a psychoanalyst still be a truth-teller, from a grand psychoanalytic theory? Can the Group Relations consultant also still be a truth-teller?

From an organizational perspective, postmodernism challenges the notions of hierarchy, of machine and open-system metaphors, authority, boundaries, etc. Does Group Relations conference structure adequately represent the organizational forms currently in use? Indeed, how does Group Relations work with the social, organizational, and psychoanalytic changes in the last half-century?

Postmodernism can be taken in an extreme form where everything is uncertain, where there is no subject or author, and truth is unknowable. However, there are more moderate psychoanalytic versions that speak about "narrative truth" rather than "historical truth" and that how psychoanalytic theories guide people to the "truth" is determined by the theory. There is subjectivity involved (Aron, 1996). And similarly, organizations can be looked at with many metaphors such as machines, prisons, brains, and organisms (Morgan, 1986). Group Relations is committed to the organism metaphor, the primary task is "what the organization needs to do to survive." Taking a moderate, postmodernist stance, what are the implications for Group Relations of the multiplicity of psychoanalytic theories currently in practice as well as the changing nature of authority and organizations? Now there are a multiplicity of psychoanalytic and organization theories based on differing historical, cultural, and philosophical premises.

Has Group Relations theory and practice changed to reflect this multiplicity, this decentering since its creation in the 1950s and 1960s? The answer to that is complex. In a paper I wrote with Karen Izod in 2004 (Gertler and Izod, 2004), we proposed that Group Relations was originally defined by an English version of psychoanalysis (Klein-Bion) and Western systems approaches. These were modernist in their assumptions of the "universal man" from psychoanalytic principles and with the use of modernist forms of organization (e.g. centralized authority, defined distribution of roles, static boundaries, etc.) and the biological metaphor of open systems. Since the mid-twentieth century, Group Relations has differentiated. Some parts of Group Relations have remained conservative in the use of the original modernist base of psychoanalytic and systems thought and other parts of Group Relations have struggled to work with and incorporate the issues and ideas of the postmodern, postcolonial era, albeit seemingly without interest in important parts of contemporary psychoanalysis and changes in organizational structures. By that I mean that the focus is more on contemporary issues of society together with a de-emphasis on incorporating the contemporary organizational issues and contemporary issues in psychoanalysis. In addition, Group Relations has become more "didactic" than "experiential," meaning "we want to teach and tell you something specific," rather than "we want to give you an opportunity to discover, without a pre-planned agenda"; a de-emphasis in creating a general opportunity for the development of a reflection/action capacity in groups, organizations and society no matter what the content. Conferences have had titles such as "European Perpetrators and Victims – Now and Then" (Khaleelee and White, 2014) and "Race and Class in Organizational Life" (McCrae, 2004).

Those practitioners who believe in the universality of human nature and structure have changed the model very little. The model is seen as timeless and adaptable everywhere. A. K. Rice would not see much different in what he proposed in *Learning for Leadership* (1965) in these more traditional conferences. I use as an example, my experience of the Belgirate Conference in 2012 where the keynote speeches (Sher, 2015; Ozdemir, 2015) described Group Relations events that incorporated Klein/Bion frameworks as explanations within a conference and the use of what seemed to be a fairly straightforward Group Relations conference structure in a change project in China. At that Belgirate conference, in the group discussion in which I participated, many people dismissed the notion that knowledge is co-created and that subjectivity plays an important part for both the consultant and the member. Also, during one of the keynote speeches at that conference, I raised a personal experience when I was lecturing in Japan about the distinctions between person-role-system. During that lecture, a psychiatrist-participant brought up the issue of the Western value of developing the "self" as against the Eastern Buddhist value of "no-self." How do "person-role-system" ideas work in a Buddhist culture? Can we so easily apply modern elements of Group Relations as a universal application of psychoanalytic and organizational theory?

Overall, my experience of the 2012 Belgirate conference was that many senior practitioners outside of the United States remained in a more modern position in Group Relations, that Group Relations was still wedded to Klein-Bion and Socio-Technical Systems. This is a one-person model where knowledge and authority is vested in the consultant and in a traditional hierarchical, open-systems perspective.

Traditional conferences still occur in the United States. But more often my experience is that practitioners in the United States have moved in another direction. In the United States, the conferences have moved toward what I think is a healing, therapeutic/reformative purpose. The conferences seem to want to "make things better," to make social progress through Group Relations ideas ("making things better" is a very American outlook in contrast to European, see Cushman, 1996). Some practitioners have incorporated conceptions of mental health and addiction as themes for conferences (Roth *et.al.*, 2015). Others in the United States have moved Group Relations conferences in a different direction by taking up the postmodern challenge of giving voice to formerly silenced social identities (McCrae, 2004). These latter conferences seem more focused on individual social/political identity but also with a "therapeutic/reformative" purpose. The focus is more on the social rather than a social-organizational-group psychoanalytic examination of leadership, authority, and experience without a specified agenda that was the original purpose of Group Relations.

Internationally, Olya Khaleelee and Kathy White (2014) wrote a paper in *Organizational and Social Dynamics* called, "Global Development and Innovation in Group Relations." In that paper, they report a survey of 49 directors from around the world with descriptions of conferences and the controversies that international Group Relations is struggling with.

The key themes that they explore concerned:

- the development of Group Relations conferences and the directors' own participation in the process, including their ideas on the evolution from hierarchical authority to collaborative pairing and shared leadership;
- differing approaches to Group Relations conferences, whether traditional, non-traditional, traditional incorporating innovation or redesign of the basic model;
- differing views on what constitutes a Group Relations model;
- the difficulties and pleasures of paired or co-directorship;
- questions about whether authority to mount conferences resides in formal Group Relations authorizing bodies, within other authorizing institutions, or within self-authorizing individuals.

Khaleelee and White speak about the tradition of innovation in other countries, where the "sacred," traditional parts of Group Relations conferences are retained. These traditional parts include:

- a formulation around boundary management;
- an idea of primary task;
- a method of learning from here and now;
- experience at both conscious and unconscious levels;
- an interest in authority relations in a temporary institutional framework.

The innovations they cite fall into four categories:

- cultural influences such as the incorporation of yoga in India so as to include a spiritual dimension;
- new events;
  - social dreaming
  - the socio-technical event
  - the market place event
- the founding of new organizations that can be "virtual" or "real";
- theme conferences – where conferences are given an identifying name to define their purpose.

They point to the rise of conferences being self-authorized rather than authorization from an institution, a move toward co-directorship and distributed leadership.

Khaleelee and White found that the directors they interviewed fall into three clusters:

- founding traditionalists who are committed to a traditional model and tended to use it with little variation;
- innovating traditionalists who largely retained a traditional model but incorporated some innovation;
- model innovators who adopted a rather different kind of Group Relations conference model.

And so they suggest that conferences across the world range from the traditional to the "innovative" based on the incorporation of cultural influence, new events, or themes. To my mind, this is similar to the recent history of Group Relations conferences in the United States.

They conclude: "Today, as group relations has globalized, the themes of conferences are also more global and therefore mobilize participants even more in their roles as citizens." While this speaks more to the social and political, I think it is somewhat different from the identity focus in the United States. Yet both seem to move away from the original focus on leadership and authority and toward a prescriptive agenda.

They give a sample of recent conference titles:

o   *Motivation, Resistance and Change in Organisations and Communities*
o   *Navigating Uncertainty: Authority and Leadership in a Turbulent World*
o   *European Perpetrators and Victims – Now and Then*
o   *Transformative Authority for Sustainable Organizations: Collaboration, Competition, and Interdependence* – the conference proposes that authority needs to be transformed toward collaboration, healthy competition, and interdependence
o   *Identity and Authority: Passion, Accountability and Leadership*
o   *What do I Stand for? Authority, Leadership and Citizenship in a Turbulent Global Society*
o   *Authority and Leadership in the Recovery from Addiction*

In their titles at least, these conferences, as in the United States, range from more traditional to more therapeutic/reformative with a lean to the latter. Another question I have is whether these conferences emphasize the postmodern social in a didactic way more than the postmodern organizational and psychoanalytic (see the fourth conference in the above list where there is a prescription for behavior). If so, why should that be? One hypothesis is that it reflects a greater concern for control over the potential for global chaos and destruction. Another hypothesis is that the incorporation of the postmodern organizational and psychoanalytic literature represents too much of a break from the past. Nevertheless, by emphasizing the issues of collaboration and identity, some of these conferences do reflect the postmodern issues of diminishing hierarchy and interdependence, at least in their titles (e.g. the "Transformative Authority Conference").

Group Relations was developed in the era of laboratory training of executives and managers (e.g. T-Groups). The original model is a temporary organization that permits the organizational and psychoanalytic experiential examination of the social, structural and the group through its thoughtful open-system design … but what about the new conferences … How do these new conferences explore the more social emphasis? I certainly want to know more about these conferences; what structures are used to match the theme? What psychoanalysis is in use and how it is used in support? What do they accomplish that could not be accomplished with the original model, especially if the original model incorporated postmodern social, organizational, and psychoanalytic frameworks? Do the theme conferences represent the blurring of the boundary between the experiencing part of the conference and the application part? Why should application be pre-established by the sponsoring institution or the director? Why shouldn't application be tied to the emergence of the content brought up in the immediacy of the conference by the members (Hayden and Sharrin, 2015)? Does the use of a theme provide a more "telling" focus? … "telling" members what to do?

So what is gained and what is lost by the "innovations?" These changes in conferences are called "innovations" by many Group Relations people, not just the authors of the paper. And it should be noted that "innovation" has very positive connotations, ("original," "creative", "inspired" are synonyms). The word could just as well be "developments" or "changes" (Sharrin, 2015). Of concern here is that these are marketing attempts to make Group Relations conferences more palatable and acceptable but with the accompanying potential of becoming more superficial and diminishing learning in depth.

Contemporary psychoanalysis and contemporary organizations

Does Group Relations more actively accept and explore the varieties of psychoanalysis and how organizations have evolved in the twenty-first century? While the Belgirate Conference in 2012 seemed modern in its thinking, what are the postmodern psychoanalytic and organization theories that could inform conferences around the world?

What follows are some of the moderate, postmodernist elements in psychoanalysis that can apply to Group Relations.

Postmodernism implies the rejection of absolute categories (e.g. good/bad, knowledge/ignorance, social progress/reversion, male/female, black/white and the classifying of one as positive and the other negative). Postmodernism also implies the rejection of absolute meanings in favor of multiplicity and/or fragmentation; and often it implies the rejection of received wisdom from authority (Levenson, 2014).

Absolute categories

Group Relations conferences bring the wisdom of the "knowing" consultant who attempts to bring to bear the pre-established system psychodynamic theories on the experiences of the Group Relations participant so as to provide meaning. There are alternatives to correct and incorrect, smart and dumb, knowing and not knowing and with valorization of the former as against the latter. Maybe organizational and psychoanalytic frameworks are simply different; maybe consciousness/unconsciousness and subjectivity exist on both sides of the consultant/member boundary; perhaps difference is defined by history, culture, and tradition. Maybe we need less evaluation. Maybe we need dialogue and conversation to create understanding.

The fragmentation of meaning

Pluralism in psychoanalysis is pretty well accepted. Psychoanalysis now has multiple narratives that govern its thinking: Freudian, Kleinian, Lacanian, Interpersonal-Relational, and the like. Those in the Interpersonal-Relational realm of psychoanalysis (like me) support a co-created experience and question the original models of a predetermined mind structure where insight is communicated through the interpretive moment. Ideally the differences in metapsychologies should be articulated and ... the relevance to the task at hand should be evaluated.

Jay Greenberg (2015) proposes that major psychoanalytic theories are composed of compelling metaphors. "Analysis recapitulates the relationship between the child and father ... analysis recapitulates the relationship between child and mother ... analysis is an encounter between two adults ... analysis is a relationship between a person who projects unmetabolized protoexperience into a receptive container." He calls these metaphors, "controlling fictions." "Controlling fictions" would include, among others, such formulations as Freud's archeological metaphors and models of the analytic conversation as one or another variant of parent-child interaction. Greenberg's controlling fictions speaks to the point of the fragmentation and multiple narratives in psychoanalytic theory.

Rejection of received wisdom from authority

The questioning of grand narratives, the awareness that knowledge can be used for subjugation (e.g. universal theories), the binary use of good/ bad has led to a rejection of "received wisdom." One can look to earlier versions of psychoanalysis where women were denigrated and homo-sexuality was pathologized, as obvious examples close to home.

The awareness of this has led to a caution in the use of grand psycho-analytic principles in American Interpersonal and Relational views. Instead there is an awareness of the subjectivity implicit in all narratives and so an attempt to "own" and discover subjectivity in the analytic process. Hence the use of the terms "co-creation" and two-person psychology, the move from "blank screen" to "participant observation" to "observing participant" (Hirsch, 2015). Analysis becomes a process of mutual discovery although with the primacy of enhancing the awareness and easing the suffering of the patient. Attachment theory and infant observation where knowledge is co-created by mother and child also has had important influence (Stern, 1985). My point in bringing this up is that there are multiple ways to "skin the cat" and those of us influenced by the North American tradition of Interpersonal/Relational psychoanalysis can potentially have a different take in working in Group Relations conferences, one not quite so objectivist and more constructivist. More in the postmodern vein...

So I wonder about the different narratives of psychoanalytic theory in Group Relation experiences. If there is a lessening of hierarchy, how is that reflected in consultant behavior? In interpretation? In the construc-tion of work processes? How is the distinction between authoritarianism and authority currently maintained?

And I also wonder about the issue of different designs and the nature of authority to represent contemporary organizations.

If what we hope for as an outcome is greater capacity to manage one's internal life to the purpose of learning and work in the world, what designs would provide that? Would it make a difference if we altered the composition of groups and events for that purpose?

In the paper I wrote with Karen Izod published in Group Relations Reader 3 (Gertler and Izod, 2004), we spoke about the differences in modern and postmodern organizations. We proposed differences in struc-ture, power, boundaries, tasks, authority, roles and leadership. We pro-posed, for example, that authority in the modern organization had clearly defined spans of control and sanctions. We proposed that authority in postmodern organizations were located more in teams and networks and the authority derived from the capacity to deliver outcomes. Similarly, boundaries in the modern organization were formally defined, transparent, regulated where as in the postmodern organization, boundaries were more blurred, informal, changing and unregulated. Tasks in the modern organization were single and discontinuous and contracted hierarchically. In the postmodern organization, tasks were multiple and negotiated with linear and non-linear structures. In postmodern organizations, the individual manages a multiplicity of roles in multiple settings as opposed to a more singular one. Wouldn't a change in design promote different, more beneficial learning? I think prospective Group Relations members would want to understand the experience that current structures provide. We need more thought about how this would work but something involving design change that represents the different organizational structures needs development. Larry Hirschhorn (2017) has contributed to this issue in his paper "Beyond BART (boundaries, authority, work, and task): Creative Work and the Developmental Project." In that paper, he shows how these basic concepts are not sufficient for post-industrial knowledge work and do not always describe organizational structures sufficiently. And so the question arises, what are adequate learning opportunities in Group Relations conferences now? Ideally, we need a program to explore these questions.

I am something of a traditionalist who sees that the original model, informed by current postmodern psychoanalytic and organizational thought, allows for the largest development of a reflective capacity for developing social, organization, and psychoanalytic understanding. Currently, I see a shift away from the opportunity to discover and the development of a reflective capacity toward a "telling" position of how things should be. I am concerned that application and conference experience is blurred. I am concerned that there is less focus on application during and after conferences. I am concerned that the focus is more toward intrapsychic and interpersonal development rather than group and organizational understanding from a psychoanalytic perspective (Hayden and Sharrin, 2015).

Why? Is there currently a need for more control, an anxiety about our loss of control, a replacement of one hierarchy of power with another, but more disguised? By this I wonder whether the directors and sponsoring institutions unconsciously push theme conferences into a defined frame. And that by doing so, these conferences are a modernist attempt to define truth in advance, to define reality for members by authority, rather than have staff and members struggle with this by themselves in the conference (Hayden and Sharrin, 2015). So I wonder if Group Relations is struggling to embrace the challenges of the postmodern world in that the variations in tradition and innovation in Group Relations *incorporate* as much as they *examine* the anxieties that the postmodern era brings, anxieties about the fundamental questions of power, hierarchy, the basis of knowledge, values, and the like.

The postmodern era brings anxieties of dislocation, an unmooring from what is known, and fears of disintegration. There is a challenge to the familiar and a challenge to an orientation that has been organizing and important in Group Relations for so many years. Also Foucault (Boyne, 1990), sees professional knowledge is professional power and a mechanism of control, and there is a lot to lose for those of us currently at the center. And so I wonder if our differences reflect our various adaptations to the postmodern situation, a need for control in the chaos. But hasn't that need for control always been the case, and won't it always be the case? Or is the sense of chaos more extreme now?

Current life reflects both modern and postmodern ideas and ideally we are inclusive, rather than binary and exclusive; ideally we enact and reflect on the enactment. That goes for traditionalists and innovators. Ideally we all take into account how anxiety operates in us, in Group Relations, and in living in the contemporary world.

Final thoughts

Recently a colleague asked me about Eric Miller and why he was important. I immediately associated to a story from *Systems of Organization* (Miller and Rice, 1967). There is an account of their consultation to a dry cleaning organization. In that account, they talk about the transaction, the boundary between customer and the dry cleaner clerk, and the psychodynamics of handing over one's dirty clothes. "Customers behaved as if they felt that the dirt in their clothes was an undesirable and dirty aspect of themselves. They relied on the cleaner to get rid of it without fuss (but not too briskly) so that they could start afresh" (p. 85). The idea that psychoanalytic ideas overlay the ordinary structural transactions of life, informed by the social, was a great insight for me at the time, one I never forgot.

And that is how I think about Group Relations still. I think that it is the overlay of psychoanalysis with structural concepts embedded in the social, that helps make sense of my world. But I think the nature of the psychoanalysis in use needs to be reflexively owned and the different dimensions of structure also need that reflexivity since both have implications for understanding experience in the current world (e.g. Larry Hirschhorn paper). And the reflexivity of experiences is supported and enhanced by the ties to history, culture, sociology and philosophy. So my call for *conceptual systems thinking*.

What do I hope members learn in Group Relations conferences? I care less about what they learn in the sense of something specific that they have been told; I care more that they learn how to learn, if they can. I don't care so much what members see in the sense of something specific they have been told, but I care they take their authority to see more (Sharrin, 2015). I care that members are able to improve reflection of their experience in the present moment, and take that recognition to better accomplish "Work" in the world. The ability to increase immediacy, intensity, and clarity of experience and putting it to good use is the "Work" I think Group Relations and Group Relations conferences offer and what I think is distinctive and of enormous benefit. To the degree we become didactic, political, in the business of persuasion, shallow marketers … to that degree do I think we have lost the essential value of Group Relations work and thought.

I think Group Relations can provide a compass for understanding the influences of the modern and postmodern world. I have tried to explain why the inclusion of an expanded map of the social, cultural, historical, and philosophical territory would be helpful.

References

Aron, L. (1996). *A Meeting of Minds*. Hillsdale, NJ: The Analytic Press.

Boyne, R. (1990). *Foucault and Derrida*. London and New York: Routledge.

Cushman, P. (1996). *Constructing the Self, Constructing America: A Cultural History of Psychotherapy*. New York: Perseus Publishing.

Gertler, B. and Izod, K. (2004). Modernism and Postmodernism in Group Relations: "A Confusion of Tongues." In Cytrynbaum, S. and Noumair, D. A. (eds.), *Group Relations Reader 3*, pp. 81–99. Jupiter, FL: A.K. Rice Institute for the Study of Social Systems.

Greenberg, J. (2015). Therapeutic Action and the Analyst's Responsibility. *JAPA*, 63(1): 15–23.

Hayden, C. and Sharrin, R. (2015). *Personal Communication.*

Hirsch, I. (2015). *The Interpersonal Tradition – The Origins of Psychoanalytic Subjectivity.* London and New York: Routledge.

Hirschhorn, L. (2017). *Beyond BART (Boundaries, Authority, Role, and Task): Creative Work and the Developmental Project.* Available at Social Science Research Network (SSRN): https://ssrn.com/abstract=2896815.

Khaleelee, O. and White, K. (2014). Global Development and Innovation in Group Relations. *Organisational and Dynamics,* 14(2): 399–425.

Lemert, C. (1997). *Postmodernism is Not What you Think (Twentieth Century Social Theory).* Oxford: Blackwell.

Levenson, E. (2008). The Engima of Transference. *Contemporary Psychoanalysis,* 45(2): 163–178.

Levenson, E. (2014). *50 Years of "Contemporary Psychoanalysis": Confluence and Influence – A Roundtable Discussion.* Held at the New York Society of Ethical Culture, 2 West 64th Street, New York: October 25th, 2014.

McRae, M. (2004). Class, Race, and Gender: Person-in-Role Implications of Taking Up the Directorship. In Cytrynbaum, S. & Noumair, D. A. (eds.), *Group Relations Reader 3,* pp. 225–237. Jupiter, FL: A.K. Rice Institute for the Study of Social Systems.

Miller, E.J. and Rice, A.K. (1967). *Systems of Organization.* London: Tavistock Publications.

Morgan, G. (1986). *Images of Organization.* Newbury Park, CA: Sage.

Ozdemir, H. (2015). Exploring Group Relations Work in China: Challenges, Risks, and Impact. In Aram, E., Baxter, R. and Nutkevich, A. (eds.), *Group Relations Work: Exploring the Impact and Relevance Within and Beyond its Network,* Vol. 4, pp. 101–124. London: Karnac.

Rice, A.K. (1965). *Learning for Leadership.* London and New York: Routledge.

Roth, J.D., Brent, C., Gold V., Harkins, S., and Robertson Jr., John B. (2015). Group Relations and Twelve-Step Recovery: Mixing Oil and Water? In Aram, E., Baxter, R. and Nutkevich, A. (eds.) *Group Relations Work: Exploring the Impact and Relevance Within and Beyond its Network,* Vol. 4, pp. 207–214. London: Karnac.

Sher, M. (2015). The Oedipus Complex, Creativity, and the Legacies of Group Relations' Intellectual Parents. In Aram, E., Baxter, R. and Nutkevich, A. (eds.) *Group Relations Work: Exploring the Impact and Relevance Within and Beyond its Network,* Vol. 4, pp. 3–20. London: Karnac.

Stern, D. (1985). *The Interpersonal World of the Infant.* New York: Basic Books.

INTRODUCTION TO SECTION II

Exploring the discourse of organization (B-A-R-T) in Group Relations

This section takes the organization and organizing of a GRC as the key unit of study and reflection. What are the elements that make up a GRC a containing space for experiential learning and how to think about the various aspects of containing?

The first chapter in this section, by Rachel Kelly and Zahid Hoosein Gangjee, talks about the Yoga Event in the Leicester conference: what it might represent and how it contributes to members' learning. They consider how we can offer events in GR conferences that are creative, relevant, address contemporary organisational concerns and still remain true to the fundamental tenets of Group Relations.

In the next chapter, Gordon Strauss, Neil Neidhardt and Victoria T.Y. Moore focus on the centrality of the role of administration and the dynamic relationship with the conference director in the delivery of a GRC. This chapter also reflects on the process of planning a workshop on administration – how the workshop was conducted and how the learning could be used in the future – profiling a process that offers essential structural support to a Group Relations Conference.

Next, Miri Tsadok and Saliem Khliefi explore the experience of clashing cultures and concepts through the lens of delivering a GRC in a war zone whereby the notion of a "safe space" is tested in new ways. Traditionally, a key challenge facing a directorial team is the requirement to create a space that offers emotional and psychological safety. For Tsadok and Khliefi there is an additional responsibility, the requirement to create a space that also offers physical safety. Is it possible to create an environment that allows participants to take the risks required to achieve new learning? What impact do the differences in heritage (Israeli and Palestinian) make to their ability to create a containing environment? This chapter explores these questions and creates the space for considering many others.

In the last chapter in this section, Jinette de Gooijer turns a forensic lens on the system relations of the institutions involved in sponsoring a conference. She considers in depth the conference itself as a container for studying institutional relations, how institutional and partnership differences play out within a directorial partnership, the differences that each organizing system brings into a partnership and how the conscious and the unconscious play out in unexpected and unusual ways.

Doing business together

Lateral and vertical relations in the institutional partnering for a Group Relations conference

Jinette de Gooijer

T his chapter explores the significance and importance of the institutional systems associated with the business of Group Relations conferences, with particular regard to conferences run as a joint venture. The focus of my discussion is on institutional partnering and the dynamics of lateral and vertical relations within a joint venture arrangement. My interest lies with the system relations of the institutions involved in sponsoring a conference, and with the conference itself as a container for studying institutional relations. I will argue that both systems are integral to the business of studying Group Relations in an experiential conference, but that it is not common to bring them visibly together in the context of the conference system.

Conceptual ideas drawn from the psychoanalytic study of lateral relations and sibling dynamics are applied to a case study of a joint venture conference held in November 2015 in Melbourne, Australia. The conference was sponsored in partnership between Group Relations Australia (GRA) and the National Institute of Organisation Dynamics Australia (NIODA). Conclusions drawn from the case look at the benefits and challenges for the design of Group Relations conferences.

Doing the business of Group Relations conferences

What does 'doing the business' mean generally and specifically to the purpose and task of a Group Relations conference? Commonly, the notion of business refers to a commercial enterprise, or if not commercial, an enterprise providing public services to a clientele. The phrase doing the business suggests people working together on the primary task of an enterprise and all the necessary operational processes, systems and technologies that go along with that. Thus, an exploration of doing the business of Group Relations conferences invites focus on the working collaboration, the containing structures and systems, and to explore how these aspects influence and are influenced by un/conscious dynamics, systems and ethics. This surely is Group Relations at work in the wider arena of our field, not just conferences.

Several questions about Group Relations, in its broadest sense, spring to mind:

* Can one do the business of Group Relations without being a member of a group?
* Is the business of Group Relations commercial? Educational? Institutional? Or something else?
* What are necessary conditions for the business of Group Relations to be successful?

I wonder, too, about whether the institutional containers we construct for doing the business of Group Relations conferences sufficiently mirror or relate to the institutions represented by the participant members. Further, I am curious about the link between the sponsoring institutional system and that of the conference; and how this becomes available for study both within and outside of the conference.

Can this business of Group Relations conferences adequately invoke, enable, evoke, provide and or provoke the necessary reality for learning about institutional systems when a conference system is so idiosyncratic in its structure and duration?

I hope these questions prompt thinking about the issues I raise. It seems important to open up the business of what we are studying when we run a Group Relations conference.

The enterprise of Group Relations conferences

The heartbeat of Group Relations conferences is people working together – they are an enterprise – with common purpose and individual ways of working towards fulfilling that purpose. A working conference is a container with the capacity to reflect contemporary organisational life, and enable the transformation of experience into learning.

The business of Group Relations conferences is to create an enterprise in which the pulse of people working together can be studied and understood, with the insights that result from this learning, to be applied to the back-home realities of work and other social roles.

What we know about participants' application of learning from a conference is that it can be individually transforming, but much less transforming (if at all) of the organisations in which they work. While the application of learning is the ultimate aim, it can be difficult to evaluate the application of individual learning to organisational transformation. Do the institutional structures set up for doing the business of Group Relations conferences play any part in the learning process? I think they do, and will hopefully show why they do in my discussion of a joint venture conference.

At this point I will just say that an institutional container is essential for holding the conference, co-sponsored or not. The conference is contained by its institutional context and the relationship between container and contained is *in* the business of the conference.

It goes without saying really that a Group Relations conference is influenced by the institutional enterprise that sponsors and authorises the establishment of the conference as a temporary organisation. Think of it as exploring the mutuality of the relationship between contained and container, so cogently described by Hanni Biran in her recent book *The Courage of Simplicity* (Biran, 2015).

Working hypothesis

The working hypothesis I explore in the ensuing discussion is:

> that all institutional relations associated with a conference need to be available for study throughout the lifecycle of the conference. These relations are between multiple sponsoring organisations and the institutional system established to

contain the conference, the institutional system and the conference organisation, and furthermore, the relations activated in the institutional event of the conference. Studying the network of institutional relations is a necessary part of doing the business of Group Relations conferences.

When a conference has multiple sponsors...

Multiple sponsorship of conferences in the history of Group Relations is common enough; they are usually conceived of as co-sponsorship, and rarely as a joint venture partnership. In conversation with Mannie Sher (personal communication, 2015), he could not recall of any conferences being run as a joint venture. Thus, the joint venture between GRA and NIODA, in running a jointly owned Group Relations conference with two directors, might be a first of its kind. Before discussing the case in more detail, I will describe the distinguishing characteristics of co-sponsored conferences and one that is run as a joint venture.

Co-sponsorship vis-à-vis joint ventures

Co-sponsorship arrangements vary as to their purpose and the investment made by the particular sponsors. Arrangements can take the form of:

- lending the authority of a brand name to a conference;
- actively nurturing an organisation to develop its institutional capacity to run conferences; and
- presence in the market for a new organisation.

Co-sponsored conferences are not structured on the basis of shared ownership. Ownership sits with one organisation and an agreement is made as to what each organisation contributes to making the conference a success (however that is defined).

The Tavistock Institute has a long history of spawning, in the best sense of the word, the establishment and growth of Group Relations institutions around the world. Some readers will be alive to the history of OFEK's establishment, written up evocatively in *Birth of an Institution* (Sher, 2007). When the Tavistock Institute building supported the initiative to establish a Group Relations institute in Israel, it was in recognition that a Group

Relations conference needs an institutional container in order to do its business. The Tavistock lent its brand and authority in a co-sponsor role in order to assist and nurture a local institution to take up the business of running a conference, or to put it more simply, for institution-building.

Co-sponsorship is a negotiated agreement between two organisations – two businesses if you like. For a local institutional container, new and vulnerable, a co-sponsor with a robust institutional system that sponsors or runs the conference can help contain the conference system. The nurturing aspects of such co-sponsorship suggest vertical relations are part of the institutional system.

At the other end of the spectrum of co-sponsorship is the case of joint owners in a partnership agreement. My idea of a joint venture is of an inter-organisational enterprise in which the parties collaborate for mutual benefit. They each contribute resources, share responsibility for the success of the enterprise and the risks. This is lateral relations at work in the realm of organisations, whereas co-sponsorship has more resonances with a nurturing parent. A joint venture evokes the idea of collaborating siblings.

Why might co-sponsorship, with one sponsor as primary lead and accountable institution, and with the other sponsor lending a hand as such, be the more common model? If one of the principles for learning from experience in a Group Relations conference is to enable the capacity to reflect contemporary life, have we in the business of Group Relations conferences got a little stuck in vertical relations? Do we shy away from the more difficult experience of lateral relations? I wonder if it is because of the anxieties lateral relations evoke – that a joint venture connects us to the dynamics of collaboration and competition, differentiation, and power.

Lateral relations in institutional collaborations

Lateral relations and sibling dynamics in organisations is receiving increased attention in the field of organisation dynamics (Armstrong, 2007; Baker, 2014; Coles, 2015; Huffington and Miller, 2008; Loughran, 1986; Mitchell, 2014; Sirota, 2012; van Beekum, 2014; van Beekum, 2016; Visholm, 2005). The dynamics of competition and collaboration, of identity formation from the basis of same and different, and securing the attention of the parent are particular to sibling relations, and may get played out in the lateral relations of organisations.

Managing cooperation and competition in lateral relations between organisations is complex. Sharing and openness, defensiveness and withholding go hand in hand. While more attention is being paid to lateral relations in the field of organisational dynamics, there is much less about institution-building or the necessary institutional conditions for doing the business of Group Relations conferences, with the exception of Mannie Sher's extensive writings on this subject (see in particular Sher, 2013a).

The dynamics of competition in the collaboration may be played out between organisations, conference directors, the staff and members. It can play out in unconscious dynamics of rivalry as evidenced in projections about in/competence, devaluing differences and questioning the other's legitimacy. Van Beekum (2016) writes of the importance of healthy parenting for containment and authority of sibling relations to manage rivalrous, murderous fantasies. In organisational terms, this points to the importance of healthy vertical relations for developing healthy lateral relations.

In the case that follows it is the two organisations involved in the joint venture – GRA and NIODA – that are required actually to provide the parenting and thus the containment for the work of the two directors and hence to the conference as a whole. In saying this, it assumes there is a sibling relationship in the field.

The joint venture conference – GRA and NIODA

Mid-2014, the two organisations formally agreed to run joint activities, with the first activity being a five-day residential conference. It was a major undertaking for a first go at working jointly, and therefore significant for the institutional relations between the two organisations. There have been other joint conferences in the history of Group Relations in Australia; mostly these had a primary lead organisation and were run more along the lines of co-sponsorship.

GRA and NIODA are closely linked in supporting the educational and professional interests of people who work in the field of Group Relations. In the case of the conference, the joint activity was based on the principle of equal ownership. The financial arrangements, however, were not equal.

GRA is a membership organisation, whose aims (inter alia) are to promote and develop Group Relations in Australia. It operates upon the goodwill of volunteers, is governed by a Committee of Management, and has sponsored a residential five-day conference every two years since its inception 10 years ago. NIODA is an education provider organisation, set up after the local university cut its post-graduate program in organisation dynamics. It employs professional and administrative staff and is governed by a Board. At the time of the conference, NIODA was seeking registration as a higher education provider and accreditation of a Master of Management (Organisation Dynamics) program.[1]

The conference had two directors (Wendy Harding, NIODA and Jinette de Gooijer, GRA), with each appointed by their respective organisations. Membership of the conference was a mix of fee-paying public registrations and a cohort of NIODA's students who were participating as part of their curriculum requirements.

The idea for a joint conference started with the two directors having an informal chat over coffee early in 2014, playing with ideas for reinvigorating Group Relations conferences in Australia, and thinking a joint conference would be a good idea. We tested the idea with our respective organisations and got a positive response. This encouraged us to prepare a formal proposal, presented separately to each organisation, which each endorsed in principle. Our proposal, a significant intervention on the local inter-organisation relational system, prompted a meeting between GRA and NIODA to formulate a Memorandum of Understanding (MoU) to guide this and other joint activities. A sub-committee from each organisation formed a working group to work on this MoU and liaise on practicalities of joint activities. Formal authorisation of the directors by their respective organisations to lead a conference followed soon after an agreed MoU was signed. The two directors also chose to abandon the nomenclature of co-directors used in the original proposal for a joint conference. The reason for this was to acknowledge the plenipotentiary authority invested in the role by each of the sponsoring organisations and mutually confirmed between the two directors. Conceptually, the conference had two directors in a lateral relationship of equal authority.

In the ensuing months, some critical events occurred which brought to light, and life, system dynamics in joint ventures, notably to do with working through institutional differences and differentiation, and the collaboration and competition present in lateral relations. That the theme of the conference was an exploration of lateral and vertical relations in the exercise of leadership, authority and power is of course pertinent to the dynamics played out over time.

It was not a smooth beginning, getting the show on the road so to speak. At one point the real and fantasised differences between the two directors, organisational identities and purposes, experiences of residential and non-residential conferences, which models of practice each was familiar with, led me to want to bail out of shared directing and go it alone, to be the director. Wendy resisted this. Her organisation had authorised her in the role of director of a conference it half owned, and it would not want its representative director to have less authority for the conference. I saw the sense in this, and got off my high horse. This brief, but significant incident played out down the track.

The first of several meetings with the conference directors was held late 2014. It was initially coined as 'the joint meeting of the representative sub-committees of GRA and NIODA for a collaborative Group Relations conference in 2015'. This first meeting was tetchy. Communications leading up to the meeting had provoked feelings of suspicion, wariness about motives, irritation and annoyance with the manner of communicating – summed up by the NIODA representatives as feeling treated like a younger sibling in the field. In fact, the two organisations are quite different in their mission and makeup. GRA made a claim for being the primary sponsor on the basis that it saw Group Relations conferences as its primary task, differentiating NIODA's educational task as primary with conferences being a component of a course program. The implication was that GRA was not seeing itself as an equal but rather as a major owner of the conference.

The reference to sibling dynamics and ownership of the conference, along with my earlier declaration to be *the* director, is symptomatic of competitive dynamics in lateral relations. Unconsciously, an attack on legitimacy and competence was in play, but we could not yet see it or wish to acknowledge it.

Meanwhile, the two directors were meeting frequently and regularly, building a working relationship, wrestling with points of difference, and in the process of doing so our trust in each other was growing. We had some real sticking points about residential vis-à-vis a non-residential conference. NIODA's students were enrolled in a non-residential conference. My strong desire was for a residential conference. A solution came in an innovation to hold the conference in an inner-city university residential college, make on-site accommodation optional, but to include events on two evenings after dinner. This helped achieve a shared, high priority goal to make the conference accessible and affordable, and to be able to offer the benefits to learning that come from the social spaces inbetween events.

Another sticking point was our mental models about equal ownership and what this looked like in practice, especially as it related to financing the conference. NIODA's budget was tied to its approved business plan; GRA's budget was more flexible and tied to cash reserves in the bank. At the time, it was more flush with funds which possibly fed into the fantasies about economic power conferring rights of majority ownership. Sirota (2012) points out that the seductive pull of power to create a vertical relationship is always present in lateral relations.

In this work together, the two directors were engaged in building the foundations of the conference institution. As we progressed in working through differences and disagreements it became apparent that our working through became a containing influence on the inter-organisational relations as manifest in the joint meetings of the two sub-committees, which was renamed at the second meeting as 'GRA/NIODA Inter-organisational Liaison Committee', but then referred to as the Joint Liaison Committee in practice.

To my way of thinking, the Joint Liaison Committee was not a governance body, but an intergroup meeting for dialogue and thinking. The directors reported on progress on matters such as conference recruitment and staffing, while individually remaining accountable to their respective organisations. Recommendations and information from the joint meeting were reported back to the two organisations for their respective Boards' and Committees' approval.

In light of the conference theme and institutional sponsorship structure, the directors were stimulated to initiate and lead a reflective session at each committee meeting on experiences of lateral and vertical relations, for the opportunity so presented to learn about inter-organisational collaboration. How to bring that into the conference and make it available for learning was a conundrum we did not resolve at the time.

While complex in its structure, the Joint Liaison Committee proved to be a necessary and valuable container for inter-organisational relations. The directors' experiences of taking up their roles responded to dynamics in the committee and influenced it in turn. As would be expected, the early stages were very much about getting to know each other. As dynamics related to fear of losing control of one's identity emerged, fantasies about and between the two organisations became more visible and were able to be worked on.

When at the second meeting of the Joint Liaison Committee the meaning of equal ownership became clearer, it helped grow understanding about the conference as an event on the boundary of the two organisations and between them – as such a third object jointly created. The conference was duly authorised to operate as an autonomous event for which the directors were jointly responsible as its management.

Lateral relations in the joint venture

The lateral relations between NIODA and GRA are dense – many members have connections to both organisations. The field of Group Relations in Melbourne has a small and active group, whose members have multiple collegial relationships. We are colleagues who work together, consult together, and run professional development activities out of different institutional containers, be they educational (universities, NIODA), professional (GRA, Organisation Development Australia), commercial (consulting practices), or personal (peer supervision groups, networking and friendships).

As briefly mentioned above, the conference theme was to explore leadership, authority and power in lateral and vertical relations at work. With this in mind, we consciously set up an institutional structure that reflected the theme directly. We were aware also of the potential risk for the institutional system and container infecting or infusing the conference, to the extent it might become a narcissistic exploration of the institutional system outside of the conference. (I have a memory of something like that happening in the final days of the Australian Institute for Socio-Analysis and its penultimate conference held immediately after ISPSO 2002 in Melbourne. My colleague Allan Shafer recalls instances when dynamics of the sponsoring organisation flooded conferences in a way that frustrated members who had nothing to do with the sponsoring organisation). It has helped me realise that a function of the business of Group Relations *per se* is to join up relations amongst the institutional systems with skin in the game, and that the work of a conference in studying Group Relations cannot be isolated from its contextual institutional system. The conference is contained by the institutional system and context; and this institutional container is influencing and influenced by the conference task.

How then to make these relations visible and available for thinking in the service of the conference task and its institutional system?

It is an abiding principle in Group Relations conferences that staff work through their own particular conceptual and other issues, just as conference members are expected to do. This principle is related to, and is in the service of, the undertaking by staff to do everything possible that pro-motes the conference's primary task and of furthering the learning of the dynamics relatedness between individuals, groups, organisations and society.

(Sher, 2013c)

Pre-conference institutional dynamics

A critical incident in the lead up to the conference alerted us to uncon-scious dynamics in the institutional system.

It was decided by the two organisations that GRA would take on the role of handling all financial transactions for the conference. The reasons for this are not entirely clear to me, which alerts me to what uncon-sciously might have informed the decision. While GRA did not require that it handle the finances, it made itself available to do this, since it did have convenient structures and processes in place for online registrations and payments.

Unconsciously, the decision may have been informed by:

1. GRA's bigger bank balance with its concomitant sense of economic power.
2. A feeling I carried that GRA was responsible for attracting the public participants (since NIODA would be bringing along a readymade membership with its students).
3. A possible reluctance in GRA to lose control of its identity as the 'primary organisation for Group Relations'.

Leading up to the critical incident, several events in the personal lives of the Directorate group meant that it met only once during a three-month period immediately after the early-bird deadline had passed. Registra-tions were looking good, and we felt very confident of a sizeable mem-bership. When we met again at the end of those three months, we discovered that the income received by GRA did not in any way reflect the number of registrations, and on closer look, invoices had not been raised, payments not followed up, and more. A rather stark reality made us exceedingly anxious, to say the least. As we explored the situation, we noted multiple unusual incidences of 'incompetence' throughout the system, focused particularly on the administrative interface between the conference and GRA's financial systems. In reflecting on what systemically might be playing out, we hypothesised that the agreement to rely on GRA as the banker for the conference was based on a number of unexplored assumptions, to which the dynamic of economic power had blinded us. We had not questioned the capacity for administrative efficiency at a time when turnover of two key office-holders had occurred. The conference directors had not articulated a schedule of delegations sufficiently. One director and the administrator were both first time in their roles. The other director had previously co-directed conferences in the university program, plus we were all relying on GRA's prior experiences of running Group Relations conferences. Personal absences of some key people meant things could not be followed up when they needed to be. We, the directors, did not attend to the implications of that, and assumed too much that the GRA institutional system had this in hand. These were some of the facts at the time.

I came in touch with my unacknowledged anxieties about wanting to be, but failing to be, a super competent first-time director; questioning my own competence and legitimacy and what had I projected onto my colleagues; plus, I have great loyalty to my own institution and felt embarrassed by its apparent incompetence. It brought me back to the earliest encounter between the two organisations and the feelings of sibling rivalry that had been expressed then but not worked through. The incident of unpaid registrations could be seen as an attack on administration in the system.

As we know, what does not get worked through goes underground and pops up elsewhere. Competition, to recruit the most members, so as to have a profitable conference and have the conference that could not be had alone, also played out as a destructive rivalry as to 'Who is the more competent and legitimate in the business of Group Relations conferences?' The result was an attack on the competence of the institutional container to contain the conference.

The lessons from this incident alerted me to the importance of attending to the real and fantasised differences between the collaborating organisations. There are significant differences between a member organisation (GRA) and an employer organisation (NIODA). The structures that bind members to each organisation are different, and the systems for ensuring continuity of operational activities are also different. A member organisation depends on volunteers for operational efficiency; people are elected to a governance role for reasons not always to do with operational capabilities. What attracts and binds people to join a member organisation are shared values and belief system. In contrast with this, an organisation employing staff to provide services functions differently. There are contracts, systems and operational policies that bind people together. Performance management processes are used to ensure consistency and efficiencies in service provision. The significance of these differences was not apparent to me when we first conceived of a jointly-run conference.

Conference system dynamics

Sher notes (2013b) that the conference director is on the boundary of co-sponsoring organisations, and in his experience, the intergroup event will reflect some of the dynamics of the relatedness between the two organisations in how the director experiences her or his role, and what may get acted out, consciously and unconsciously. Such dynamics of relatedness were borne out during the system relational event of the conference, designed to provide opportunities to study and experience the relationships and relatedness between all parts of the conference. The task of the event was defined as: 'To study the exercise of leadership, authority and power in the lateral and vertical relations of the conference system as it is experienced as a whole, in its context and between and within its parts; and to share learning from this study, during the event, in whatever creative ways you choose.'

As is usual, members formed into small groups and occupied the allocated working spaces, with the exception of one group who found themselves without a room, and chose to work in the open space of the foyer outside the main room. While many of the other groups remained in isolation (secure and chummy), little intergroup interaction seemed to occur. When it did occur, the quality of the interaction was described as invasive, often limited to data gathering, and no observable sharing of learning occurred. However, the group in the open space did explore the authority structures of institutional relations with management and other groups and held a system meeting, at which all were invited, to share their learning. In effect, this group created a 'third space' where the task could be explored.

Another interesting occurrence in this event was the actions of the consultants group to hold a social dreaming matrix, with an overt intent to proactively sell their consulting services to the working groups. Every member attended the matrix. It seemed that in the institutional system members could share dreams (unconscious learning), but the deliberate work of sharing conscious learning was more difficult. The actions of the consultants' group to convene a matrix without any prior discussion with the management group (comprising the directors and administrator) was observably competitive and felt to be an attempt to establish an alternative management.

The group structures manifesting in the system relational event mirrored to some extent the sponsoring organisations' structure of relations for managing the conference. Figure 2.1.1 depicts this working structure. The two organisations connected in a matrix of vertical and lateral relations, but what is clearer to me now post-conference is that the inter-organisational relations were held in a third space, outside of the conference boundaries. The third space was held by a *liaison* group. Two organisations and two management groups were both governing the conference. Our idea that the system relational event could explore the dynamics of lateral and vertical relations and not be contaminated

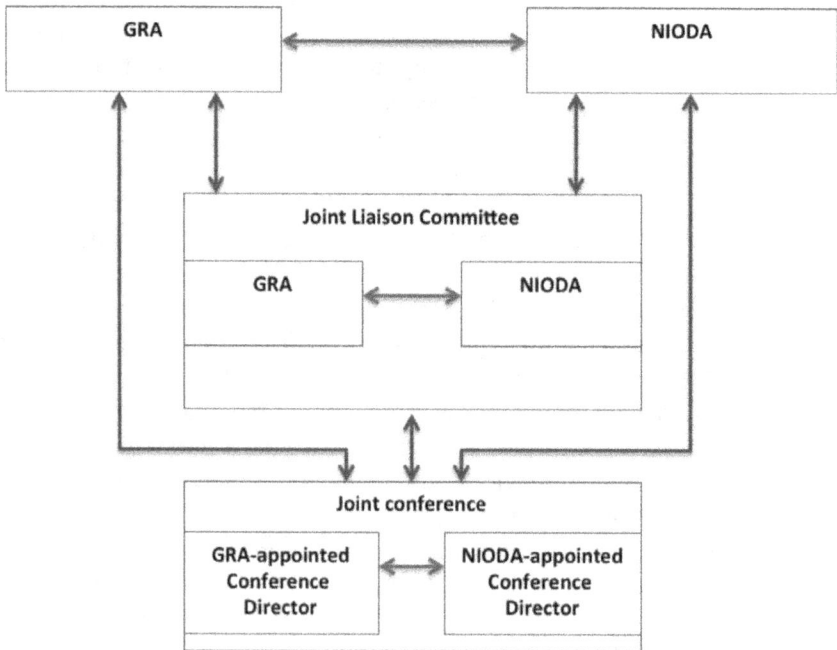

Figure 2.1.1. Inter-organisational liaison structure.

by the relatedness the two sponsoring organisations was naïvely hopeful. The event clearly revealed what was jointly held and could be
explored collaboratively (authority structures), and what was separated
and difficult to explore (competitive authority).

There is more to be said on this dynamic as it relates to lateral and
vertical relations, but I will need to leave that for a future paper.

Conclusion

Why set up a joint venture at all? There are obvious external benefits in:

- pooling scarce resources to achieve common aims;
- enhancing the ability to attract a large enough cohort of members to
  be able to have a large study group and system events of real
  significance;
- the kinship ties formed through collaborative work, especially in
  Australia where there are only two or three organisations focused
  on Group Relations; and,
- in the context of organisational work in the marketplace, a joint
  venture provides direct experience of issues facing our constituencies
  (students, consulting clients, professional members) in inter-organisational relations, partnerships and joint ventures, competition and
  collaboration between groups in the same organisation or across
  other boundaries.

Institution-building is an important part of the business of doing Group
Relations conferences. GRA and NIODA built institutional containment
through a joint institutional structure for containing the conference enterprise, by working on pre-conference dynamics in the institutional system
and in staff meetings, holding a series of pre-conference staff meetings to
build the conference institution, and ultimately in a post-conference review.

I have argued that the sponsoring organisations in a joint venture also
need to work through their own particular conceptual and other issues.
This assists the relatedness between the organisations and the conference
to be well-coordinated and aligned. Additionally, when staff work together
through their particular issues before the conference, they make a significant and valuable contribution to building a conference institution that is a
good enough container, and which they collectively own.

Through my experience to date of a joint venture and reflecting on its system dynamics, I have discovered the significance of the relations in the institutional system of a joint venture and their influence. In the work my colleagues and I did on establishing a good enough container for the conference, I came to realise that the conference is not an isolated object for providing opportunities for learning about institutional relations. This becomes even more significant when the institutional relations are between multiple sponsors of a conference.

There are *more boundaries* in a joint venture, *greater complexity* to manage, *multiple projective material* in the system – lateral and vertical relations are in play at the same time. The conference is a third object between two organisations; it is in a matrix of relations. If we are to do the business of Group Relations conferences, mindful of un/conscious dynamics, systems, and ethics, there is a requirement to bring institutional relations more to the fore – to include in the task of working conferences, spaces for studying the dynamics of the institutional container and the object or conference it contains.

Acknowledgements

I am grateful to colleagues who have helped my thinking in preparing this chapter. In particular, Mannie Sher, Gabriela Barrial and Rosemary Viswanath who agreed to be interviewed; Avi Nutkevich and Allan Shafer for reviewing early drafts; Louisa Brunner and Julian Lousada with whom I shared the terrors and excitement of being one of the keynote speakers at Belgirate V. Louisa initiated our coming together as a small group to contain our feelings and experiences of our roles. It made a world of difference. Finally, this chapter could not have seen the light of day without the opportunity to work in a joint venture conference. I treasure the collaboration I experienced with my colleagues to bring it to fruition, in particular Wendy Harding and Fred Wright, and members of the Group Relations Australia and National Institute of Organisation Dynamics Australia management committees.

Note

1.   NIODA successfully achieved accreditation later in 2016 for its Masters of Leadership and Management (Organisation Dynamics) program.

References

Armstrong, D. (2007). The dynamics of lateral relations in changing organizational worlds. *Organisational & Social Dynamics*, 7(2), pp 193–210.

Baker, J. (2014). Sibling relationships at work. *Psychodynamic Practice*, 20(1), pp. 28–39.

Biran, H. (2015). *The Courage of Simplicity: Essential Ideas in the Work of W. R. Bion*. London: Karnac Books.

Coles, P. (2015). Sibling rivalry at work: from family to groups. *Psychodynamic Practice*, 21(3), pp. 254–263.

Huffington, C. and Miller, S. (2008). Where angels and mere mortals fear to tread: exploring 'sibling' relations in the workplace. *Organisational & Social Dynamics*, 8(1), pp. 18–37.

Loughran, E. L. (1986). *Consulting to Interorganizational Systems*, Springfield, MA: Center for Organizational and Community Development, University of Massachusetts and Center for Human Development.

Mitchell, J. (2014). Siblings and the psychosocial. *Organisational & Social Dynamics*, 14(1), pp. 1–12.

Sher, M. (2007). Birth of an institution: early correspondence leading to the establishment of OFEK and Tavistock group relations in Israel. *KAV OFEK*, 8(Nov.), pp. 1–18.

Sher, M. (2013a). *The Dynamics of Change*, London: Karnac Books.

Sher, M. (2013b). From groups to group relations: Bion's contributions to the Tavistock 'Leicester' conferences. *The Dynamics of Change*. London: Karnac Books.

Sher, M. (2013c). Group relations conferences: reviewing and exploring theory, design, role-taking and application. *The Dynamics of Change*. London: Karnac Books.

Sirota, J. (2012). Some reflections on the experience of Belgirate III: tradition, creativity and succession in the global network from a lateral perspective. I: Aram, E., Baxter, R. & Nutkevitch, A. (eds.) *Group Relations Conferences: Tradition, Creativity and Succession in the Global Group Relations Network, Volume III*. London: Karnac Books.

van Beekum, S. (2014). The Oedipal as a defence against the sibling. *Organisational & Social Dynamics*, 14(2), pp. 367–378.

van Beekum, S. (2016). The murderous sibling. *Transactional Analysis Journal*, 46(Jan.), pp. 26–38.

Visholm, S. (2005). The Promoted Sibling: Sibling dynamics – a new dimension in the systems psychodynamcis of organizations. *ISPSO Symposium 2005*. Baltimore.

The Yoga Event

An important here-and-now event in the Group Relations conference bouquet

Rachel Kelly and Zahid Hoosein Gangjee

One of the issues in the business of offering Group Relations conferences (GRCs) is: how do we offer experiences that are creative and relevant yet ensure that these are true to the fundamental tenets of designing and conducting GRCs. The Tavistock Institute has been offering the Yoga Event at the Leicester conference for the past 10 years and this chapter seeks to clarify some fundamentals about the nature and purpose of yoga; its contribution to members' learning; what it might represent within the conference, coming out of the myths and fantasies expressed and some of the resistances it faces. This chapter seeks to show how the central principals of yoga and GRCs are essentially similar.

The Yoga Event has been part of Group Relations conferences in India for a long time, in fact it is provided by nearly all of the Indian GRC institutions. It was first introduced into the Leicester conference in 2008 by Eliat Aram who had been to a Group Relations conference in India and experienced the Yoga Event there. She decided to invite Gouranga Chattopadhyay to lead it the first time. Rina Tagore led the second event in 2009 and since 2010, one of the authors of this chapter, Rachel Kelly, has led it. So, in 2015, provided for the eighth time, it has now become one of the traditions of the Leicester conference, at the heart of Group Relations.

A Group Relations conference is devoted to *experiential learning in the here and now*, about group and organisational behaviour, with a particular emphasis on the nature of authority and leadership. Its purpose is educational. In other words, it is designed as a temporary educational organisation, which can be studied experientially as it emerges, evolves and comes to an end. The primary task of the conference has not changed substantially throughout its evolution but various nuances have been explored throughout the life of Group Relations. Miller, in the Leicester Model says that he and others envisaged coming up with an ultimate unifying theory of human behaviour, which could be developed and tested within these conferences i.e. there has always been an interest in integration, without quite knowing how.

Some of the basic tenets of Group Relations include *relatedness* – how influence is used amongst individuals and groups; the processes by which individuals and groups establish their identity; and the process of finding meaning and expressing oneself and becoming part of a group. All these are constructs of our minds – not just a group or organisation as construct but our ideas about ourselves, realising our differences whilst at the same time realising we are of the group. How the individual is involved in these dynamics is a central question of a Group Relations conference. How aware we are of oneself and being able to manage this/lead oneself directly correlates with the group's ability to be aware of itself.

Other tenets include Bion's basic assumptions that groups make: fight/flight, dependency, pairing – which are used as *mechanisms against anxiety and uncertainty*. The group-as-a-whole engaged on the group task and simultaneously possibly being undermined (although not necessarily) by one of these basic assumptions, at any given moment.

Understanding the idea of *boundaries* – time boundaries, space boundaries and the regions between systems are where finding your *role*, either as member or staff, can become clearer, learning ways in which to access your personal *authority* in a group and the nature of the *organisation* in the mind.

The individual can be thought of as an *open system*. Our personal systems are complex and multidimensional. We need to consider all the components that make up our systems: physical structure, physiological processes, the content of our minds, our ideas and attitudes toward our surroundings and our sense of longing for connection to something greater then ourselves. Each Group Relations conference has its own design and there have always been developments in the design of the Leicester conference throughout its history. So Harold Bridger, for example, developed the double-task conference in the 1950s, as an alternative to the current Leicester Model. The introduction of the A and B groups and the Training Group and subsequently in the later 2000s, Emerging, Furthering and Advancing Praxis groups take account of the fact that people come to the conference with differing Group Relations experience. The Training Group was first introduced at Leicester in 1963. Review and Application Groups and Role Analysis were introduced in other conferences later on and the World Event and Design Event instead of the IE and IGE have been offered in various conferences much more recently. So, the model is always evolving – being thought about afresh, and innovations introduced.

Let me bust three myths about what yoga isn't: yoga, particularly in the West, is often thought of as being about exercise, fitness, stretching or relaxation – this is partially true in that a side effect of practising yoga is that you may feel somewhat exercised, and/or fitter, stretched, or relaxed. Is it just for the young and bendy? Well, practising it will help you feel younger and more flexible, whatever your age. But this is only a part of the story.

By the same token, yoga is not just about the body – the mind/body/ spirit are one and the same – we don't function without all three. In Ancient Greek, the word 'psyche' (i.e. what we now think of as the mind) meant both breath and blood – the spirit of life. One of the eight elements of yoga, is Pranayama – the extension of the breath. It is a combination of two Sanskrit words: Prana meaning life force or spirit and Ayama meaning extension or control through practice. So, Pranayama is practising the conscious awareness of the breath and this underpins the whole of yoga – a psychophysical method.

Since antiquity, with the increasing frenzy and constant change of modern life, we seem to have lost this ancient wisdom. Descartes in the early 1600s brought into focus the prevailing concept of the dominance of the mind: not just separate or different from the body but in a hierarchy where the mind is more important than the body, *the mind is the person*. This mind/body dualism – a split that has become such a powerful cultural concept, so embedded it's rarely questioned, is only now being brought to the fore in the cultural mainstream with recent advances in neurobiology and curiosity about the way the brain works and the nature of consciousness. A person is not a brain which happens to be carried around in a meatsuit. You, your consciousness is a whole-self phenomenon/construct – it is your sensory perception of yourself in relation to the world around you.

Yoga is a lot more than the practice of the postures – this is just one element out of eight in the Yoga Path as outlined by Patanjali in the Yoga Sutras (Satchidananda 2012), a series of aphorisms, about 2,000 years ago (yoga itself is more than 5,000 years old – for a very long time it was passed down orally). Practising all eight elements together by degrees, helps you to consciously control your mind in order to reach a state of freedom from its ceaseless activities, judgements and assumptions, ultimately helping you to see reality for what it is and not what your mind makes it out to be. The postures emerged as people observed nature: the strength and resilience of a palm tree in a storm; the self-containment of an eagle; the stable, rooted and historic nature of a mountain; the flexibility of the snake: all spine; the potency and power of a roaring lion; the delicacy and poise of a crane and the freedom and joy of a laughing baby; and they invented postures to mirror them in order to gain their qualities – leadership qualities.

So, these postures (and the other seven elements) are vehicles for developing an insight and intimate knowledge of how your whole system functions and using tools of practice to clarify and fine-tune it. It is learning through experiencing the postures about how to be in the here and now. There is no destination; there is only now. It is about developing the capacity to be with one's own fluctuating experience and to stay in a position of not knowing i.e. always in a learning stance (Miller, 1989). This is the practice of mindfulness, bringing the uncon-scious to consciousness, an ability to stick to the task and stay in role i.e. being present in each moment during each posture as a member or staff member, not being distracted by competition, either with yourself or others.

Bion refers to Keats' 'negative capability' – 'when a man is capable of being in uncertainties, mysteries, doubts, without any irritable reaching after fact and reason', and links this to the idea of being without 'memory and desire' in group work; Izabel Menzies-Lyth talks of how difficult it is to actually stay in this state of mind. Practising yoga aids staying in this state of mind. It is about coming back to neutral, to a state neither trying to do or be something else but neither is it being passive. Physically this could be described as a state of active non-doing, a dynamic tonus without tension. You are less likely to be swayed by the slings and arrows – being more your authentic self, coming back to the uncarved block (Taoist concept of *Pu*), unfettered by habit. Bion, (incidentally, born in India), was concerned with understanding reality and that you can only do this through your sensory perception i.e. your whole self.

'I found myself numerous times working in sessions and afterwards feeling in a painful state of not knowing what on earth was going on' (Menzies-Lyth, 1989). Yoga helps in making this state less painful and more manageable, become more at ease with the unknown, so that it's possible to work in that state (deepening and stabilizing it), rather than becoming paralysed or having another reaction.

The fundamental tenet of yoga is that there is only one indivisible cosmic force – everything living and non-living is part of this universality. Reality is fundamentally unknowable and different from conceptual thinking which expresses not reality as it is, but how it appears to us and how we relate to it. Quantum physics is only now catching up with these ideas. Yoga is about facilitating change that translates into living a more balanced, joyful and fulfilling life. It is about gradually becoming more aware of your whole self, so the *quality* of your thinking changes, allowing yourself to become more internally quiet, less anxious, allowing things to percolate through you, becoming less attached. You can become a witness to what is going on, starting with the internal and moving to the external. You develop insight through a type of binocular perspective, i.e. in the sense of having two 'eyes': one eye with yourself at a distance, bringing yourself under scrutiny, the other on your context (to begin with, you and your relationship with your mat).

Paying attention to your internal self, your feelings, allows them to be more available to you – a heightening of consciousness. The practice of asana, the postures, is to pay attention i.e. to be aware of your body/mind responses to the postures. At the same time, to feel stable and comfortable when performing the posture. And also to be able to breathe comfortably in it.

The emphasis is always on the breath (pranayama) – following your breath rather than straining to do the posture 'right'. Where a posture is experienced as difficult or boring there is an opportunity to practise with the internal, becoming more and more subtle, increasing presence of mind, as opposed to the physical challenge of a difficult posture.

For one member the Yoga Event signified true internationalisation. For him, it provided a proof of primacy of role over authority. It is no coincidence that we have metaphors like: 'having backbone' and 'being spineless' – the spine is the first structure that forms inside the womb, from this, the body and limbs sprout. The spine supports us from behind but in our 'go-getting' world, we are often tilting forward, interested only in the front of our bodies. For Jung, 'behind' symbolised the region of the unseen and the unconscious. The sinuous spine in yoga is the centre of our anatomy allowing the free flow of life force energy – the fractal of the Axis Mundi, the ancient pillar that supports the world.

The Yoga Event has evolved but the following resistances have been noticed/spoken about in most if not in all of the Leicester conferences to varying degrees. However, in Indian conferences, resistance is encountered much less because yoga is more culturally acceptable, part of the heritage – the exception might be in the business world.

In the conference, the Yoga Event may bring up shame about the body because many modern cultures glorify the young and thin. There can be shame that the aging body can't do what we think it should be able to, shame about what appears to be the uncontrollable nature of our bodies.

Where a modern lifestyle has become predominantly sedentary, it can be a shock suddenly to be required to stay in a particular position on the floor or move in a particular way. The slow pace and emphasis on the breath may appear appropriate for older people and beginners but this pace also exposes, so at some level it's obvious to you when you're fluffing a movement. The pace can also be considered not active enough – some consider yoga simply as a form of physical exercise and take the opportunity to go to the Sports Centre to work-out or have a run instead.

Inspiration and expiration: the Yoga Nidra (conscious sleep to allow a holistic, whole-self-understanding of the previous postures) evokes the idea of death – at the end of each session it is performed in the corpse posture, lying down, still. Many modern cultures keep death at a considerable distance and fear of death can be present at all ages. However, the Yoga Nidra is easily the most popular part of each session – the bliss of the final 'end relaxation'. But again, because it is particularly about the here and now, it can be difficult – you are hovering between consciousness and unconsciousness and, if not paying attention, it's possible to go to sleep for the whole time.

Others consider yoga as a form of religion, referencing the chanting of OM (which evokes the universal vibration but also happens to be a religious symbol for various sects and religions of Indian origin); the hands together 'in prayer', particularly in what has been described as the 'ritual' at the beginning and end of each session.

Conference staff may have had some experience of yoga previously but more often do not, mirroring the experience of many members coming to their first GRC. Staff may feel ambivalent around not being able to do postures *correctly/properly* so where is or how can they find their expertise in this event? Can the staff be in a learning position in a Group Relations conference?

The consultant staff are also sitting in the body of the conference, on their mats amongst the members. Chairs, and who sits where and next to whom, are particularly significant in Group Relations conferences. Culturally the chair through the ages has been imbued with significance – it often reveals social status and represents role. Being asked to sit on the floor and use mats could be construed, unconsciously, as communicating disrespect. Chairs can also be considered a sedative – the verb *sedate* meaning to calm comes from the Latin 'to sit' and we are trained to sit up straight, and settle down in our chairs throughout school. Sitting calms, the option of not having chairs could be inviting revolution. New brain research shows that learning increases with physical activity i.e. when the whole self is being used. We are made to move so static chair sitting maintains power relations and keeps radical ideas safely contained.

In the Yoga Event, there has always been an option to use a chair, placed either at the side or back of the room, for whatever reason.

In the conference, there are two demonstrators on either side of the leader and where women only have been the demonstrators, they have been thought by some as 'models'. It is important to have one/two male demonstrators, if not a male leader, which would encourage some of the male members. Yoga is a very female activity in the West (cf. with India where it's been adopted by the army for example).

Where the leader of the event has been female for the past seven years, particularly where there is a female director of the conference as well, there can be ambivalence about female leadership which is then directly expressed by opting out. Equally, where the leader is non-Indian there have been enquiries why an Indian leader has not been chosen – questioning the legitimacy and qualifications of a non-Indian leading the event.

In fact, all the above resistances have caused the Yoga Event to be seen by some as more 'optional' than other events (despite all Group Relations events/groups being completely optional for members of course). It's thought of as a personal experience rather than a collective inspection/reflection on our relationship first, with ourselves, then, the mat, and then gradually moving outward, the group, and the rest of the world. Any absences can and should be interpreted systemically and can certainly be worked with in the staff meetings – the challenge is how to work with this more directly in the collective of members and staff.

One member's feedback was for a plenary where absences would be highlighted in the way they are in the LSG. The emphasis can be on working with the body/mind/spirit – the body in particular in the presence of others – reminding us of the body of the organisation.

There is also the issue that the group-as-a-whole phenomena cannot be interpreted in the same way as in other events; i.e. there's no opportunity to directly interpret in the session itself. It has been discussed whether to have 10 minutes at the end to talk about each session but not actioned.

Conclusion

The Yoga Event is an integral part of Group Relations conferences – it has an important function, for the integration of mind/body/spirit, and the understanding of the whole self. Without it there's a focus on the mind as dominant. We communicate at least as much non-verbally as verbally – and this is particularly important in groups.

The practice of increasing conscious awareness; finding your authority, physically; building finer balance; managing reactions; a binocular viewpoint, can only increase members' learning for the whole conference.

There are inherent tensions in that it's not always apparent to members what the relevance is and opting out of the Yoga Event can be a vehicle for the expression of dissatisfaction with other parts of the Group Relations conference.

However, yoga in the West is comparatively young, but it is becoming increasingly mainstream and with new conference members who don't 'know' what Group Relations is all about, there is a likelihood that the event or similar psychophysical events will remain and evolve in the Leicester conference and other Group Relations conferences around the world.

Acknowledgements

Eliat Aram
Gouranga Chattopadhyay
Rosemary Viswanath

References

Chattopadhyaya, G. (2007). Unpublished paper on yoga.

Cranz, G. (1998). *The Chair*. New York: Norton.

Feuerstein, G. (1989). The Yoga-Sutra of Patañjali: A New Translation and Commentary.

Menzies-Lyth, I. (1988). *The dynamics of the social: selected essays*, vol 2. London: Free Association Books.

Miller, E. (1989). The Leicester Model, Tavistock Occasional Paper No. 10.

Sri Swami, Satchidananda (2012) *The Yoga-Sutras of Patanjali*. Buckingham, VA: Integral Yoga Publications.

Administration

Where the business of Group Relations begins and ends

Gordon Strauss, Neil Neidhardt and Victoria Te You Moore

Introduction

A dministration in the context of a group relations conference (GRC) is often thought of in terms of the role and duties of the conference administrator, but this view is too narrow. Anyone who has worked as a conference administrator or directed a GRC knows that the administrative process begins before the administrator is selected, is extensive during the pre-conference period, continues and may expand during the conference itself, and often is not complete when the GRC itself has come to an end. For a function as critical to the success of a GRC and one loaded with all of the issues about which group relations teaches—leadership, authority, boundaries, tasks, roles and how these are affected by unconscious psychological processes—it is striking how little attention administration receives.

Although there is some group relations literature that deals with conference administration explicitly (e.g., Gold et al., 1993; Nahum and Shafer, 2000; Shafer, 2006), it is small. Often, what is most notable in articles or chapters about GRC experiences, is how little is said about the conference administrator, even when one might expect the working relationship of the administrator to the director to be examined. A recent example is the chapter in the previous volume of this series (Aram et al., 2015) about co-directorship experiences in GRCs over a 20-year period (Josselson et al., 2015). Missing from the recollections of co-directing by seven very experienced GRC directors was any discussion of how or whether co-directing affected the conference administrator and the working relationship between director(s) and administrator.

The relative invisibility of GRC administrators and their work is understandable. Done well, GRC administration allows members and staff at a GRC to focus on their work within the conference with less anxiety about many boundary issues: Have the members paid their fees? Have they arrived and registered? Have accommodations for staff (and members if the GRC is residential) been arranged and assigned? Have the folders for members and staff been assembled? Have the staff meals been planned and the food ordered? Are the rooms at the conference site sufficient and do they have the proper number of chairs, and are there sufficient times for meetings of the director, administrator and others on the administrative team to meet during the conference? These are only a partial list of tasks commonly delegated to the GRC administrator.

However, there is a price for the relative invisibility of the administrator in a GRC. The administrator (or those working on the administrative staff in larger GRCs) may be taken for granted, and over time the role may be denigrated. Sometimes this is from a seeming hierarchy of conference roles: being one of the staff consultants may be viewed as more desirable (and therefore more important). In the US, there is a long history of individuals who aspire to be consultants starting out as conference administrators or assistant administrators; their being an administrator was often seen (both by them and others) as a necessary step, a "paying your dues," while awaiting the chance to become a consultant on staff. Fortunately, this view of administration is not universally held; there have always been a (small) number of individuals who approached being the administrator as their GRC "role of choice."

In contrast to training opportunities for individuals wishing to learn about or hone skills as small group consultants that have been available (at least in the US) for more than 30 years as well as similar educational events for learning about consulting to large study groups or even serving as a conference director, we are not aware of any similar educational events related to GRC administration until we and colleagues conducted the first such workshop in 2013 (GS and NN were two of four staff at that workshop and Victoria Te You Moore (VTYM) attended the workshop as a participant).

In this chapter, we will start with a more comprehensive look at GRC administration, briefly review the process of planning the administration workshop and then describe how the workshop was conducted and what we learned that may be useful in future workshops. Ms. Moore will address the workshop experience from the perspective of one who attended and also speak to how she used the workshop experience in subsequent GRCs where she served as the administrator.

GRC administration

Authorization and roles

Initially authorization will come from a sponsoring organization and most often will be specifically for the director. The director will usually select the administrator, though for some GRCs the sponsoring organization will also select the administrator. Either way, the director-administrator team must negotiate their roles: what tasks get delegated from the director entirely to the administrator, what gets shared, and what remains only with the director.

What we hope becomes clear when reading this list of administrative tasks is that these tasks range from the relatively straightforward and comparatively simple (such as receiving payment or checking members in at the start of the conference) to tasks that cannot be done alone or without the cooperation of others (such as monitoring for distress or casualties).

Tasks

Pre-conference

1. Design of the conference
2. Staffing and pre-conference meetings, including consulting to the staff-as-a-whole as a part of the conference Directorate, and to the administration team as the head of the team
3. Conference location, including preliminary room assignments for major conference events

4. Lodging for staff (and membership, if residential conference)
5. Organizing meals, snacks, and refreshments for staff and membership
6. Budget
7. Recruitment
   a. Designing, producing and distributing the conference brochure
   b. Setting discounts and scholarship (bursary) amounts
   c. Active solicitation of members
   d. Receiving applications and payments
   e. Bringing members across the registration boundary, managing boundary interactions that occur, and consulting to the membership at this boundary when relevant
   f. Establishing a waiting list if applications exceed space
   g. Reducing staff and renegotiating space and food contracts if enrollment is substantially below budget
8. Obtain authorization on behalf of conference to give continuing education credits
9. Help obtain conference sponsorships

On-site but pre-conference

1. Conference event schedule
2. Staff arrival and check-in
3. Staff meetings including a tour of the conference facility
   a. Coming together as a staff and beginning to examine staff dynamics
   b. Assigning small and large study group teams
   c. Assigning members to SGs and review/application groups
4. Member check-in/registration
5. Managing communication between the conference and the hosting organization(s) (e.g., catering, facilities, security personnel) and between the membership and the staff
6. Care and feeding of staff (this carries into the conference)
7. Care and feeding of members (if GRC is residential or if some meals are part of the conference)

Intra-conference

1. Conference opening

2. Staff meetings
   a. Whole staff meetings and reports
   b. Staff sub-group team meetings
3. Being on-call to members at all times and attending to members and staff during breaks
4. Role transitions
   a. If director is in LG
   b. Whole staff into and out of institutional event (IE)/world event
5. Taking in/integrating the evolving conference process and dynamics
6. Providing for staff R & R after evening staff meetings
7. Monitoring for distress/casualties among members or staff
8. Member-staff "social hour" after all "here-and-now events" are done
9. Final conference plenary
10. Managing boundary crossing out of conference at its end (both members and staff)

Post-conference

1. With members
   a. Possible application learning
   b. Possible issuing of continuing education credit certificates
2. With staff
   a. Payment/travel reimbursement
   b. Possible further processing and reflecting on the conference
3. With sponsoring organization (and conference facility)
   a. Settling finances
   b. Final report on the conference

How the administrative tasks get divided between the director and the administrator will vary; the experience of the director will certainly be a factor, but the experience and perceived competence of the administrator will often play a bigger part. How is a novice or relatively inexperienced administrator supposed to learn how to assume the role with competence?

The traditional and usual answer is to learn by doing, ideally by being an assistant administrator to someone with more experience who can show the novice "how it's done." That approach used to be more or less the way people learned to be GRC consultants to large or small study groups: you went to GRCs, observed and experienced what the consulting staff said and did (and how they spoke their consultations), made inferences about what the consultant thought, felt and meant, and then, when given the opportunity to be on a GRC staff, you used your experience, taking up the role basically in imitation of what you had seen, and heard. For close to 20 years the A.K. Rice Institute for the Study of Social Systems (AKRI) has worked to develop a program to better prepare those who aspire to work in GRCs. So far, though, learning the role of conference administrator isn't part of that training program.

Evolution of the workshop on administration

Starting in 2012, four members from the Midwest Group Relations Center (an AKRI affiliate center) plus four other AKRI members began a series of conference calls with the goal of designing a workshop for GRC administrators. The group included three former directors of the AKRI annual conference, two former administrators who had worked on the AKRI annual conference multiple times each and three individuals with other GRC administrator and/or consultant experience. The planning for the workshop was conducted during and between a series of conference call "meetings." For a portion of the planning process in 2012, we divided into two groups of four and interestingly one group focused somewhat more on the psychodynamic aspects of the administrator role (e.g., thinking of the administrator as a consultant to the boundaries of membership and staff) and focusing on the unconscious processes that tend to occur between administrator and membership, administrator and staff and administrator and director. That group felt strongly that the workshop should not to focus on the nuts and bolts of administrative work that could easily be read about or learned in a course, for example, for event planners. The other group emphasized learning about creating and sustaining a partnership with the director, about effective boundary work with staff, members and representatives of the host site and about taking up a role in experiential events, especially the IE.

We also considered the denigration or demeaning of the administrator role. We recognized that at the level of observable process, sometimes this is by other staff, sometimes by the members and sometimes by the administrator him- or herself. Failing to get the administrator's report at breaks is one way in which a director can demean the administrator's role. The wish to be a consultant and viewing the administrator role as only a stepping stone to that role on staff is one way an administrator can denigrate their own role. Treating the administrator and the administrative staff like maids and butlers can be a process that comes from members or staff. (Marc Kessler, a member of the planning group who had many years of GRC administrator experience, had an interesting observation: "I learned that the major role of the administrator is to create a space in which the other players, both staff and members, can do their work. The 'maid and butler tasks' are part of that role, and they have to be taken up. If the administrator despises that part of the role, the work becomes intolerable. Obviously, it is not all that the roles are, but let us not neglect it, and not neglect to instruct those taking up the role that it is an important and valuable part.")

We had begun thinking the workshop would be for conference administrators, but over the course of 6–7 months, we came to the first of two important ideas for the workshop: that our focus would be on administration—the Administrator-Director team as well as the administrative functions within a conference—not on the administrator role alone.

The other major challenge we faced was how to bring experiential learning to the workshop. The challenge was how to avoid having it seem (too) contrived. Early on we thought about using a panel of experienced directors and conference administrators, perhaps to include one or more "case" presentations for discussion with the workshop participants. Another idea was to conduct consultations in the open with administrator/director pairs (thinking we might have such pairs from upcoming conferences attend the workshop). What we settled on—experiential pair exercises in which pairs or threesomes would take turns role-playing the conference Administrator or Director (or Associate Director if a threesome) grew organically from the earlier decision to focus on the administrative team. As we progressed in our thinking, we developed yet another idea: to relate GRC administration to administrative roles and functions outside the world of group relations.

We decided to offer the workshop in conjunction with the September 2013 AKRI Dialogues (a meeting for all AKRI members where ideas and applications relevant to the theory and practice of group relations are presented; it is held every 18 months). There is a tradition of pre-meeting workshops and we anticipated that the administration workshop would be 1.5 days. Our original title was "Conference Administration: The Essential but Often Denigrated 'other,'" but it became instead "The Administrative Mashup: A Dialogue Between Transformational and Transactional Leaders, Between Zombies and Vampires." Eight people enrolled but only six attended. We had four staff (we had planned on five, but one had to withdraw due to illness).

The administrative workshop

The workshop schedule is shown in Appendix A. In what we called the Introductory Mashup, we welcomed the attendees, introduced ourselves and reviewed the workshop learning goals and objectives. These can be summarized as

1. Gaining a clearer conception of Administration in GRCs
    a. The role of the administrator
    b. The role of the director
    c. The administrative team
        i. Its dynamics
        ii. Its role in managing multiple boundaries
2. Providing conceptual tools for thinking about the conference as a total entity
3. Reflecting on the often-experienced denigration of administration within GRCs

We then engaged the participants in a discussion of their goals in attending the workshop as well as their experiences in the administrator or director role as well as their experiences of and associations to administration in GRCs. The workshop began at 11 am and after a 90-minute opening plenary session, we continued the process of less formal introductions by having a joint participant-staff lunch.

The afternoon of the first day was devoted to the first two of three pair exercises. The pair exercises were the real heart of the workshop; they were intended to be experiential role-plays in which each member of the pair was either in the role of administrator or director. After 15 minutes in one role, they would switch roles. After the second 15 minutes the pair would get feedback from the staff member who observed them and begin to discuss the process. Then all pairs and staff gathered together to further review the issues raised by the exercise (see Appendix B). Examples of the tasks or problems presented in the pair exercises included dividing a hypothetical GRC membership of 40 into four small study groups (the pairs were given a printout of the membership with information about, age, race, gender, title/degree and previous GRC experience plus indication of the eight students and their instructor who were part of a leadership class that uses group relations as a model); a scenario in which the director is concerned about competitiveness between the administrator and the associate administrator and its impact on the administrative team and on the conference; a scenario in a residential conference in which a member begins to act bizarrely—retreating to his room, expressing grandiose ideas such as, "I have finally grasped the essence of group relations and have become the spiritual son of Wilfred Bion"—and members are approaching the administrator with concerns about him and whether he should be allowed to remain at the conference.

The second day of the workshop began with the third pair exercise, and then we concluded with two one-hour plenaries. The first we called "What Could Go Wrong?" in which the staff shared experiences of dealing, as director or administrator in a GRC, with unexpected developments. We concluded with an exercise we called "Top Ten Things…" in which the participants as a group developed a list of the qualities of a good GRC administrator and administrative team. It also allowed the participants to begin to articulate what they had learned in terms of key concepts. Participants were asked to complete an evaluation of the workshop.

While most of those who came to the workshop had already served as an administrator or a director at a GRC, our co-author Victoria T.Y. Moore had not (yet). In what follows, she reflects on her experience both at the workshop and in applying its lessons subsequently.

A participant's perspective

I attended the 2013 Administration Mashup Workshop at the AKRI Dialogues having recently been hired in my first conference administration role, as the Assistant Director for Administration (ADA) for the 2014 Group Relations Conference on Authority and Leadership in Recovery from Addiction in Chicago. My group relations experience at the time was limited. I had been a member at the 36th Annual Northwestern University Group Relations Conference: Authority, Leadership and Diversity in Groups and Organizations. I had also been a student and subsequently a teaching assistant for Sonny

Cytrynbaum's graduate group dynamics course at Northwestern University.

The Administration Mashup workshop was a formative experience for me. It shaped how I conceptualized and took up the ADA role. Even though my understanding of and approach to the role continues to evolve as I continue to take it up in different conferences, I still draw from the foundational learning I gained in the 2013 Administration Mashup Workshop. Every conference stretches a different part of my understanding of the ADA role, but I can still anchor my learning in the role in the workshop that the staff presented.

The next section examines how the Administration Mashup workshop helped inform my taking up of the ADA role at each of the three subsequent conferences on which I worked. Across all of them, I have kept the stance that the administrative role is a valued and important part of the conference. That the administrative role is a rewarding and hard-to-fill one and not something to be devalued, is an idea that the Administration Mashup workshop showed me early on in my group relations work. I have also appreciated the design of the workshop to make space for director-administrator pairs to attend. This design enabled me to broaden my mental model of the administrator's relationship to the director. It also helped me learn from the workshop participants who had directed, as well as from watching the here-and-now dynamics of the participating director-administrator pair.

Chicago 2014 GRC on authority and leadership in recovery from addiction

I served as the conference's Assistant Director for Administration and oversaw an administrative team of three experienced administrators, including one of the co-presenters of the Administration Mashup workshop.

Boundary

Participant discussion during the Administration Mashup workshop laid the foundation for my learning around boundary management and boundary flexibility. In particular, I recall a participant raising the question of when an out-of-the-box boundary decision is considered "corruption vs. flexibility." Being more comfortable with a more rigid interpretation of boundaries myself, I began to appreciate, through the Administration Mashup work-shop, the possibility of some flexibility around the boundaries.

Task

One workshop participant had conceptualized the task of the ADA as "holding the body of the conference" while that of the Director as holding the conference in the mind. The ADA makes sure that the body of the conference – and the bodies at the conference – are cared for so that the mind can work. This conceptualization helped inform my mental model of the tasks of the Director-ADA pair, although how much this division of labor helped build an integrated, cohesive container for the conference, and how much it engendered a split between the mind and body of the conference, I am still not sure.

Role

The workshop exercise in which participants brainstormed ideal qualities of an administrator gave me the conceptual framework for two qualities that I would go on to develop and appreciate as an ADA for this conference. The first quality is developing my trust in the director and exercising my loyalty to him and to the conference. The second quality is developing a tolerance for ambiguity and accepting my powerlessness over things I do not know or cannot control. For instance, when I was tasked with creating the first draft of small study group and review/application group assignments for the membership, I found that I could not do so despite having data on the membership from overseeing registration as well as some theoretical knowledge of SSG and RAG composition. While I was a newcomer and stranger to every staff and member of this GRC, most of its staff and participants were not strangers to each other. A GRC with this theme had been held several times in the past, and in its current year. I was the only new staff member. Some of the staff and members also had current and historical dual relationships and thus could not be in the same SSGs or RAGs. The Conference Director and other staff members with patients in the membership made significant changes to the ADA's proposed SSG and RAG assignments without much explanation as to why.

Another example of my powerlessness over things I could not control was how I was regarded by another GRC system. I was a graduate student and group dynamics TA of a man who directs another annual GRC in the Chicago area, which was sponsored by my graduate program. By becoming the ADA for a competing GRC system, I was seen as a "rogue" student by the director of my graduate program and had email privileges revoked after I used my university email account to promote this competing GRC.

One workshop presenter's comment that "it's harder to find a good administrator than a good consultant" helped me value and appreciate the roles that I and my administration team were taking up in the staff-as-a-whole. I was also able to develop a deeper level of compassion for the members of my team and for their varying strengths and limitations.

Beijing 2014 GRC on authority and leadership in recovery from mental illness and addiction

I served as an Assistant Director for Administration under an Associate Director for Administration. During the conference itself, the Associate Director for Administration authorized me as the lead administrator while she herself took on a non-administrative role on another team. In my new role, I oversaw a team of two other Assistant Directors for Administration who were full-time employees at the conference's host institution and who did not partake in any staff meetings during the duration of the conference. As such, I was in many ways the sole administrator on staff during the conference.

Authority

From my workshop notes, I have written: "parallel process: authority issues in one direction (bottom-up) may speak to authority issues in another direction (top-down)." There was much ambiguity around my top-down authorization from the Director. Instead of authorizing me in a particular role (administrator or cultural interpreter), the Director asked me whether I would be flexible until closer to the conference date, and then taking up whatever role was needed. I agreed. The ambiguity in authorizing the administrative team also showed up in the fact that the team's lead was the Associate Director for Administration, and every member on the team was called an Assistant Director for Administration. This title inflation was confusing in that everyone was referred to as an "ADA"; it was also confusing in that it was difficult to identify where the authority lay at any given moment in the conference. This ambiguity in authorization of the administrative team I attribute to the Director (top-down).

In a parallel process, there were many bottom-up challenges to the Director's authorization from the Associate Director for Administration and the administrative team. The Director tasked the Associate Director for Administration to be the head of both the administrative team and the cultural interpreters' team. The Director also tasked me, a member of the administrative team, to mentor my Associate Director for Administration as she was new to group relations work. The Associate Director for Administration was thus authorized and de-authorized in her role as head of the administrative team. This confusing setup likely contributed to the Associate Director for Administration "abandoning" the administrative team and working only with the cultural interpreters' team. She put me in charge of the administrative team and its tasks for the duration of the conference, but I lacked the formal authorization to make decisions.

My authorizing-deauthorizing continued in that the other two administrators, whom I was tasked to "lead," were staff members working for one of our host institutions. They were performing duties for their full-time jobs while assisting with administrative tasks when asked, so they were not available for administrative or all-staff meetings. They did not take on a full conference staff role thus did not authorize the conference Directorate – or me – to consult to them on unprocessed dynamics. They also frequently deployed a "shadow" administrative team (facilities personnel at this host institution) that spoke and answered to them and not to any other conference staff member. This "shadow" team also was not available to attend any staff meetings. When the host administrators and their "shadow" team experienced burnout from undigested conference dynamics, they came to me with their displeasure, not in their roles as administrators for the GRC, but in their roles as staff of the host institution of the conference, with threats of consequences for the conference. These authority issues were difficult to experience, but provided memorable lessons to learn.

Role

I experienced what someone from the Administration Mashup workshop called "the isolation of the director." In addition, I experienced the isolation of the director-administrator pair from the rest of the conference such that various projections and dynamics of the conference system are located in this pair rather than shared and metabolized by the staff system. As previously mentioned, during the conference proper I was effectively the only full member of the administrative team. The Associate Director for Administration had left me in charge while she tended to the cultural interpreter team. A woman who worked as administrator during the months leading up to the conference switched roles to work only as a cultural interpreter during the conference. The other two administrators were full-time staff members at one of our sponsor institutions. They, along with the "shadow" administrative team that worked for them, did not take on the full conference staff roles as they did not agree to the staff contract with the Director to attend staff meetings, to examine group dynamics and authority relationships, or to stay past the hours of their day jobs to support this conference. Given the lack of available administrators to take up the administrative role during the conference, and the lack of direction and consultation from the Associate Director for Administration, I found myself working mostly alone directly for the Director, in the isolation of the director-administrator pair. Case in point, there were two conference hotels, and the Associate Director for Administration had assigned me a room in the same hotel as the Director, while assigning herself a room in the other hotel, along with the cultural interpreter team. As such, I was the one sitting with the Director in our hotel lobby at night, helping him update drafts of his opening statements and other conference documents, even though in the past this has been the role of the head of the administrative team.

Boundary

According to a brainstorm exercise during the workshop, one quality that the administrator wants in a director is "respect for the administrator's limits and space." In this conference, I learned experientially how challenging it can be to hold the boundaries and be a container for the conference in my role as administrator when my role boundaries are shifted around on an ad hoc basis by the Director or the Associate Director of Administration. Both the Director and the Associate Director of Administration assigned me the additional and last-minute role of temporary cultural interpreter during parts of the conference. And I obliged. Learning from my experience in this conference, I try to be more clear and strong when asserting my needs and limits to the Director and to the Associate Director for Administration.

Schaumburg, IL 2015 GRC on authority and
leadership in recovery from addiction

Role

The value I place on the administrative role, which I internalized thanks to the Administrative Mashup Workshop, was reciprocated during the last staff meeting of our conference. A consultant-in-training remarked she was jealous of the administrative team and wished she had been on it. The idea that an administrative team could be a desirable place for someone seeking a staff position rather than just a necessary step to something greater is something I am glad that one more person shares.

Conclusions and future directions

One goal we did not achieve was to use the workshop to explore how GRC administration compares (and/or contrasts) with administration outside conferences. It is our collective impression that lessons learned from group relations administration experiences would have a number of applications in the worlds of business, education, healthcare and social services as a minimum. If future administration workshops were longer, it would seem logical to focus on the application of processes and learning in ways analogous to the approaches used in GRCs.

We view the administration workshop that we conducted in 2013 as a pilot study. In retrospect, it was fortunate that the numbers were small: among other things, it allowed us to have each of the pair exercises observed by a staff member. Overall, we view the initial attempt to provide structured yet experiential learning about administration and the administrative roles in GRCs a success (the evaluations by other participants were similar to Victoria's, though without the benefit of two additional years to test its value). While the workshop could be squeezed into a single 11-hour day, we think the overnight break was valuable, both for staff, who met in the evening to review the workshop's progress, and for the participants who had more time to process their first two pair exercises before doing the final one. We hope others in group relations with an interest in conference administration will feel inspired to explore and extend our model.

Appendix A

The administrative mashup: a dialogue between transformational and transactional leaders, between zombies and vampires

Workshop schedule

Day 1

9:00–10:30	Staff meeting
11:00–12:30	Introductory mashup: you and us
12:30–1:30	Lunch – staff and participants together
1:30–3:15	First pair exercise
3:15–3:45	Break
3:45–5:15	Second pair exercise
5:30	End of first day
6:30–8:00	Staff meeting

Day 2

7:30–8:30	Staff breakfast meeting
8:30–10:00	Third pair exercise
10:00–10:30	Break
10:30–11:30	"What could go wrong?"
11:30–12:30	Top ten things…
	Wrap up

Appendix B

The pair exercise

Each 90-minute pair exercise gives each member of the pair a chance to be in the role of Administrator and Director. A task will be presented from each of three phases of a group relations conference:

1. Pre-conference long before the conference will begin
2. Pre-conference, but at the conference site shortly before the start of the conference
3. During the conference

During the first 45 minutes of each pair exercise, one of the pair will be in the Administrator role for 15 minutes while the other is in the Director role; they switch roles in the next 15 minutes. They will be observed by a member of the workshop staff, and during the final 15 minutes, preliminary feedback and discussion will occur.

The second 45 minutes is a plenary discussion of the exercise, where we will have a chance to discuss and explore the different choices each pair made in addressing its task.

Acknowledgement

The authors would like to acknowledge and thank Charla Hayden and John Robertson for their participation as staff at the 2013 Administration Workshop. We also wish to recognize the work of the planning group: Paula Cramer, Charla Hayden, Edward Klein, Marc Kessler, Neil Neidhardt, John Robertson, Gordon Strauss and Kevin Wilson.

References

Aram, E., Baxter, R. and Nutkevitch, A. (Eds.) (2015). *Group Relations Work: Exploring the Impact and Relevance Within and Beyond its Network*. London: Karnac.

Gold, V., Haywood, M., and Lee, E., (1993). Internal caring: the role of administration in Tavistock Group Relations Conferences, in K. West, C. Haden, and R. Sharrin, (Eds.), *Chaos & Community*. Proceedings of the Eleventh Scientific Meeting of the A.K. Rice Institute.

Josselson, R., Khaleelee, O., and Sher, M. et al. (2015). The experiences of co-directorship in group relations conferences, in E. Aram, R. Baxter and A. Nutkevitch (Eds.), *Group Relations Work: Exploring the Impact and Relevance Within and Beyond its Network*. London: Karnac

Nahum, T. and Shafer, A. (2000). The role of the "conference Administrator". Paper presented to the 2nd Scientific Conference of the Australian Institute of Socio-Analysis, Canberra.

Shafer, A. (2006). Multi-level application of group relations conference learning: staff, members and sponsoring organizations, in L. Brunner, A. Nutkevitch, and M. Sher (Eds.), *Group Relations Conferences: Reviewing and Exploring Theory, Design, Role Taking and Application* (pp.1123–1138), London: Karnac.

A conference in the shadow of war – a sealed room or a safe area?

Miri Tsadok and Saliem Khliefi

The title of this lecture came up long before we knew what we are going to say and how this chapter would evolve. At the beginning, right after the conference, we knew two things: first, that leading this conference during the war was challenging in a unique way. Second, that the images "sealed room" or "safe area" came up during the conference as a metaphor for the questions we were dealing with. A "sealed room" and a "safe area" are concepts that belong to the terminology of war-time Israel. The "sealed room" is for protection against chemical weapons; the "safe area" is for protection against conventional weapons.

17 July 2014 saw the beginning of Ofek's Hebrew language Group Relations conference, entitled "Authority, Leadership and Role – to Lead, to Surrender, to Change."

Tzuk eitan (called internationally "protective edge"), a military operation which later developed into a full blown, bloody war, with its terrible cost to the Middle East, had begun a week before. The days before the conference were accompanied by alarms and rockets landing almost all over Israel, while at the same time Israeli air-craft were heavily bombing Gaza.

Doubts and hesitations filled us: should we insist on holding the conference under these circumstances? There were logistical questions: we were not sure how many; there would be cancellations among the participants: people called up to the army; people who wouldn't leave their families in this vulnerable situation and others who would not feel like they could be available mentally for this kind of activity. We faced logistical difficulties concerning the staff as well – one of our consultants could not make himself available for work since his son, an officer in the military, was scheduled to go into Gaza; our administrator had a role in the emergency services of the municipality and was not sure until the last minute if she could and should take up her role in the conference. But above all, there was a more basic question: Would it be possible to build an effective space for learning and reflection? Would it be *right* to continue "business as usual" while such massive destruction was taking place? Weren't we at risk of creating a "sealed room", or on the other hand failing to build a "safe area" to work?

We will try to link our assumption is that this dilemma touches on a much broader topic. We will explore the role of Group Relations theory and practice and relate it to the wellbeing of society in general and specifically in times of social crisis as we describe the processes before, during and after the conference.

Organizational and theoretical background

Ofek's Hebrew language Group Relations conference is like the "younger brother" of the annual international conference. It takes place once every two or three years. Its duration is 4–5 days and the language spoken is Hebrew rather than English. These attributes – the Hebrew language and the shorter duration – make the conference significantly more convenient to participants as well as staff. They might also contribute to the very unique identity which this conference has developed in the course of its existence. Among other things, it is more attuned to issues that Israeli society is preoccupied with at the time of its happening.

At the time of writing the brochure, months before the conference, we obviously did not anticipate that war would break out. We were concerned with the crisis of trust between the Israeli people and their leadership. In the brochure we prepared, we wrote:

> The conference takes place in Israel in 2014, a time of general economic growth and stability, alongside socio-economic gaps which are deepening ...incidents of corruption and status abuse undermine trust and

raise the question if there is, or could there be, a leadership that justifies followership and surrendering to leadership.

The issue of leadership and surrender had an impact on our choice of the conference's theme: *authority, leadership and role – to lead, to surrender, to change*. It stemmed from the idea that much emphasis is put on leadership but not enough attention is given to the conditions which are needed in order to follow. As Obholzer and Miller (2004) noted: "For the organization to be creative it requires followership to be an active process of participation in the life of the common venture" (p. 33), i.e, the opposite of passive and submissive compliance.

One of the key concepts we defined in the brochure was the pair: leading and surrendering: "Every process of change requires a leading movement, but at the same time it requires the counter-movement of surrender and followership." A study conducted by the Weizmann Institute and recently published under the title "Crazy Ants Have Some Serious Lessons for Society" illuminates the issue of leadership and followership from a different angle. The researchers investigated the behavior of ants when introduced to the common task of carrying a piece of food. This task requires the cooperation of dozens of ants. Hours of observation revealed that an amazing balance of conformism and individualism enabled the achievement of this task. The researchers described it as a leadership that is based solely on the competence relevant to the task in the moment; a few seconds after the leader loses her ability to direct, another ant emerges to take up the leadership role. What fascinated us in these findings, was the evidence that the knowledge regarding potential leadership exists and circles around within the system, enabling the transition of roles.

The term "surrender" was introduced to psychoanalytic discourse by Emanual Ghent (1990).

Ghent's basic idea is that surrender, is a state of free movement, of being in the moment, totally in the present: "Its ultimate direction is the discovery of one's identity, one's sense of self, one's sense of wholeness, even one's sense of unity with other living beings" (p. 109).

This idea corresponds with the term "organization in the mind" coined and elaborated upon by David Armstrong (1997). Armstrong developed the idea "that emotional experience is very rarely located within a purely individual space" (p.3) and that the organization exists within the person-in-role: "I seek to understand these experiences as expressing the client's relatedness to the organization, as saying something about the organization-in-his-mind, not just metaphorically but literally" (p.4). What underlies both is the notion that the individual does not exist in a "sealed jar," the experiential acknowledgment of this is the basis of surrender.

Back to our term "safe area": we are talking about a state or space that is both the precondition and the product of surrender. We could imagine a spiral process in which a good enough setting enables the reduction of resistance and facilitates a process of self-discovery that is less defensive.

We suggest that the primary task of Group Relations conferences is to build a safe area that enables the exploration of the experience of the individual in relation to his or her environment. A safe area is, in a sense, a possible place to play within. Play, as Winnicott taught us, is an essential element in our development. The ability to play is based on the possibility to move freely between the sphere of reality and the sphere of the imagination. One can let oneself express wishes and drive playfully, only if one can be sure that there is someone who stands guard and makes sure the game is not going to become an existential danger. Existential danger is the ant-thesis of the 'play experience'.

In his article *Dreaming, Fantasying, and Living,* Winnicott (1971) differentiates dreaming from fantasying, a distinction that helps us to clarify the difference between a "safe area" and a "sealed room": dreaming, he says, belongs to the realm of real living and relates to real objects, while fantasying or day dreaming, "remains an isolated phenomenon, absorbing energy but not contributing – in either to dreaming or to living"(p. 31). _When describing the early childhood of the patient, the subject of the article, Winnicott says that although he could identify some difficulties in the early relationship with the mother and the father as well, the developmental failure was mainly due to the fact that the patient, being the youngest child, entered the group of elder brothers. The little girl "found herself in a world that was already organized before she came into the nursery" (p 34). Thanks to her talents and high intelligence, she had managed to fit in, but without being able really to contribute and influence the group play. Her fitting in was on a compliance basis: "The games were unsatisfactory for her, because she was simply struggling to play *whatever role was assigned to her*" (p. 34).[1]

In line with these ideas we would suggest that without the ability to invent and create our role in play, we could not have real contact with life; in other words, it is taking the role as an act of surrender that enables us to play, dream and live.

Winnicott clarifies that despite the subtle and somewhat evasive difference between dreaming and fantasying, these two are entirely different modes of relating to life and creation: "It will be observed that creative playing is allied to dreaming and to living but essentially does not belong to fantasying" (p. 37).

Holding the conference in the shadow of a war – the dilemma

In the case of this specific conference the challenge was double: first, how to build a safe area in spite of the "noise" of the outside reality or, in Winnicott's terms, the danger of impingement that would intrude on the potential space. Was it relevant in the reality of war?

A week after our conference took place, a workshop was scheduled to take place as part of the P.O.C.D. (program in organizational consultation and development). The leading staff member from abroad canceled his participation. He cited safety considerations at first, but later on he admitted honestly that he could not come in the present circumstances of violent reality. He was unsure of the value of Group Relations work in this context. One could argue with this conclusion, and many staff members and students were hurt by his decision. We imagined that the decision itself was accompanied by feelings of distress on his side. One might see this refusal as an alternative to our decision to hold the conference, an echo of our doubts at the pre-conference stage: Isn't it arrogant and presumptuous to insist on holding the conference in these circumstances? Aren't we at risk of day dreaming or fantasizing?

In retrospect, we believe that it was the right thing to do. By holding the conference, we created and protected an island of sanity in a state of insanity.

We will try to describe the process we went through, each one from his or her perspective, with the intention of bringing it as close as possible to the actual experience. To that end we will switch between two modes of stories: Miri's story and Saliem's story.

Miri's story

Looking back, I wonder when it all began … It is not easy to set a starting point. Was it the first day of the conference when I was standing in the reception area, welcoming the participants on their arrival, all excited, matching each name that I knew from a list to the face who was now in front of me?

Or, perhaps it all began when I first took the role of consultant in a conference, years ago? Or even earlier when I first participated in a Group Relations conference?

I have decided to start from the time that the Ofek Board approached me and asked me to take the role of directing the upcoming Israeli conference (over a year before the actual conference). It was a surprise but I was ready to meet the challenge. I did not have previous experience in directing a conference, nor of being an Associate Director and yet, I felt it was the right time for me.

I approached Saliem and invited him to be my Associate Director. We had worked very well together in the past and I have great respect for him, although deep inside I was also pleased that this conference would be directed by an Arab-Jewish team. At the time, I had no idea how meaningful and precious, this would be.

Although the reality of war and violence is unfortunately well known to us in Israel, the breaking out of the war caught me unprepared. I was outraged! How in one fell swoop my painstaking work of almost a year would be destroyed. I met full on the experience of the devastating destructiveness of war and its utter opposition to the work of living.

The atmosphere of the days before the conference were heavy with tension between Arabs and Jews. A terror event of kidnapping and then murder of three Jewish boys shocked the country. Gangs of extreme right-wing nationalists (*lehava*) were storming the streets, attacking people with an Arab appearance. Demonstrations protesting against racism were held. I felt the urge to participate in these demonstrations. Not surprisingly, this claim for peace was countered by anger from others. The police barely succeeded in preventing an escalation of violence. At a certain moment, while standing there, surrounded by this angry and screaming crowd, I felt anxious, helpless and furious. I realized then that what prevented me from conducting myself with tolerance and peace was the fear I experienced. The screams were mostly coming from youngsters whom I would identify as "deprived youngsters." Some of them I could have met in different circumstances as direct or indirect clients. But at this moment they were my enemy, an enemy I could not and would not have discourse with (Erlich 2013).

I do want to suggest that Group Relations conferences are an opportunity to create a safe area for talking with the enemy – not necessarily the political enemy but enemies of various kinds that we instinctively want to get rid of, or to ignore.

We had hoped that the conference would attract Arab participants. If it had, we could say that we were building an island of peace and tolerance. Common exploration of the group and the inter-group processes in such intensive encounter would be a satisfactory achievement.

Unfortunately, we did not succeed in recruiting even one Arab participant, Saliem will relate to this and to his experience as the sole Arab at this conference.

Now, I would like to describe a critical event which concerns the question of "safe area" versus "sealed room":

During the third large-group session, I was standing by the door, in my role as "gate keeper," responsible for closing the door at the designated time. Two minutes before, Ruth came rushing into the room, slamming the door in my face. Haim Deutsch, the third consultant, who is an observant Jew, and Saliem were already sitting inside. I joined them silently, but inside felt shaken. The talk began. A young participant shared her dream about a king who was attacked by his people right after the coronation ceremony. While she spoke, there was much movement in the room, as people were trying to fill empty seats. (This motif accompanied us throughout the large-group sessions; there always was at least one empty chair.) A man who was seated by an empty chair said he felt lonely. A woman volunteered to move next to him but by doing so, she created another empty chair and another participant said: "now I am the one who is left out." The words "outsider" and "lonely" were introduced into the discourse of the group.

At one point, a male participant recalled the scene of the opening plenary of sub-conference A: "It was like religious ceremony. I felt like turning upside down their chairs and calling towards these eight consultants who sat like idols: what is this idolatry? I felt like shattering the golden calf." There were laughs of appreciation. I commented: "I could tell myself that the talk was about those eight and not about us, the three consultants in the room, but I could not ignore the slamming of the door that I witnessed at the opening of this session, an act that suggests anger towards the authority in this room, here and now." The laughing continued but gradually subsided and turned into silence. Then, a painful cry from Ruth penetrated the silence: "I cannot stop thinking that while we are sitting comfortably here, thousands of citizens in Gaza are losing their houses and are being evacuated from their homes. How can we sit here, knowing that this is going on around us now?"

It seems as if that cry came right from the core of our common worry, of creating a bubble, a "sealed room" dominated by an omnipotent and egocentric fantasy.

Actually, we could identify the precursor of this cry in the conversation about the king who was attacked and the urge to shatter the golden calf. I tried to give an echo to this cry and suggested: "It seems the group is asking what kind of authority allows all that? The authority outside and the authority within? How can we trust authority?"

It was a painful moment for us all. Various voices were raised as a reaction to this claim, nods of agreement along with disagreement: "but this is always true, terrible things happen all the time, should we stop everything?" And later: "it is a pity that the government is not sitting here in this conference; they desperately need it."

It is worth mentioning that Ruth, "the voice of protest," collapsed physically from dehydration on the last day of the conference and required urgent medical assistance. This precipitated a meaningful drama on the boundary of my role. When I heard about her physical state, I had the urge to go to her room and check directly how she was doing. The administrators held me back assertively saying: "this is our role, not yours!" They were right and helped me keep myself within my role. In retrospect, I think that my difficulty might be linked to the fact that a part of myself identified with this protesting voice. I guess there was a similar voice within myself as well, that had the urge to stop everything and to declare: no more play, we cannot continue business as usual!

Almost a year after the conference, following a meeting with Saliem to prepare for our lecture, I had a dream: we are both at a conference, in a hall that is built like a small amphitheater, surrounded by a green and cultivated lawn and ancient buildings. It resembled an archeological site. The group atmosphere is stormy and the conference seems on the verge of explosion. I urgently approach a participant who is trying to present her work and say to her: we must work on your pairing state! I am aware that while I intervene in this way, I myself am pushing my partner aside. But my words work like a magic; she accepts them and I announce to the rest of the group that we are taking a short break and will continue shortly.

To my great relief, I see that the people who were beginning to leave the conference were calming down. I know I had succeeded in stopping the break up and in making us return to work.

It seems that the dream expressed a sense of emergency that requires a sharp and precise action but at the same time creates space for reflection (we need to work on your pairing state).

The transformation that took place in the dream from leaving as an act of breaking up, to leaving for a break in the work is the essence of building the safe area.

Of course, the dream also reveals something of Saliem's and my dilemma while working together at the conference and while preparing the talk: how to work separately, but retain togetherness at the same time.

Saliem's story

I was raised as an Arab. A fact I didn't know in my childhood; it was something I had to discover (and explore) with time. Discovering that I am an Arab led eventually and inevitably to discover other, non-Arab sectors, one of them being "Jews" and this drew me into the heart of the most complex relations between these different groups. I grew up in a home that did not emphasize the identity issue, in a world where people are equal, similar, with no differences, a kind of an ideal world or perhaps a utopian one. However, in time, and with exposure to the unavoidable reality, I had to understand that things were more complicated than they seemed, and what could I do? There were people with different identities, including Jews. And that is how a lifetime of "coping with the conflict" began.

Being a Jew has many connotations and associations for an Arab; conquering, oppressing, controlling, and "bad." At the same time being an Arab evokes many images that did not fit with what I felt is an Arab. These associations confused me because they contradicted the values that I was raised with. But in order to belong and feel related and comfortable, I had to conform and adopt to one specific view, and in this way attempt to spare myself the struggle of coping with contradictions.

Later on, this confusion became stronger. I could see the situation from a more complicated perspective. The Jews that I met, I noticed, did not exactly fit the images I had of them. I felt more and more confused. My search for the truth led to increasingly perplexed feelings and sometimes to anger. It was like being stuck between two worlds. The more ambivalent my feelings towards the conflict became, the harder was it for me to belong: I could not be fully an Arab, but I couldn't fully belong to the Jews either. Was this an identity crisis? I didn't know, but then I consoled myself with the thought that the world was confused, not me.

Within this complicated situation, I made my way living in two worlds: having relations with people from the "other side," adopting strategies like avoiding politics and trying to demonstrate the "other side" of the Arabs.

It was with this background and with the desire to contain complications and to minimize the gaps between people, or perhaps within me, that I was exposed to the "Group Relations" method.

As with every conference, the challenge that I faced was recruitment. I believed in my abilities to make people interested as I believed in the conference, the attitude, and the perspective. But most importantly, I believed in the personal input and the experience that this conference would allow participants to gain. I naively believed that "of course, all my friends will take part." I prepared a long list of friends, people I know, professionals, and potential members from my society, and the marketing process began.

I faced the first challenge: how to market the conference? What to say? Where to start? I phoned lots of friends, professionals and those I thought might be interested. People seemed to be curious and willing to participate; they asked about the date and other specific details, so I was sure many would come. It is going to be a successful conference! I did it! I congratulated myself.

As time passed and the political situation worsened, I noticed that the people I had spoken to did not register. A feeling of discomfort and difficulty enveloped me. Was it the right time to follow up and call people? Was it really the right time to create a dialogue with the other side? I started to make follow-up calls to the interested people while feeling embarrassed but intent on succeeding.

I remember this period as a very difficult one; most of those that I talked to apologized but did not register; my self-confidence was undermined, and I was filled with frustration and feelings of disappointment. Important issues came to my mind: I had invited Arab participants to a conference with Jews in order to create a dialogue and to learn, while feelings of hostility and fear surrounded both sides. Feelings of aggression prevailed. Very soon I understood that I would be fulfilling the role of the missionary, and the fact that I agreed to be part of it was conceived by some Arabs as compromising and legitimizing the other side's policy. People didn't want to forgive or have a dialogue and learn; they only wanted to fight and boycott.

Taking part in a dialogue in a conference was conceived as renunciation of one's principles, or one's identity. As one of my colleagues said: "A dialogue in a war that we won't win? Why participate?"

Alone and lonely I attended the conference, an Arab, the only Arab who agreed to participate. It was really difficult. I didn't know how it would affect me. Would the participants ignore or notice me? Would it be comfortable for me to be ignored? Would they fight me? Would I be the enemy? Was I participating to change the image of the Arab (the friendly Arab)? Would I endure the difficulties? I felt that being an Arab at the conference became my entire existence; I lost my other parts.

Several more challenges were waiting for me at the conference, for example, the large group. The group was huge in my eyes, while I was feeling lonely and confused sitting in the middle, thinking which place should I take? What connotations will be associated with me? My eyes looked into the participants' confused eyes, trying to find a logic and words to intervene, to speak out loud my loneliness, alienation and the feeling of being different, not always succeeding.

Slowly, within the emotional storm, and when personal and emotional stories that echoed my feelings were told, I felt more and could feel their feelings and find myself in them, or find theirs in me. That created a sense of safety and connectedness to the group.

From that safe and close position I created within me in the group, and the discussions about the war and differences, my Arab identity started to grow and revive itself. It impacted my perception, my understanding of the group process, and shaped my thoughts.

The following example will help me to explain the process I went through among the group:

During the second meeting of the large group, a religious participant, despite his efforts not to, eventually found himself sitting next to Haim (who is as mentioned above was an observant Jew). When I listened to him I had various feelings and thoughts. I was jealous of Haim as someone found him as his safe place. I felt alone and wondered whether someone would find in me a safe place as well. I was frightened of staying outside, or to being tagged as "bad," or "not relevant." The gap between Haim and me got wider, yet between Miri and me it got smaller. It is difficult to describe. I did not want to be irrelevant and left out; I wanted to fight Haim maybe in order to win Miri. Feelings of aggression overwhelmed me. In that moment, another participant commented that she preferred to sit next to an Arab consultant rather than a religious one.

I was surprised. It felt good to know that my identity resonated with the participants. I could reunite with the group. I had a better hold on my feelings but still I couldn't collect my thoughts with any understandable reason. Was it a complement? It was really nice to hear, but still, as Miri intervened later, it may have also been an attack on the Arab consultant.

Slowly, I found myself connecting between the external and the internal realities, between the war "outside" and my imaginary war, the one between Haim and me, between my different identities, between the participants. In other words, the war outside lived also within us; it existed between Haim and me; it existed between the participants and the staff, and between the participants and themselves.

One of the thoughts I had during the session was about us three consultants, from different backgrounds, sitting together, having the same role and the same task. I wondered how the participants perceived us. A previous experience may illuminate the question.

When I was at school, we had several meetings with Jewish students. Before the meeting, we had to go through a preparation process with Arab and Jewish facilitators. I always fantasized that the facilitators enjoyed a peaceful relationship between themselves, but we the students did not. Maybe this experience shaped my understanding of the participants at that moment.

Back to the group – the experience of splitting between me and Haim, could be seen as an attempt to bring the external reality into the group. We, as staff, were possibly perceived as a "model of peace," of co-existence, not interfering with one with the other, working together in harmony, and sticking together to the task; this may have aroused envy in the participants as if we were creating a work of art, that others in the room were not able to do. Perhaps splitting the facilitators was an attempt to transcribe the reality, the social construct and the external war inside the group, as if we the consultants had to fight between us, because there was no place for peace during these stormy days. The external stress was transcribed to the internal sphere in order to balance between these two spheres.

Conclusion

We have tried to illustrate that leading the conference in these circumstances was accompanied by the risk of creating a "cocoon," a "sealed room." In analogy to the position of the mother in the face of her baby's distress we associate our stance in the conference to Bion's description of the emotional position – open to the storm but able to think the distress and contain it (Bion 1967).

The challenge we were facing was how to hold the war outside in our minds without denial on the one hand, and without submission to its destructiveness on the other. Did we meet this challenge?

It is not easy to answer this definitively, but it seems that it was possible to reflect and explore the inter-group processes in a way that could rise above the splitting mode of "them and us."

At the conference, as opposed to the demonstration that we described before, we think we succeeded in creating a space for a discourse about various kinds of experiences: of alienation and estrangement; of the dark skinned with the foreign accent, of the orthodox Jewish woman, and the one who simply felt himself an outsider in the group. The issue of "otherness" came up and was expressed in various ways in the different units of work in the conference.

The transformative movement was symbolically expressed in the last large-group meeting by the participant who previously declared her aversion to religious people. She sat next to Haim and said with a smile on her face: "I chose to sit here."

In his article *Discourse with the Enemy*, Shmuel Erlich (2013) relates to this shift as the transition from the narcissistic dyad to the Oedipal trio in which there is space for the third to exist:

> "The Oedipal trio signifies something quite different. it says, "you too are human, *although* you are different from me." It is therefore *inclusive* and allows diversity in sameness."

> (p.98, emphasis in the original)

We would like to end with a quote from a poem written by Tich naht Hahn, a Zen Buddhist teacher from Vietnam who lives in France. The story around the poem is that it was written as a reaction to a terrible event of rape and violent attack on a boat of refugees from Vietnam. Tich naht Hahn went into the woods and after being there three days, he returned with this poem:

> I am the twelve-year-old girl,
> refugee on a small boat,
> who throws herself into the ocean

after being raped by a sea pirate.
And I am the pirate,
my heart not yet capable
of seeing and loving.
— —

My joy is like Spring, so warm
it makes flowers bloom all over the Earth.
My pain is like a river of tears,
so vast it fills the four oceans.
Please call me by my true names.

Note

1. It is interesting to note that in this article, the etiology of this tendency (absorption in fantasying) is rooted in disturbed relations with a group.

References

Armstrong, D. (1997). The "institution in the mind", reflection on the relation of psych-analysis to work with institutions. *Free Associations* 7(1).

Bion, W.R. (1967). *Second Thoughts*. London: Karnac.

Efrati, I. (2015). Crazy Ants Have Some Serious Lessons for Society in https://www.haaretz.com/science-and-health/crazy-ants-have-some-serious-lesson-for-society-1.5387955

Erlich, H.S. (2013). Discourse with the enemy. In *The Couch in the Marketplace*. London: Karnac.

Ghent, E. (1990). Masochism, submission, surrender: masochism as a perversion of surrender. *Contemporary Psychoanalysis*, 26.

Levy, J., Kaplan, O., Nutkevich, A. and Tsadok, M. (2006). Learning from experience, and the experience of learning in the academic setting. In E. Aram, R. Baxter, and A. Nutkevitch (Eds.), *Group Relations Conferences, Tradition, Creativity and Succession in the Global Relations Network*, Vol. 3. London: Karnac.

Obholzer, A and Miller, S. (2004). Leadership, fellowship, and facilitating the creative workplace. In C. Huffington, D. Armstrong, W. Halton, and J. Pooley (Eds.), *Working Below The Surface. The Emotional Life of Contemporary Organizations*. London and New York: Karnac.

Winnicott, D.W. (1971). Dreaming, fantasying, and living: a case-history describing a primary dissociation. *Playing and Reality*.

INTRODUCTION TO SECTION III

Exploring the discourse of business in Group Relations

This section picks up the theme at the Belgirate V conference about "doing the business of Group Relations" (GR). What all of these chapters share is the energy and creativity that "the business of group relations" can engender, including the challenges, the pleasures and the risks.

In the chapter that opens the section, Louisa Diana Brunner invites us to consider not only what we are doing when we conduct a GRC, but more broadly what we are doing in and with GR as an international community. She is clear that what we are *not* doing is anything that meets her definition of a business. In exploring what she calls "enterprises of passion," she touches on or introduces themes which show up in many of the other four chapters in this section.

The chapter by Eduardo Acuña and Matías Sanfuentes traces the history and development of GR in Chile during and after the era of the Pinochet dictatorship. The authors illustrate both the role of cooperation as well as the limiting effects of competition within GR. Also to be noted in this chapter are the risks that Acuña and his colleagues ran in putting on GRCs and integrating GR thinking into their business school curriculum in an era of political repression.

The chapter by Seth Harkins and his colleagues gives a detailed and fascinating account of the 2014 GRC held in Beijing, China. First, the development of a new GRC role – the cultural interpreter – represents a true innovation of conference design. However, like many innovations, this one was accompanied by many challenges, most of which played out in the realm of role and task boundaries. The other unique aspect of this chapter are the accounts by several of the authors about how their conference experience as multi-ethnic staff members led them to reflect on the (group) dynamics of multi-ethnicity.

The chapter by Barbara Lagler Özdemir and Hüseyin Özdemir does something all too rare in the GR literature: present the experience and learning from a series of GRCs "in the real business world." Their focus is on in-house GRCs conducted with their corporate and OD clients, all of whom are top and senior executives. They summarize their work with clients in 11 in-house conferences in six countries over the past 14 years.

The final chapter in this section, by Ugo Merlone and John Wilkes, addresses some of the themes introduced in Louisa Diana Brunner's section-opening chapter. Why have the number of GRCs fluctuated? Why have the number of GR organizations grown to more than 35 worldwide (see their Table 3.5.1)? What is the role of covert competition? In an effort to examine these questions – couched within a hypothesis based on the Tragedy of the Commons – they devised an experiential learning exercise which they piloted at the A.K. Rice Institute Dialogues meeting earlier in 2015 before using it at Belgirate.

Group Relations conferences

Can enterprises with passion become businesses?

Louisa Diana Brunner

Introduction

Nearly 20 years ago I attended my first Leicester Conference as a member. At the time I did not know anything about Group Relations conferences, I had gone to Leicester to train on leadership and authority. It was such a shock to find myself in that unexpected setting. That conference was an epiphany for me, the start of my Group Relations conferences experience as participant and staff, and the approach has become a great passion.

I learned three important things at that Leicester Conference. First of all, always ask yourself why you have been called to do a certain task at a particular moment and in that specific role. Second, work with your own experience. Third, if you formulate and offer a hypothesis, you need to sustain it with thorough evidence.

Turning to the first question, I have asked myself why I was invited to present a keynote in that moment in Belgirate. The first answer I gave myself is that because I am Italian the invitation is in recognition of the land where the Belgirate Conference takes place[1] and of the Italian Group Relations community. We were a very small Group Relations community when we started in 1998, now thanks to all the hard work of many colleagues, we are well established in the international community.

The second answer I gave myself to why me at that particular moment, is that I work mainly in the business world and the word business was in the title of the fifth Belgirate Conference and I could contribute from this perspective.

At the Belgirate Conference, I did not give a traditional lecture, but I presented a PowerPoint presentation which included two videos. This chapter is built on that presentation. Like the presentation in Belgirate, it is a sort of research diary on some themes that have preoccupied me through the years. In preparing the presentation and this chapter, I was inspired, on the one hand, by cummings[2] (1991) who said 'Let me cordially warn you, at the opening of these so-called lectures, that I haven't the remotest intention of posing as a lecturer. Lecturing is presumably a form of teaching; and presumably a teacher is somebody who knows. I never did, and still don't, know. What has always fascinated me is not teaching, but learning...'. So also for me learning from the experience of writing, presenting and from colleagues' suggestions was the main aim. On the other hand, Erlich-Ginor (2006) suggests that Group Relations conferences are 'Tools that are useful in creating potential spaces and in the service of generating meaning. Group Relations provide containers for play and exploration in the area of learning about authority, leadership and organization ... through playing and creativity.' So, I positioned the presentation at Belgirate as a playful exploration rather than as an attempt at a definitive theoretical academic exposition.

The presentation and this chapter are not specifically on conference experiences, but about us, as a whole Group Relations community of practice. The initiating idea was that I feel that as Group Relations community and practitioners, we are going through an identity crisis which affects many dimensions of our work:

- Businesswise, on how to position Group Relations conferences in the global and globalized training and consultancy context and market.
- Organisationally, from a hierarchical vertical oedipal to a more lateral egalitarian culture.
- Conceptually, in terms of controversies among the disciplines involved in Group Relations, e.g. psychoanalysis, systemic thinking, organisational studies or others.

- There is a tension about how much to retain from tradition, how much to be open to innovation and to be 'contaminated' by other ideas and perspectives (Erlich-Ginor, 2006). Khaleelee and White (2014) argued that the 'Group Relations model is under development ... the tradition is in transition because society is in transition ... authority and leadership struggles seem to be at the heart of the world changes' (Khaleelee and White, 2014, p.424).

As a consequence of all this and of the great changes in society, I feel passionately that we – Group Relations Practitioners or Community – are stuck in an image of ourselves or in an understanding of ourselves which blocks us both in learning and in doing business.

In this chapter I will first describe what I mean by *enterprises with passion*. Then I will discuss my hypothesis that Group Relations conferences are not business but *enterprises with passion* and that this does not allow further development especially for new audiences and markets. I will argue that our inability to address openly the experience of competition undermines our potential to move forward. I will present some evidence about this hypothesis from some specific issues: recruitment, international versus national conferences, staffing, and ambivalence and ambiguity in relation to the aim of the Group Relations conferences. I will also suggest that friendships, often deep and intimate and at the same time quite complicated, play an important role in our community and impact our culture and that of our organisation, although we do not acknowledge it publicly. Finally, inspired by the Milan 2015 Universal Expo and its symbol the *Tree of Life*, I will suggest the need for more understanding and management of the Group Relations community and network as a whole. I will conclude with some considerations on the experience of presenting in Belgirate.

Enterprises with passion

The title of the fifth Belgirate Conference was *Doing the Business of Group Relations Conferences: Un/conscious Dynamics, Systems and Ethics*. So my first question about Group Relations conferences was: are we really doing business or something else (e.g. enterprising, mission, friendship) – and why? So, I developed the idea that more than businesses, Group Relations conferences are *enterprises with passion*.

The word enterprise derives from the French *entreprendre*, and means to undertake (Kets de Vries,1996b, p.856), to begin something. According to Soanes and Stevenson (2006, p.202) an enterprise is a 'venture, project', which implies initiative, energy and passion. They (Soanes and Stevenson, 2006, p.70) also suggest that the idea of 'business' (in English) is about 'occupation, trade, craft' and therefore exchange (e.g. money or buying and selling) and establishment. So the *'entre-prendre'* dimension is more about action through an energy from inside while the 'business' one is about exchange or exchanges. *Entreprendre* has more to do with the creation of new endeavours while businesses seem more established.

At the conference in Belgirate, I showed a video in which I presented *A year of enterprises with passion – November 2014–2015*. It shows the sequence of conferences around the world, with their titles, dates and locations. It was the first time that a series of Group Relations conferences had been collected in that way. In preparing the presentation I was led by the hypothesis (see section 1) that all these conferences compete with each other and that this reality is not addressed and discussed sufficiently in our community. We compete quite destructively (rivalry) inside our community instead of collaborating to compete constructively outside to attract new audiences, have better economic returns and a 'louder voice'.

The word 'competition' comes from late Latin *competere* – *cum* (with) – *petere* (directed to, searching). It means to meet, to contend – a race, act of competing, encounter. It implies a direction, a purpose to compete for. The word conflict, on the other hand, derives from the Latin – *conflictum* – fight, crash, battle, contrast, rivalry.

Family business is a reference point for me intellectually and emotionally, since it is an area where I have worked and researched for many years. As I will argue in section 4, I would not say that the Group Relations community is similar to a family business. Nevertheless, I want to quote Miller and Rice (1988) on competition in family business because it seems relevant to my hypothesis. On the one hand, 'The driving force of industry and commerce in a capitalist economy is competition: competition for capital for investment and competition for customers. . .' (Miller and Rice, 1988, p.199). These authors also suggest that in such a competitive environment external enemies are used by groups to keep them together. Although it is not openly acknowledged, competition reverberates inside the organisations through 'competition for jobs, for wages and salaries, for status and power' (Miller and Rice, 1988, p.199). Cooperation can be a means for coping in such a competitive context. On the other hand, Miller and Rice

(1988, p.199) suggest that in 'contrast, the driving force in a family is its unity – unity based on repression or denial of internal conflict ... Competition between members must be kept low' (Miller and Rice, 1988, p.199). In a family business often, the internal needs of wellbeing and emotional support of the family are not compatible with the competitive demands of the market. This can be managed quite easily when the company is profitable and the external conditions allow it, and a 'family business sometimes can afford to ignore its competitors ...' (Miller and Rice, 1988, pp.199–200) but '... any reduction in business success may jeopardize the fragile defence against conflict...'. For a long time Group Relations conferences were successful, but I feel that now Group Relations conferences are in a challenging phase, for example in terms of recruitment of members since nowadays there are more opportunities to attend Group Relations conferences, as will be discussed in section 3.1. Our community is in quite a vulnerable place and defences against internal conflict are used.

From a psycho-dynamic perspective, therefore, it seems to me that, on the one hand, as a community we oscillate *between a basic assumption and work group 'pairing' mentality* (French and Simpson, 2010)[3] of the enterprising dimension in conceiving, designing and launching the conferences. On the other hand, we are infused with a me-ness/one-ness culture (Lawrence, Bain, and Gould, 1996) that also leads to the narcissism of the small differences symptom (Freud, 1917). For example in some conversations we name a conference according the director's name or as *my conference*. Or some intense discussions take place on who has devised an event or has offered a hypothesis or tiny differences in the design of the Conferences. I feel that there is a shortage of real collaborative experience among conferences and sponsoring organisations, beyond co-branding which in most cases seems more a marketing feature than deep cooperation. De Gooijer, in Chapte 2.1, outlines the challenges of such collaborative experiences. Furthermore, beyond the opportunity offered by the Belgirate Conferences, I feel that there is a lack of real common endeavours and related structures in order to move from an *enterprises with passion* culture to a more business-like one. I will discuss this further in section 5.

Evidence of competition

To support my hypothesis, I will present further evidence about competition in our community from four different perspectives, which are:

- Recruitment
- International versus national
- Motivation to be on the staff of Group Relations conferences
- Ambiguity and ambivalence about the primary task

Recruitment

Membership recruitment is the prerequisite to run a Group Relations conference. Without members a conference cannot take place.

My impression is that we are all competing inside our community for members: we are all fish in the same pond. This internal-intra competition can contribute to our losing sight of what people in the market really want and need in a changing global context. The following vignette clearly illustrates the competition between conferences.

> One morning in May 2015 I was working on the Belgirate presentation. I had in front of me the printed list of the Group Relations conferences from the Tavistock Institute website. A potential member, Nick (the name is a pseudonym to preserve anonymity) called to say that he could not go to the AKRI conference in Boston nor could he go to Ireland in June and wanted to know where he could go to a Group Relations conference. I had also sent him the flyer for the learning from action conference in Italy in October, an application of GR methods for Therapeutic Communities. He said his summer holidays were at the end of August, so, unfortunately, he could not go to Leicester for this reason. I checked the list to see where he could go, I felt like the best travel agency. I suggested that he should go to Goa in India since the dates were fine. He was enthusiastic and said he had never been to India. Then I felt guilty that perhaps he might not go to the Italian conference, since I am Italian and an honorary member of the sponsoring organisation, the Il Nodo Group and the Director is a friend. So I suggested that he could go to both. He said that he had already called the Nodo Group for more information, and I felt relieved.

It could be that this potential member is problematic himself. But as this vignette shows, it is difficult from a potential member's perspective to understand the differences between Group Relations conferences. The conferences are different in terms of the titles, brochures, communication and marketing, location, staff and fee. Certainly the language can be an important variable for a member. If it is an international conference a basic knowledge of English is a prerequisite. From my personal experience, location and staff are influential in a potential member's choice, more than other aspects such as the title or the conference events. But only thorough research would make it possible to understand better the impact of all these variables on members' choices.

On the other hand, from a potential staff point of view or as a member of the sponsoring organisation, I asked myself which are the main criteria for inviting a member to participate in a conference. My understanding is that the main concern is how the potential member can benefit in terms of learning and professional development. But I wonder if I have in mind all my affiliations or commitments, for example, if I am a member of staff of a conference and am invited by the director to recruit, will I be neutral and will I really be able to understand the potential members' needs? Furthermore, a colleague, who was on the staff list for the first time, recently wrote to me begging me to recruit at least one member, so that her attendance could be confirmed, and eventually also be eligible to come to the Belgirate Conference. All this raises ethical issues. It is fully understandable that a director asks a staff member to recruit, but I wonder if that is the condition for being on the staff. Personally, I think that the invitation to be on the staff should not be connected to recruitment, but on staff skills and competence.

On a similar matter – not openly spoken about, as if it were a taboo – my feeling is that in terms of our culture, the success of a conference director is evaluated on the number of participants attending the conference. Although this is not always true, I have often felt that low recruitment is perceived by directors as a narcissistic injury, all of which can get into the recruitment dynamics.

International or national conferences?

In my experience, there is a tension between international and national Group Relations conferences. This is also more extensively discussed in Chapter 1.1.

It seems that in our community there is a hierarchy in Group Relations conferences. The international dimension of the conferences is an asset and an important achievement for each Group Relations local community or sponsor. It is a *first class* conference, attractive and flamboyant, and fully recognized. But international dynamics are very different from national ones, although they are inter-penetrated. My impression is that if a conference is not international, or marketed internationally, it is considered a *second category* type of conference, therefore less attractive, less seductive and glamorous. Furthermore, national conferences are often treated as a training opportunity for new directors.

As an example, a recent Italian Group Relations conference had three international staff and ten international members. This was an excellent result, after many years of trying to establish the conference as an international one, an achievement that was also due to the great energy and marketing competences of the director. What I heard about the conference was very interesting and meaningful. In a private communication Ilana Litvin,[4] an international staff member at that conference, wrote to Luca Mingarelli, the director of that conference, about the conference dynamics. 'Globalization and its Zeitgeist encourage unions, alliances, mergers, dictate collaborations and treaties, at the same time harbouring dangerous forms of isolationism and separatism. We live in an era with constant oscillations between union and splintering... tension between union and merger on the one hand, and splitting and isolation on the other, a tug of war between hope and paranoia, between powers which wish to work together constructively, and those which fear loss – of identity, of resources, of power, and therefore undermine unions and emphasise differences'. The basic assumption which best describes this global sense of threat is me-ness/oneness...'. Litvin's description is very accurate and insightful about the global tensions in which we are all immersed. I also read that conference report[5] which was very interesting but the Italian context was hardly mentioned. I also asked some staff members and participants what emerged with regard to the Italian context dynamics and I did not get any convincing answer. The dynamics were essentially international as described by Litvin.

This reported experience made me think about how the strong effort for internationalization can lead to forms of homogenisation. An Italian, an Israeli, an American, or an Indian conference are inevitably very different from an international conference in Italy, in Israel, in the USA, in India, with obvious marketing implications. But putting it more psychoanalytically and associatively, I hypothesize that this homogenisation looks like a form of emulation. Klein (1988) suggested that emulation can be a defence against envious feelings – and I would add against the anxiety of healthy competition in our community. The risk is of losing sight of the local dynamics and opportunities and not understanding the social context in this race to establish an international conference. In some countries, a solution is to have a national and an international conference; nevertheless the hierarchy persists, perhaps unavoidably.

I do not think that homogenisation is a phenomenon which affects only Group Relations conferences. The tension between global/international and local, is something not fully addressed sociologically or psychologically. Again I am not going to propose a solution to this issue, but I just want to point it out.

3.3 Why do we work on staff of the GRC?

There are two matters which could make a Group Relations conference a business: the profit for the sponsoring organisation and staff fees. As this type of information is difficult to collect, it seems as though money may be the dark side of Group Relations. But my feeling is that profit for the sponsoring organisations is a matter which is more or less dealt with, although one could discuss what percentage of the margins on profits of the conference turnover can be taken by the sponsoring organisations. However, staff fees are a sort of taboo and a real issue. Certainly, money is not a motivator to be on the staff, since the role is usually underpaid in comparison with any consultancy on the market. An example of the complexity of the staff fee issue can be seen in an email I received after being on the staff of a five-day conference.

> Dear Louisa,
>
> I am pleased to let you know that you will receive a fee of €700 for your participation... This provides me with the opportunity to express my gratitude and appreciation for your personal contribution to the meaningful and significant work done in this conference. Clearly, the importance of your contribution is not reflected in the fee, which, as you know, is essentially determined by the conference budget...

I thought this mail was very well written and generous; I really appreciated it. But why should a director write such an email to a staff member? I felt a sense of guilt and shame in the words which I thought were problematic in respect of the task.

But being invited to be on the staff is a highly competitive endeavour since the opportunities are quite limited, therefore a very scarce resource. I will not discuss the criteria by which staff members are invited, because it is beyond the scope of this chapter, but I will focus on the motivation to be on the staff. To help me think about this issue for this chapter, I had some conversations with other Group Relations staff colleagues and friends about their motivation to work for a Group Relations conference. I was also interested in understanding this, considering that the conference staff fees are low especially with respect to business standards.

Although the number of people I contacted is a very limited sample and this is not scientific research, I organised the data I was able to collect using McClelland's (1988) three categories of *power* (individual and social), *affiliation* and *personal achievement*.

All these statements are convincing, real, and present at the same time, and others could be identified. But what mostly surprised me were the affiliation and personal achievement dimensions. All the issues described in the chart are mainly internally driven and motivate staff to work on the conference nearly for free. It is more or less voluntary job, with reimbursement of expenses. This also leads to the question about who can afford it in terms of personal earning, suggesting that it is impossible to make a full-time career out of this work. I hypothesize that 'sentient pay-off' explains why staff are willing to work at conferences for so little. But the prevalence of an inward-driven motivation instead of an outward-driven motivation, towards the market or more socially engaged activities, as it emerges from Figure 3.1, can be risky because the assumption could be

Table 3.1.1.   Types of motivation to work as Group Relations staff.

Power (individual and social)	*Affiliation*	*Personal achievement*
Influencing society, having an impact	Part of a community of practice	Find the intimacy and closeness experienced in the conferences
Exploring society – a laboratory of social identity	International dimension and working with interesting colleagues	Self- development of the staff
A mission: spreading our values (ideology) or active citizenship	A "family" deep friendships	A continuation of our own learning experience – on going training
The prestige of being on the staff and recognized	Travelling opportunities	Mutual self-help

Elaborated from McClelland's Human Motivation Theory (1988).

that our motivations coincide with potential members' motivations, or that what is good for us is good for members. This could also lead one to ask oneself whether the conferences fulfil members' needs or staff needs? And what is a Group Relations conference from an epistemological point of view? My understanding from the classic Rice (1965) is that Group Relations conferences are basically an educational methodology conceived as training in leadership, authority and group dynamics and *beneath the surface* unconscious processes. This is done through a residential method and on the assumption of the creation of a temporary organisation which mirrors real-life organisational experience[6]. In political terms, Group Relations is part of the post-war emancipation movements of industrial democracy and participation. It was also a time of economic boom and growth, when the market would easily absorb new products and it was enough to say that my product was the best. At that time, those who had good ideas and creativity could say, 'I like my product and I put it on the market, as I like, and the client will like it too.' In the contemporary world, in all profit and non-profit businesses, we live in a dictatorship of consumers or clients, in the sense that companies and institutions are very sensitive to consumers' or clients' feedback and needs, for example through continuous surveys and exit polls. I am not arguing that we need to be dependent on those very controversial means, but perhaps we need to approach these issues in a more business-like manner. Perhaps we need to study who our competitors are or whether our product, which we love so much – those *enterprises with passion* – are understood and are convincing for our contemporary potential clients, in order, perhaps, to market them more effectively beyond our closed circles. In this context, also the issue of the staff job as a form of volunteering should be rethought. Without losing the dimension of passion and enthusiasm, it would be important to find ways to pay the staff according to their real market value.

3.4 Ambiguity or ambivalence about the purpose of Group Relations conferences

In their research paper, Khaleelee and White (2014) portray global development and innovation in Group Relations in terms of the tension between tradition and innovation through research based on interviews with conference directors. Building on that paper, again as in section 3.3, the question which arises is what, in essence, is the real purpose of Group Relations conferences?

I identified two main aims:

- An educational aim – a training event focusing on leadership, authority, roles, groups and organisations through the study of unconscious processes (Rice, 1965).
- A political or social involvement – influencing society, having an impact (active citizenship), a laboratory of social identity through the study of unconscious processes (Erlich *et al.* 2006; Litvin and Bonwitt, 2006).

I see these two purposes as two lines of business which are both intertwined and present and I feel an ambivalence and ambiguity in the way they are pursued within the conferences' design and process.

To better understand my statement that the purpose of Group Relations conferences is both ambivalent and ambiguous, I will briefly look at these two aims, the educational and social and political involvement, to clarify why I think that they are ambivalent and ambiguous.

The educational aim

In my view, as Rice (1965) addressed it, the original education aim of Group Relations conferences was to *learn for leadership* and authority, in groups and organisations. A leadership training based on a psycho-dynamic systemic approach which, differently from other methodologies, takes into account also *beneath the surface* unconscious processes. My feeling is that this leadership training purpose is less explored now in itself organisationally, but it is combined with societal issues. The evidence is in the titles of many Group Relations conferences (e.g. see video *A Year of Enterprises with Passion – November 2014–2015* where there is often reference on the social context). Although it is an interesting phenomenon, I feel that this could be misleading, ambivalent and can be confusing for members in terms of the aim. A clear straightforward focus on leadership, authority, role and organisation, is still a strength of our methodology.

I hypothesize that the need to broaden the theme of the conferences and also include contextual issues is a consequence of today's complexity of the nature and paradigms of leadership which have evolved following changes in organisations and in society. This challenges the practitioners' work in the field and is disorienting because new ways of approaching leadership are necessary. For example at Miller's and Rice's time, leadership was motivated to maintain a balance in the achievement, power and affiliation dimension (Mc Clelland,1988) and the relationship and relatedness between leaders and followers were valued and respected. Today's research suggests instead that there has been 'a steady increase during the past decades in the number of managers for whom achievement is the primary motive' (Sprieier *et al.* 2006, p.1). Petriglieri and Petriglieri (2015, p.1) argue that leadership is an individual asset. It is perceived as an instrumental 'set of skills', a 'personal virtue', and 'a goal focus-activity'. This culture has led to *dehumanization of leadership* (Petriglieri and Petriglieri, 2015, p.5) where leaders are disconnected from the followers and the environment and are not trained to address the issues of 'for what purpose and on whose behalf ' (Petriglieri and Petriglieri, 2015, p.42). The *dehumanization of leadership* helps managers affirm precarious identities and avoid disturbing affect attendant to the experience of leading' (Petriglieri and Petriglieri, 2015, p.23) through instrumental behaviours, a loss of sensitivity, of the emotional and symbolic dimension and a disconnection 'between the inner and social words' (Petriglieri and Petriglieri, 2015, p.23). As an antidote to such a situation, Petriglieri and Petriglieri (2015) suggest that a systems-psycho-dynamic approach can help in understanding what is going on *beneath the surface* in contemporary corporate leadership and how humanization of leadership could be possible. This is nothing really new for Group Relations practitioners. This is our approach. But if we believe that this is true, as I do, this is a wonderful business opportunity for all of us to engage in, but we need to move forward to be prepared for such a challenge.

On the one hand, we need to adapt our model design to contemporary leadership and organisational needs and issues as described above. On the other hand, also on the basis of my experience of working in a business school, I think we need to find ways of approaching the business world with much more strength and conviction and sales skills and we need to adapt/translate our language for this type of audience. It is a challenging task, but we need to take it upon ourselves instead of letting ambivalence and ambiguity in the purpose prevail.

Political or social involvement

Political and social involvement were inherent in Miller's and Rice's ideas. My understanding is that the initial idea or epistemology behind a Group Relations conference in their thinking (Miller and Rice, 1967) was that learning about leadership, in a cascade manner, can also change organisations and society. This could also take place as a consequence of the awareness of conscious and unconscious processes. In the interview I conducted with Eric Miller (Brunner, 2002), I felt he was quite lukewarm about the conference as a societal laboratory and he said 'the extent with which these kinds of phenomena will emerge within the conference does not necessarily depend on the external situation in general, but it is influenced by how much, or how little, containment is provided by the conference Director and Conference Staff' (Brunner, 2002, p.161). But what was described by Miller and Rice in 1967 and by Miller in 2002 belong to different historical periods. Nevertheless, I tend to agree with Miller, but as described above, the trend in Group Relations nowadays is to bring society directly into the conference theme and in a way force it in, which is ambiguous.

From a political/social perspective, the question which arises is how a small training event can change society, especially in a world like ours in such disarray. A common way of looking at it is with a systems approach, and the idea that the fractal can represent the whole. So, if we take this idea into consideration we can assume that what happens in the microcosm of a conference mirrors societal dynamics, and the resulting understanding will spread out. For example, if we are more aware of our role as citizens, we can create better societies. Therefore, for most of us, the assumption behind the idea of the impact on society is a generic one about changing society and about values in terms of vision, the search for new understandings and sometimes an ideology, but it is often very limited in terms of action. A strong personal, political and social involvement and action are necessary to move forward from a specific training event such as a Group Relations conference to a real change in society. There are very few cases (too few) of such changes, for example the work of Brendan Duddy (Guardian 2008) as the secret negotiator in Ireland or Renate Groenvold Bugge (2015) in Norway, but they are too few and more should follow, if this aspect of Group Relations is to be better illustrated and understood.

To conclude this part, the two aims, educational leadership training and political and social involvement can both be integrated or can compete with each other. However, from a business perspective the lack of clarity as to whether it is leadership training or something else does not help in marketing and selling our product. The consequence is that the general aims of the conferences appear confused and in competition for the 'outside' world audience, that is, for those who are not already familiar with the Group Relations way of working. Personally, I feel more comfortable in suggesting an ordinary Group Relations conference as a form of educational leadership training when recruiting participants. Obviously, it is different for a thematic conference exploring identity or societal issues.

I hypothesize that the all-inclusive, undifferentiated, ambiguous, and ambivalent nature of the common aim, incorporating both leadership training and the impact on society, is defensive. On the one hand, it could be seen as a defence against engaging with the market creatively and competing openly with our competitors in the leadership domain, such as other training centres or business schools. On the other hand, it prevents us from being really politically and socially active, by using Group Relations conferences thinking as a tool intended to have a real viral impact. Furthermore, probably this has to do with the fact that the method of *working with experience* was a unique innovative feature and asset of Group Relations in the post-war climate when it was conceived and developed and had a subversive dimension (see Chapter 1.1). Now, however, *experiential learning* in different versions beyond the psycho-dynamic systemic tradition has expanded enormously (e.g. outdoor, case studies).

A community of practice reflecting family or friends?

In section 2, I quoted Miller and Rice (1988) about competition in family business. I am aware that, among others, the metaphor of the family or family business is quite commonly used in our community. For example, Khaleelee and White (2014, p.416) suggest that the Group Relations culture 'naturally has resonances with family dynamics...' But I am not completely sure that the metaphor of family or family business, which is quite intuitive, represents the reality of our community. As mentioned in section 1, for nearly a year I shared my ideas about this presentation with Robert French, to whom I am extremely grateful for his attention[7] and amazingly generous support. In a private conversation (21 September 2015) he suggested that 'running alongside the competition within the Group Relations world there is also a strong thread of friendship – and of course one impact of friendship is the envy that it can set up. Another is the impact of betrayal, which I think has had a big impact on Group Relations (the setting up of different organisations all over the place...)'. The type of relations that we establish in our community are about different levels of personal relationships, in the sense of friendship, peership and partner-ships, and also loved, hated and envied colleagues.

As mentioned above in Figure 3.1 about staff motivation, we tend to reproduce or we search for the experience of intimacy and closeness experienced in the conferences which can be related to family culture but also to something else such as friendship or peership. Friendship is different from family. In the real world today, many start-ups are born out of friendship or partnership. Some develop and others fail. Friend-ship, with the exception of some authors such as French (1998, 2007) or French *et al.* (2009), is a dimension which has not been sufficiently explored. It is easier to think about family, because we are more familiar with it. A fundamental difference is that we do not choose our family nor do we choose our peers in school, in the military, or who will be with us at a Group Relations conference, unless we are the director. But we choose our friends. We are not obliged to be friends or to work with somebody we do not like. In the family there are both the oedipal and sibling dimensions, while in friendship there is mostly a sort of sibling, fraternal, lateral and hopefully egalitarian type of relationship.

The theme of friendship leads us to the issue of horizontal and vertical relationships and different ways of taking up roles and authority in contemporary organisations. In the family, both are present in the par-ental and sibling relationships. Khaleelee and White (2014, p.424), suggest 'Basic authority and leadership struggles seem to be at the heart of all the changes in the world; issues of authority have not left us and will not leave us. Oedipal issues in relation to authority do not disappear and will not disappear; it is only a matter of what form they will take, and this is where our tradition can be of help: sorting out the new forms of the basic authority and leadership dilemmas.'

Friendship pertains mainly to the horizontal and lateral dimension which is a territory in organisational life that has only recently received attention. Armstrong (2007, p. 194) suggests that lateral relations are 'a relation between collaborating persons, role holders, groups or teams that is unmediated by any actual or assumed hierarchical authority'. The issue is how can we be *emotionally present*, how can we live within these new forms of organisational life in which we are immersed also in our Group Relations community. It means dealing with 'themes of anxiety and vulnerability, in the dismantling of prior expectations and assumptions, both conscious and unconscious, and in the face of what might be termed the nakedness of being on one's own, with colleagues' (Armstrong 2007, p.195). All this is not an easy task, as we often see in Group Relations, both for staff and membership groups in the Inter-Group event or in the institutional event where the relationship is more of a peer type then in other events of the conference. A loosening of the hierarchical boundaries exposes all to more anxiety and vulnerability and this is not always easy to confront and, in some circumstances, is not well contained by the staff and can be risky.

I hypothesize that the recurrence of the family or family business metaphor in our community, which I still value as one of the possible interpretations, is a defence against coming to terms with what Armstrong (2007, p.199) suggested as a 'heightened sense of vulnerability', anxiety and fragility, which we all feel so threatened by. By the way, to add threat to threat, the family is profoundly changing and perhaps in our family metaphor we still have a 'family in the mind' that is disappearing or does not exist anymore.

Much more could be said about a horizontal/lateral culture and a vertical one, but I just wanted to point out that this is an issue in our community. In any case, horizontal and vertical dynamics are dealt more in depth in Chapter 2.1.

The Milan Universal Exhibition (Expo) 2015 and the Tree of Life

Khaleelee and White (2014) are convincing when they talk about the franchising model in the development of Group Relations conferences; the evidence is that the only place where you can get the fullest picture of Group Relations conferences globally is on the website of the Tavistock Institute.[8] Some people have talked about colonialization of Group Relations. This is probably linked to the fact that Group Relations conferences were established in Great Britain by the Tavistock Institute, and Great Britain is a nation which has a long tradition of colonialism.

I work mostly with the business world where the dark sides are often ignored, denied and strong emphasis is on the future and positive thinking. Therefore inspired by this and heading towards the end of this chapter, I want to suggest an idea about the future through a metaphor and a different experience. During the Belgirate Conference, before I started the presentation, I showed the film of the *Tree of Life* at Milan's Universal Exhibition, Expo 2015, which closed five days before the

Conference began.[9] The first historical world exhibition was the 1851 Great Exhibition in London. After it, over the years many universal exhibitions were organised in the significant cities throughout the world: Vienna, Melbourne and Paris which, for example, bequeathed us the Eiffel Tower, built especially for that occasion. In 1928, 31 countries from all over the world signed a convention that regulated the organisation of all such events and established a common body, the B.I.E. (Bureau International des Expositions). Today the B.I.E. has 154 member-states globally, which are well aware of the political and communicative power of these exhibitions that represent a worldwide opportunity to exchange the scientific and technological development. Addressing the Expo history, I asked myself if the Belgirate Conference could be a sort of Expo for Group Relations conferences as a place to meet and share. But something is still missing for us.

To go a step further, the symbol of Milan's Expo 2015 was the 'Tree of Life' or the cosmic tree. Myths about the tree of life exist in traditions across the whole world. For example, in the Jewish tradition, the Tree of Life called Etz Chaim represents beauty, protection and wisdom, figuratively the Torah. In the Christian tradition, it is associated to the idea of paradise in the Apocalypse or Book of Revelation. In the Islamic tradition, in the Quran, they talk of the 'Tree of Immortality'. Indian tradition, according to its earliest writings, represents the cosmos in the form of a giant tree.[10]

Getting the Milan *Tree of Life* at Expo 2015 established was a difficult, confusing, and complicated process. For example, there was the risk of it not being ready in time for the opening of Expo 2015, due to corruption among the construction tenders and builders. Nevertheless, it was almost a miracle that the Expo took place. The *Tree of Life* was there and in my opinion it was the best element of Expo 2015.

Looking at the picture of the *Milan Tree of Life* in Figure 3.1.2, I want to point out the energy which emerges from *beneath the surface* and manifests itself at the base of the tree via the fountains. This water springing out from the earth made me think of our conferences, the *enterprises of passion*, with all their energy, initiative. But in the *Milan Tree of Life* the trunk of the tree gets narrow and gives me an idea of the narrowness when one is stuck where I have hypothesized we are at present. Finally, the *Tree of Life* opens out again as branches which are connected through joining dots, connections, which look quite structured and organised, and no longer spontaneous free initiatives.

Figure 3.1.1. The Milan Expo 2015 *Tree of Life.*

Using this metaphor, I want to suggest that we too as a community of practice should get more organised/structured and that this is a possible option/direction to reflect on and to pursue. There should be more collaborative initiatives that are formally structured and organised, which can support our work both scientifically and in terms of marketing and recruitment. Belgirate is a first step in my view, but perhaps we still need to move forward. For example, Expo established a common body the B.I.E., as a common regulatory structure. We could think of something similar and coherent in our business. Looking again outside Group Relations circles, when we consult the family business and the family, where the ownership has grown and become much more fragmented through the generations, we suggest structured family assemblies or meetings with all the family members attending. These are beyond the formal governance boards or executive committees. There is a need for an organised, structured container to help the different family generations, on the one hand, to know each other better and, on the other, to feel safe if conflicts (including trans-generational ones), tensions and rivalry emerge. The ultimate aim of these events, which have an emotional management component in their design, is also to help improve the business.

Ultimately what I want to emphasise is that, as a community of practice, we need this structuring/organising element, to enhance collaboration and cooperation. It represents an enormous cultural change, but if the life of these *enterprises with passion* is not regulated, the risk is that they could go wild and prove unable become businesses, and that intra-community competition could also kill us and the wonderful training tool that we can offer.

Conclusion

In this chapter I have tried to illustrate some of the challenges that I feel our community needs to deal with. As mentioned above, this is not a scientific document, but more a diary of free associative thoughts or an observation/consultative report based on my personal experience and exchanges with colleagues.

As a conclusion I want to address my experience of presenting during the Belgirate Conference.

Initially I had decided not to give a traditional lecture, but a Power-Point presentation with a video which I felt was more coherent with what

I wanted to suggest. I wanted the communication medium to be more contemporary and more from the business school. I took the risk of presenting in a different way and obviously I was very anxious about how people would react. Luckily, the conference management scheduled my presentation for the evening of the first day. I thought immediately that a PowerPoint presentation with two videos and music could keep the audience awake and I was relieved. It was coherent with the content which I was using to address our community as a whole.

The choice of a more creative keynote, perhaps nearly a show, had many challenges which I had not realized when I started working on it.

- Although from the beginning I was aware that not having a 'real' paper would involve more work afterwards, when I had to write this chapter, I underestimated the amount of work involved in the PowerPoint/video presentation itself. Keeping together content and communication medium was very demanding in terms of workload and mental space, although also a lot of fun. The detail was extremely complicated, and it included going to Belgirate to try out the technology in the plenary room. Having to rely on it, I had to be sure that the hall could support it. This created another element of anxiety and complexity. It made me think of how much we need to invest to get out of our comfort zone. Furthermore we often think that technology can make our life easier, but it is not always the case. I learned that one cannot improvise in a new territory, while wanting to be professional.

- During the presentation, the reaction of the audience to the video 'November 2014 –2015. A year in the life of *enterprises with passion*' (as mentioned in section 2, showed a historical sequence of the conferences worldwide) was different from what I expected. I presented the video because I thought that it was the evidence of the competition between conferences. Instead my experience was that colleagues were keen to see all the conferences globally together, or happy that theirs was mentioned. The video, also through the seductive help of images and music, gave the idea of a very powerful global network. I associated the audience's reaction to that of to the famous 1985 song of the charity USA for Africa 'We are the world'. People's focus was on the pride in seeing the global dimension and the spread of the conferences finally put together. Although I felt the pride was well-deserved and significant, this audience's reaction was slightly illusionary in the dynamic of the 'here and now' and a way of defensively hiding the competitive dimension which could not be acknowledged collectively. The pairing and one-ness mentality seemed to prevail. Furthermore, my impression was that the audience enjoyed the overall presentation. Many people came to talk to me after it, saying that they liked it. But I asked myself how much they really understood of it. Did they like the presentation or the show which I had been able to mount? I had the feeling that it managed to create a good positive atmosphere for the conference, probably a feeling of belonging. During the conference the presentation and some ideas in it were referred to in several instances, which I do not deny. But I felt it did not have the impact in terms of content and debate that I hoped it would have. It must be said that it was the first time that a keynote speech was addressing issues of our community as a whole and not only of the conferences which I felt was daring and risky. I was also anxious about the authorisation for doing it.

• The aim of my presentation, and hopefully of this chapter, is to alert our community. It is a call for reflection, but also for action. On the one hand, perhaps my anxiety led me to take extreme care in terms of the packaging and of building the show, because I felt that it had to be nearly a perfect container since I was going to talk of competi-tion, which I think is a controversial subject in any community. On the other hand, such a presentation was an attempt to show that one can also present difficult issues with different media and languages in a more contemporary and easy way, also keeping the layman and -woman in mind. As McLuhan (1962) suggested 'the medium is the message' in the 'global village'. The presentation confirmed my idea of the need for a different language. Nevertheless, I think that different languages lead to different understanding, interpretation, and perhaps manipulations, so the human condition of avoidance of pain remains unavoidable and new emotional defences are evoked and installed.

Before and during the conference and when writing this chapter, when sharing ideas with Julian Lousada and Jinette de Gooijer, the other two keynote speakers to whom I am very grateful, has been fundamental. Asking for help and collaboration was a necessary choice to try to implement, and not only theorize, what I was trying to suggest through the presentation/chapter. Three keynote speakers can inevitably have very strong competitive opinions on which is the best paper. But the experience of collaborating, sharing the three papers/presentations, our anxieties, bewilderment, being there one for one another before, throughout, and after the conference was an amazing and nurturing experience. First of all it gave a sense of coordination, harmony, and integration in the content, but it has also been a support system. It presents the strongest evidence in the 'here and now' that collaboration is one of the best antidotes to competition for us as individuals and also if we want our conferences to make the transition from *enterprises with passion* to *businesses*.

Acknowledgement

I am grateful to Eliat Aram, Gordon Strauss, and Yossy Triest for having invited me to deliver a key note paper at the fifth Belgirate Conference, and for their support throughout the experience. The long conversations and generous exchanges behind the scenes with Robert French to whom I am very grateful have been fundamental to my Belgirate presentation/chapter.

My gratitude goes also to all the directors who invited me to join the staff of Group Relations conferences, to the sponsoring organisations that appointed me as a director, to all colleagues and participants I have worked with over the years. Thanks to all these encounters I was able to build such a valuable personal and professional experience.

Notes

1. In 2002 Avi Nutckevitch and Mannie Sher were looking for a location for the first Belgirate conference which should have been in Israel. It could not be held there as it was the time of the second Intifada, so Avi Nuckevitch asked me to help him. I did not find the Belgirate location; it had been used for the Italian Group Relations Conference for some years and was found by Elio Vera. So we should all be grateful to Avi Nutkevich and Elio Vera for such a beautiful place.

2. I am extremely grateful to Robert French who supported and helped me in such a generous way first in preparing the Belgirate presentation and then in writing this chapter. The quote from e.e. cummings, as with many others I will refer to in the chapter, is part of many email conversations with Robert French who said that 'cummings always used lower case for his

name – and often didn't use capitals at all, but played around with punctuation and lay-out very creatively' (email 16 September 2015).

3. French and Simpson suggest that Bion's original terminology of 'basic assumption and work *group*' can generate confusion since in reality he describes 'two *mentalities*' (French and Simpson, 2010, p.1861). According to French and Simpson both *basic assumption mentality* and *work group mentality* can be characterized by pairing, flight and fight and dependence dynamics. *Work group mentality is* connected to purpose, task, and external reality, while *basic assumption mentality* is related to fantasy.

4. I am thankful to Ilana Litvin for this.

5. I am very grateful to Luca Mingarelli for sharing it with me.

6. It was inspired by the mid-twentieth century group dynamics laboratory experiences such as Bethel, Maine and the National Training Laboratories, Kurt Lewin's (1943) thinking about field theory, the psychoanalytical thinking of Klein (1959), Bion (1961) and systems thinking (Bertalanffy, 1950).

7. French and Simpson (2015) address in depth the theme of attention in Bion.

8. http://www.grouprelations.com

9. YouTube link: https://www.youtube.com/watch?v=jhsce15byHc. Downloaded on 6 February 2017.

10. R. French, email of 21 September 2015.

References

Armstrong, D. (2007). The dynamics of lateral relations in changing organizational worlds. *Organisational and Social Dynamics*, 7 (2): 193–210.

Bion, W.R. (1961). *Experiences in Groups and other Papers*. London: Routledge.

Brunner, L.D. (2002). Groups and work in the past and at present. Conversation with Eric Miller. *Organisational and Social Dynamics An International Journal of Psychoanalytic, Systemic and Group Relations Perspectives* 2(2): 156–171.

cummings, e. e. (1991). *The Charles Eliot Norton Lecture. I: six nonlectures.* Cambridge, MA; Harvard University Press.

Erlich-Ginor, M. (2006). Structure and design of group relations conferences: issues and dilemmas. In Brunner, L.D., Nutkevitch, A. and Sher, M. (2006) *Group Relations Conferences: Reviewing and Exploring Theory, Design, Role-Taking and Application,*. London: Karnac Books, pp. 30–43.

French, R. (1998). *Friendship: the human capacity for drawing boundaries and crossing bridges*. Annual Symposium of ISPSO (International Society for the Psychoanalytic Study of Organizations), Jerusalem, Israel, 1–3 July 1998: Drawing Boundaries and Crossing Bridges – Psychoanalytic Perspectives on Alliances, Relationships and Relatedness among Groups, Organizations, and Cultures Relationships, and Relatedness between Groups, Organizations, and Cultures.

French, R. (2007). Friendship and organization: learning from the western friendship tradition. *Management & Organizational History,* 2(3): 255–272.

French, R., Case, P. and Gosling, J. (2009). Betrayal and friendship. *Society and Business Review,* 4(2): 146–158.

French, R. and Moore, P. (2004). Divided neither in life, nor in death: friendship and leadership in the story of David and Jonathan. In Yiannis Gabriel (Ed.), *Myths, Stories, and Organizations: Pre-Modern Narratives for Our Times.* Oxford: Oxford University Press, pp. 101–115.

French, R. and Simpson, P. (2010). The "work group": redressing the balance in Bion's experiences in groups. *Human Relations,* 63(12): 1859–1878.

French, R. and Simpson, P. (2015). *Attention, Cooperation, Purpose. An Approach to Working in Groups Using Insights from Wilfred Bion.* London: Karnac Books.

Freud, S. (1917). *Mourning and Melancholia.* In Freud, S., *The Standard Edition of the Complete Psychological Works of Sigmund Freud* 14, London: Hogarth, pp. 237–258.

Freud, S. (2001 [1913]). *The Origins of Religion Totem and Taboo, Moses and Monotheism and Other Works.* London: Routledge.

Groenvold Bugge, R. (2015). Using an organisational perspective to intervene when disaster strikes: learning from experience following the terror attacks in Norway on 22 July, 2011. *Organisational and Social Dynamics An International Journal of Psychoanalytic, Systemic and Group Relations Perspectives* 15(1): 101–116.

Hoggett, P. (2014). Learning from three practices. *Journal of Psycho-Social Studies,* 8(1): 179–196.

Khaleelee, O. and White, K. (2014). Global development and innovation in group relations. *Organisational & Social Dynamics* 14(2): 399–425.

Kets De Vries, M.F.R. (1996a). *Family Business: Human Dilemmas in the Family Firm.* London: Karnac Books.

Kets De Vries, M.F.R. (1996b). The anatomy of the entrepreneur: clinical observations. *Human Relations,* 49(7): 853–884.

Klein, M. (1959). Our adult world and its roots in infancy. *Human Relations,* 12: 291–203.

Klein, M. (1988). *Envy and Gratitude and Other Works, 1946–1963.* London: Virago.

Lawrence, W.G., Bain, A. and Gould, L. (1996). The fifth basic assumption. *Free Associations,* Vol. 6, Part.1 (No. 37). Process Press.

Lewin, K. (1943). Defining the field at a given time. *Psychological Review:* 292–310. Republished in *Resolving Social Conflicts & Field*

Theory in Social Science, Washington, DC. American Psychological Association, 1997.

Litvin, I. and Bonwitt, G. (2006). Sexual abuse: application and adaptation of basic Group Relations concepts, technique and culture to a specific social issue. In Brunner, L.D., Nutkevitch, A. and Sher, M. (2006) *Group Relations Conferences: Reviewing and Exploring Theory, Design, Role-Taking and Application*. London: Karnac Books, pp. 47–60.

McLuhan, M. (1962). *The Gutenberg Galaxy: The Making of Typographic Man*, 1st ed. Toronto: University of Toronto Press, reissued by Routledge & Kegan Paul.

McClelland, D.C. (1988). *Human Motivation Theory.* Cambridge: Cambridge University Press.

Miller, E.J. and Rice, A.K. (1967). *Systems of Organization. The Control of Task and Sentient Boundaries*. London: Tavistock Publications.

Miller, E.J. and Rice, A.K. (1988). The family business in contemporary society. *Family Business Review,* 1(2): 193–210.

Petriglieri, G. and Petriglieri, J. (2015). *Can business schools humanize leadership?* Working Paper Series 2015/18/OBH. Insead, the Business School of the World.

Rice, A.K. (1965). *Learning for Leadership. Interpersonal and Intergroup Relations.* London: Tavistock Publications.

Soanes, C. and Stevenson, A., eds. (2006). *Concise Oxford English Dictionary.* Oxford: Oxford University Press.

Sprieier, S.W., Fontaine, M.H., and Malloy, R.L. (2006). Leadership run amok the destructive potential of overachievers. *Harvard Business Review,* June 2006.

The Guardian (2008). Disobeyed orders and a dangerous message. Brendan Duddy, a secret link with the IRA, recalls his risky contacts with a British official known as 'Fred' [Accessed on 10 May 2016].

Von Bertalanffy, L. (1950). An outline of general systems theory. *British Journal for the Philosophy of Science,* 1: 134–165.

Political, ethical and historical dilemmas in building a Group Relations institution

Eduardo Acuña and Matías Sanfuentes

This chapter describes the building of an educational institution in Group Relations (GR) in Chile, whose embryonic beginnings date back 30 years, a period during which the institution experienced incremental transformations that enabled its existence today. The chapter also includes the study of political, historical, and ethical dilemmas that GR promoters have faced throughout the years in the process of making this activity a legitimized training space for Chilean audiences.

The development of GR in Chile was based on the models of the Tavistock Institute conferences, whose theories, structures, and learning methodologies were adapted for local application in accordance with the conditions of Chilean society and organizations (Bridger, 1990; Miller, 1990 a, b). From the inception, the building of GR was rooted in the School of Business of the Faculty of Economics and Business (FEN, as abbreviated in Spanish), University of Chile, a public entity where GR has been gradually incorporated in the education of professionals in the field of Human Resources. The foundation of GR is the result of initiatives developed by a group of professors associated with the Business School. Occasionally, international collaborations from consultants, teachers, and institutions with expertise in psychoanalysis and organizations have helped to invigorate local conferences.

The chapter has two objectives: one is the understanding of the institutional history of GR, between 1983 and 2015. To this effect, a chronology was established allowing a retrospective outlook of the main circumstances, events, and actors who participated in the unfolding of that history. This outlook shows how the institutional development was affected by vicissitudes and changes that took place at the university and the FEN, which were closely related to the transformations experienced by the Chilean society during Pinochet's dictatorship and the transition to democracy. This evolution was also affected by the strong impact of neoliberalism on the Chilean economy, and particularly on university education. The second objective is to elucidate the most relevant dilemmas that GR promoters had to face to give continuity to those activities. Through a retrospective outlook, the political, ethical, and historical dilemmas that affected the GR's evolution within the faculty are distinguished. The leitmotif of these dilemmas had been to achieve a GR identity legitimized by university authorities. This has been a complex task because of precarious conditions in terms of resources and very asymmetrical power relations at the School of Business. Although these dilemmas have had a stronger influence during specific chronological stages, they also revealed themselves in the course of other periods, thus causing the intersection of historicity with new temporal horizons.

The elaboration of this chapter is mainly based on two theoretical perspectives: historical institutionalism and psychoanalysis. First, historical institutionalism contributes to the notion that institutions are the product of a distinctive past created by individuals and groups that influence the changes that occur throughout the years. This perspective emphasizes that institutional changes depend on the political context and the characteristics of organizations. These changes are driven by organizational actors in accordance with their political power. The transformations can follow either a radical and abrupt or incremental and discontinuous strategy (Hall, 2010; Mahoney and Thelen, 2010; Suddaby et al., 2014). On the other hand, the psychoanalytical perspective emphasizes how unconscious processes in individuals and groups can have dysfunctional effects in the understanding and establishment of organizational changes. This line of thought reflects some of the literature that shows how the organization's history harbours unconscious aspects that have an impact on the current exercise of roles and strategies of organizational life (Chapman and Long, 2008; Krantz, 2001; Levy, 2011; Long, 2004, 2006; Sievers, 2006, 2015).

The study employs a narrative methodology to explore the historical process of GR institutionalization at the FEN's School of Business and the key implicit dilemmas at play in that historicity (Piper-Shafir et al., 2013; Suddaby et al., 2014; Yates, 2014). The narrative is essentially based on the experiences and recollections of the authors of this document and of conference consultants during the promotion, maintenance, and application of GR. As part of the research, some of the Business School's records, which provided information on the execution of the conferences, the design of activities, participants and consultants, were also examined. Likewise, the narrative employs data found in documents, journals, and books referring to the historical context of Chilean society and the FEN (Departmento de Economía, 2009; Montecino and Acuña, 2013; Salazar and Pinto, 1999). Lastly, the narrative method incorporates the hermeneutic interpretation to study the various emerging contents emanating from the different texts employed as sources of information (Alvesson and Sköldberg, 2004).

The chapter is structured as follows: first, a chronology is presented describing the history of the conferences' process of development. Subsequently, the most significant dilemmas present during that process are identified and explained. The chapter ends with conclusions regarding the most outstanding meanings in the establishment of the conferences at the FEN.

Chronology of the building of Group Relations conferences

Driving force context: Tavistock Institute (1983–1984)

One of the authors of this chapter (E.A.) participated, between 1983–1984, in a 'Programme on Action Research' at the Tavistock Institute, where he was trained in psychoanalysis and organizations.

Participation in that programme was prompted, to a significant extent, by the intervention conducted by the military dictatorship and right-wing political groups at the FEN. This intervention supported, through teaching and research, the neoliberal entrepreneurial revolution in Chilean society (Clavel, 1984; Departmento de Economía, 2009; Palma, 1974; Selume, 1986). In these circumstances, the Department of Labour Relations and Organization (DERTO being its Spanish abbreviation) – to which E.A. was academically affiliated – was subjected to continuous and severe warnings of its imminent closure, because the faculty's highest authorities deemed that DERTO's academic focus and work did not add value to the neoliberal revolutionary strategy. In such an antagonistic atmosphere, E. A. requested and obtained DERTO's and the faculty authorities' approval and support to attend the programme at the Tavistock Institute, arguing that the institute's experience on socio-technical changes would allow incorporating new approaches to DERTO activities.

The studies carried out by the Chilean participant at the Tavistock Institute involved access to knowledge of psychoanalysis and its applications in groups and organizations, learning about the socio-technical approach, industrial democracy, and the use of experiential learning and action research. This knowledge revealed an epistemological paradigm radically different from conventional university education in social sciences and management (Palmer, 2002). The programme also provided the student with an opportunity to have his first experiences in the field of GR, by participating in small study groups and in two conferences, one conducted by Eric Miller, on 'Creativity and Destructiveness in Groups' and in a residential conference led by Harold Bridger on 'Institutions for Transitional Learning: the Double Task Method'. During the student's sojourn at the Tavistock Institute, Eric Miller was his tutor.

Experimenting with Group Learning: the Double Task Model (1985–1992)

When E.A. returned to DERTO, he found a dispirited group, whose identity as a department was continuously questioned by the faculty authorities, thereby hinting at its imminent closure (Pedrero and Trincado, 2014). This human context reflected a resistance to receive and assimilate the Tavistock theories and methodologies, even more so when psychoanalysis and its applications to the world of management were totally alien to this academic community. Differentiating himself from this prevalent trend, a young professor showed interest in learning and applying those ideas, which would be decisive in the establishment of future GR applications.

In 1986–1987, DERTO was finally closed down. Simultaneously, it was decided that some of its professors could become part of the Business Department, creating the area of Human Resources Management. E.A. and the young professor mentioned earlier, were assigned to that department (Pedrero and Trincado, 2014).

In 1988, the two professors mentioned above conceived, organized and conducted two diploma programmes, one in Human Resources Management, and the other in Organizational Development and Change, which were offered as annual specialization programmes for professionals. Between 1990 and 1992, the directors of those diploma programmes decided to include experiential workshops in Group Relations, where they also acted as consultants. The Double Task Model was used in the workshops.

In 1989, the faculty invited Frank Heller, a Tavistock consultant, to present a seminar on 'Technological Change, Decision-making and Parti-cipation'. As a consequence of the seminar, the British Council in Chile approached the faculty with the proposal to sponsor an action research project in a Chilean company addressing the seminar's subject. The project enabled the exchange of formative experiences between Tavistock consultants who travelled to Chile and faculty professors that visited the institute in London. As part of the project, in 1992 Eric Miller travelled to Chile, where he carried out different academic activities at the faculty, which helped to disseminate the socio-technical ideas and the Leicester conferences educational model. Miller's work was crucial to the atten-dance of four people – Chilean professors and consultants – at one of those conferences (Pedrero and Trincado, 2014).

The collaboration between the Tavistock Institute and the faculty had a special political significance because it took place when the first demo-cratic government had been established after the dictatorship. Relation-ships with the institute, particularly due to its international reputation, were a boost to the faculty's morale, so harshly shattered by the dictator-ship's repression and ideology (Montecino and Acuña, 2013).

Incorporation of the conferences at the School of Business's Institutional Framework (1993–2004)

The participation of Chilean professors and professionals in the Leicester conference made it possible to have a group of consultants to conduct the conferences in GR, which were incorporated in the institutional framework of the School of Business through the diploma programmes in Human Resources Management and Organizational Development and Change.

The GR method that began to be used in the conferences had the Leicester conference as its main model, focusing on the learning of uncon-scious processes in the 'here and now', in small and large study groups, in review and application groups, and in the use of plenary sessions at the beginning and the end of each conference. Working with the Leicester model was complex for the group of consultants since they felt overwhelmed in their ability to contain the participants' anxieties and to make interpretations that would contribute towards learning. For the consultants, conducting the intergroup event according to the Leicester model was a somewhat sophisticated job. Therefore, during many years, these activities were carried out using the Double Task Model. The consultants previously trained at the Leicester conferences were reluctant to support the conferences at the faculty. This forced the incorporation of psychologists among the staff, who showed interest in the model after completing some of the diplomas, and thereby had previous experience in Group Relations. Two residential conferences were held annually, one for each of the diplomas, attracting in each case between 30 and 40 participants.

In 1998, Eric Miller was invited for the second time to visit the faculty. On that occasion, Miller acted as a consultant to the University of Chile Council, and led two seminars on the theoretical and methodological contributions of psychoanalysis to the management of post-industrial organizations. Miller's sojourn and the work done while in Chile gave support and legitimized the integration of the conferences at the Business School.

This stage coincided with the three successive post-dictatorship democratic governments during which the country's economic development was given significant impulse. This boost meant a large increase in the demand for professionals qualified in Human Resources and Organizational Change, in the context of the challenges presented by post-industrialism and globalization. This in turn enabled diplomas and conferences to have a permanent and large demand for enrolments that guaranteed continuity to the educational activities.

Consolidation of the model (2004–2015)

During this stage, a consolidation of the model took place that has guided the formation of conferences at the School of Business. In this consolidation, various situations converged, contributing to that achievement.

The working model used in the conferences was aligned very similarly to the Leicester model. In particular, this involved implementing the intergroup event and the review and application groups, ending the previous eclecticism of using the Double Task approach for these activities. Furthermore, conferences became more complex when the institutional event was incorporated.

The group of consultants was strengthened by an increase in the number of professionals qualified to perform those functions. The group diversified with the inclusion of women consultants making the group, which primarily consisted of men, more evenly balanced. The staff increased its psychoanalytical orientation, because the majority were psychologists with psychoanalytical training and experience in GR. Some of them had participated as members of the Leicester conference.

Before 2007, the diploma programmes lasted for a year but, thereafter, the number of classes was reduced to almost half, and the programme began to have a duration of one semester, conducted twice a year. Conferences were also conducted twice a year, keeping the residential nature of the events. These conferences attracted participants in both diploma courses. The number of conference participants has fluctuated between 40 and 60 individuals.

The consolidation of the conferences' model has also resulted in colla-boration established with internationally known colleagues such as, John Newton, James Krantz, Susan Long, Burkard Sievers, Rose Mersky and Paul Hoggett, who visited the FEN bringing knowledge and methods for the development of GR. Also, in the international sphere, relations were estab-lished with ISPSO and OPUS, and as a result of those international ties, the 31st ISPSO Annual Meeting took place at the FEN in 2014. In 2010, the FEN's School of Business began offering a Master's programme in Human Resources Management and Organizational Dynamics. The conferences have been an essential aspect of the programme.

During this stage, three books were published in Spanish, which were a significant support for students' learning after the conferences. One book compiles some of Eric Miller's seminal writings (Miller, 2005) another refers to Coaching and Role Analysis (Acuña and Sanfuentes, 2009), and the third includes works on Socio-Analytical Methods (Acuña and Sanfuentes, 2013).

Another element that contributed to consolidate the model was the incorporation of M.S. as full-time professor at the Business Department. He has worked uninterruptedly in the conferences since 2004, contributing to develop the model and also lecturing on one of the diploma programmes. His joining the department provided new sources of collaboration and internal political support to strengthen the implemented changes. As from 2010, M.S. was director of one of the two annual conferences, which involved materializing the transition of leadership, which until then had been solely performed by E.A.

During this stage, democracy continued to strengthen, and for the first time after the dictatorship, in 2010 the country was governed by a coalition of right-wing parties. The political environment was turbulent, with strong social movements protesting against the extreme social costs of neoliberalism and globalization. At this stage, the model of the entrepreneurial university had a strong influence. This type of model assumes that faculties, schools and departments must look to autonomous financing of their activities.

Dilemmas

In the light of the historical account of the building of the conferences, the authors of this chapter reflected on the principal dilemmas they have faced during that construction (Acuña, 2013; Erlich-Ginor, 2006; Krantz, 2001; Long, 2004; Martin, 1992).

A fight for identity: between disdain and recognition

Political circumstances surrounding the genesis of the conferences created traumatic losses for DERTO's collective academic identity, as well as for its professors. These events were the expression of institutional disdain, first when totalitarianism at the FEN violated, in a generalized and reiterated way, and sometimes with violence, the professors' human rights. Subsequently, the authorities arbitrarily abolished DERTO, which thus lost its juridical status of a university institution, and then devalued its academic activities, which for decades had enjoyed legitimacy. Lastly, when without any consultation and also arbitrarily, the authorities decided the assignment of DERTO professors to the Business Department. All these changes resulted in suffering, humiliations, and moral shame for the professors, with the aggravating pressure of having to keep such vicissitudes to themselves, without the chance to mourn collectively. In this context, some of the professors assigned to the Business Department fought for identity recognition taking into account the teachings of the Tavistock Institute (Honneth, 1997; Hogget, 2009).

Between the politics of salvation and revelation

In the will to fight for recognition of identity, E.A. decided to confront the dilemma between the politics of salvation and of revelation, according to the idea set forth by Lawrence (2000). Salvation politics meant maintaining a conservative pattern by adhering to organizational theories and learning methods that tended to reify the institutional order, highlighting the determinant role of managers or consultants who, with authoritarian paternalism, defined guidelines to be obediently followed by workers regarding organizational improvement proposals. By contrast, revelation politics referred to the dilemma of opening to the internalization and practice of the Tavistock's educational perspective, which stood out for its emancipatory principles of working in groups and organizations. Revelation politics conceive organizational members as having the capacity to exercise personal authority for their own management in roles according to their work experiences in organizations, while at the same time these capabilities provide a view of the system that enables coordinating roles at a group level and at the level of the whole organization (Lawrence, 1979). This dilemma posed the quandary of maintaining the positivistic and functionalistic perspective predominant at the Business School, or else, give way to a new epistemology, which fostered the development of experiential knowledge based on Group Relations activities. The stance vis-à-vis the dilemma was a fluctuating one, above all because putting into practice the revelation politics was an enormous challenge and risk due to the restrictions in knowledge and experience of the initiative's promoters.

Tavistock's orthodoxy: inhibitions and incentives to creativity

Here we refer to how the orthodoxy of the Tavistock paradigm, and most particularly its conferences, has become an inhibitory institutional burden, and at the same time a stimulating incentive to the process of building the conferences.

Studies at Tavistock implied assessing the learning obtained there as an organization ideal (Schwartz, 1990), which compelled E.A. to consider the dilemma of what to do with such knowledge: to undertake academic actions under very precarious conditions and that could hardly be assimilated to that working ideal; or else, to bury such learning by repressing it, forgetting everything learned at the Tavistock. The solution to the dilemma was ambivalent. Propelled by the political conditions and the need for survival, a conservative option was taken after a few years. That option was strongly reinforced by the discouragement arising at the time by the existing difficulties of creating a local conference with a minimum consistency to the work ideal represented by Tavistock's orthodoxy. That self-imposed pressure for quality was extremely paralysing, since behind it lay a narcissism that illusorily searched for perfection according to foreign standards that had no relation whatsoever with the situation and conditions faced at the FEN (Schwartz, 1995). The sense of reality, driven by work pressures, finally asserted itself and ended the paralysis, which meant that two professors from the Business Department decided to implement workshops on GR in the already created diploma programmes in Human Resources Management and in Organizational Development and Change. This decision was able to moderate, to a certain extent, the frightening burden of being faithful to the ideal of Tavistock's orthodoxy.

This dilemma has been constantly present in the building of the conferences. Even today, when conferences are aligned with the Leicester model, the tension between making improvements to the educational activities and taking this orthodoxy into account persists. That tension has had the virtue of promoting continuous learning, and over time, it has allowed the consolidation of an autochthonous authority that values the differentiated and distinct identity achieved with local conferences.

Authorization and disavowal of experiential learning

During the development of the conferences at the School of Business, a constant political tension prevailed regarding the use of the experiential learning method vis-à-vis the already established method at the School for the Education of Managers. Such tension implied a challenge in the sense of finding a stance that would allow using and maintaining the experiential method in a jointly functional and balanced way, without excessively infringing the established institution for the creation of knowledge in management (Hoggett, 1998; Long, 2004).

The conferences and the experiential learning method achieved their positioning by managing ambiguity (Feldman, 1991). This managing took into account interpretations that are neither clearly consistent nor clearly inconsistent, regarding whether the conference method undercuts the established institutional framework, or contributes to its conservation. We pointed out how this ambiguity is supported by some interpretations that favour the authorization of the conferences. One of these interpretations resides in the trust that the School of Business has in the conferences' directors, whose authority is acknowledged, in their capacity as faculty professors, to ensure that educational activities are being carried out within a framework of respect for the school's institutional order. Another interpretation that authorizes carrying out the conferences is their financial self-sustainability and the generation of earnings over time, which is understood as a sign of preference by the market. On the other hand, the legitimacy of the conferences was also strengthened by the integration of their authorities into an international, academic and professional community, identified with the practice and development of psychoanalysis in organizations, which meant the acknowledgement, by that community, of the work performed in Chile through the conferences. This recognition is interpreted by the School of Business as an international acknowledgement of the conferences' value.

The link between the Group Relations conferences' institutional framework and the Business School can be described through what Bion (1962, 1970) designates as a 'commensal relationship'. This type of relationship is defined as the link between two objects that are dependent on each other for the creation of a third one that will benefit both parties. Beneficial objects that have emerged from this link include the learning acquired by its members, the prestige of the programme, and financial gains, among others. However, the degree of contact and interpenetration between both parties is superficial, and a rather detached tolerance predominates that is sustained by the mutual benefits obtained from such a relationship.

The contradictions of a captive membership

A significant dilemma faced during the building of the conferences was that participants came mostly from the diplomas' academic programmes, and more recently, from the Master's programme. Both the conferences and the following theoretical lectures constitute a minimum course that participants are required to complete to receive the corresponding accreditation. As a result, the majority of students have no independent motivation to participate in the activity, but rather, they do it because the conferences are part of a programme that includes other associated subjects. While this has allowed captive participants running the conferences for many years, it has also generated ethical dilemmas that collide with the assumption of personal authority that is at the base of the GR model. Thus, although one is aware that participants have mostly benefited from these learning instances, this is achieved by imposing a method that often can generate conflicts in student participation. We have faced these dilemmas by holding the ambiguity upon which we build up the conditions to work. Moreover, we actively support the students' awareness of the conference's emotional and behavioural consequences. Finally, we make it explicitly clear that the quality of people's participation during the conference is not evaluated.

Linked to the above, as a team we faced the dilemma of expanding these educational events within the institutional boundaries of the School of Business, aiming to reach public and private organizations in the context of current complex globalization conditions. This dilemma sets forth, above all, the uncertainty of whether opening boundaries will find the necessary legitimacy in those external audiences to guarantee their financing and earnings, both so highly valued by the School of Business. The expansion of boundaries also presents the challenge of adapting the conferences' methodology to the requirements of external audiences while remaining faithful to their theoretical and epistemological principles.

Conclusions

This chapter provides information about the construction of GR in an educational institution in Chile, rooted since its inception in the School of Business of the FEN, University of Chile, where the institution experienced incremental transformations that enabled its existence to date.

This construction took place through a gradual incorporation of GR into the institutional framework of the Business School. Conference promoters, from a subversive stance, had to overcome very adverse conditions both at a political and a resources level, in particular during the dictatorship, so that their undertaking would prosper. Years later, with the coming of democracy, the promoters were able to strengthen their political stance and have access to resources that allowed them to consolidate the conferences as educational activities in programmes for professionals in the field of Human Resources.

Conference promoters had also to overcome ethical dilemmas with respect to whether it was proper to carry out such activities in the face of limitations in knowledge, experience, and consultants. In the end, the promoters took the risk of putting them into effect, with the conviction that the conferences were unprecedented contributions to the study of management in Chile. The risk was taken through keeping a balance between the need to innovate by using new theories and methods of learning and the formal framework of the Business School. In this respect, the collaboration of international colleagues was essential to increase that learning.

The relationship and relatedness with the Tavistock Institute was transcendental in the building of the conferences, with leading members of the institute providing seminal contributions on GR. They were the anchors upon which conference authorities and consultants in Chile could base the development of activities, first, by resorting to the Double Task Model and then, by working with an eclecticism that combined aspects of the Leicester Model and the Double Task Model, to finally adhering only to the Leicester method. The relatedness with the Tavistock was an encouragement to the learning and increasing improvement of the conferences, and at the same time, was a self-imposed factor of thoroughness so that achievements would be of a quality reasonably similar to the institute's standards.

References

Acuña E. and Sanfuentes, M. (2009). *Coaching: análisis del rol organizacional.* Santiago: Editorial Universitaria.

Acuña, E. and Sanfuentes, M. (2013). *Métodos socio-analíticos para la gestión y el cambio en organizaciones.* Santiago: Editorial Universitaria.

Acuña, M. E. (2013). Memorias volectivas. In S. Montecino y E. Acuña (eds), *Las huellas de un scecho. Anales de la Universidad de Chile. Edición extraordinaria con motivo de los 40 años del golpe de estado,* pp. 351–385. Santiago: Universidad de Chile.

Alvesson, M. and Sköldberg, K. (2004). *Reflexive Methodology.* London: Sage Publications.

Bion, W. (1962). *Learning from Experience.* London: Karnac

Bion, W. (1970). *Attention and Interpretation.* London: Tavistock Publications

Bridger, H. (1990). Courses and working conferences as transitional learning. In E. Trist and A. Murray (eds), *The Social Engagement of Social Science, Volume I. The Socio-Psychological Perspective,* pp. 221–258. London: Free Association Books.

Bridger, H. (2009). To explore the unconscious dynamics of transition as it affects the interdependence of individual, group, and organizational aims in paradigm change. In Sieverset al. (eds), *Psychoanalytic Studies of Organizations,* pp. 51–65. London: Karnac.

Chapman, J. and Long, S. (2008). Role contamination: is the poison in the person or the bottle. *Toxic Leadership,* 15(3), 40–48.

Clavel, C. (1984). La Universidad de Chile: 50 años de historia académica. *Revista Paradigma,* 29, 6–41.

Departamento de Economía (2009). *Economistas de la U, una biografía 1934–2009.,* Santiago: Universidad de Chile, Facultad de Economía y Negocios.

Erlich-Ginor, M. (2006). Structure and design of group relations conferences: issues and dilemmas. In L. Brunner et al. (eds), *Group Relations Conference,* pp. 30–43. London: Karnac.

Feldman, M. (1991). The meanings of ambiguity: learning from stories and metaphors. In P. Frost et al. (eds), *Reframing Organizational Culture*, pp. 145–156. London: Sage.

Freud, S. (1919). Lo ominoso, *Obras completas*, tomo 17, pp. 215–251. Buenos Aires: Amorrortu.

Hall, P. (2010). Historical institutionalism in rationalist and sociological perspective. In J. Mahoney and K. Thelen (eds), *Explaining Institutional Change Ambiguity, Agency and Power*, pp. 204–223. New York: Cambridge University Press.

Honneth, A. (1997). A society without humiliation? *European Journal of Philosophy* 5, 3, 306–324.

Hoggett, P. (1998). The internal establishment. In P.B. Talamo, F. Borgogno, and S.A. Merciai (eds), *Bion's Legacy to Groups*, pp. 9–24, London: Karnac.

Hoggett, P. (2009). *Politics, Identity and Emotion*, Boulder, CO: Paradigm Publishers.

Krantz, J. (2001). Dilemmas of organizational change: a system psychodynamic perspective. In L. Gould et al. (eds), *The Systems Psychodynamics of Organizations*, pp. 133–156. London: Karnac.

Lawrence, G. (1979). A concept for today: the management of oneself in role. *Exploring Individual and Organizational Boundaries*, pp. 235–249. London: Karnac.

Lawrence, G. (2000). The politics of salvation and revelation in the practice of consultation. *Tongued with Fire Groups in Experience*; pp. 165–179. London: Karnac Books.

Lawrence, G. (2008). The presence of totalitarian states-of- mind in institutions. ARCHIVE. Retrieved from http://human-nature.com/jraj/lawren.htlm 30 August 2008.

Levy, J. (2011). Memory Lost and Memory Found: a reflection on the place of memory in the group relations network and conferences. In L. Gould et al. (eds), *The Reflective Citizen*, pp. 65–81. London: Karnac.

Long, S. (2004). Building an institution for experiential learning. In L. Gould et al. (eds), *Experiential Learning in Organizations*, pp. 101–136. London: Karnac.

Long, S. (2006). Drawing from role biography in Organizational Role Analysis. In Newton et al. (Editors). *Coaching in Depth: The Organizational Role Analysis Approach*; pp. 127–143. London: Karnac.

Mahoney J. and Thelen, K. (2010). A theory of gradual institutional change. In J. Mahoney and K. Thelen (eds), *Explaining Institutional Change*, pp.1–37. New York: Cambridge University Press.

Martin, J. (1992). *Cultures in Organizations. Three Perspectives*. Oxford: Oxford University Press.

Miller, E. (1990a). Experiential learning in groups I: the development of the Leicester Model. In E. Trist and H. Murray (eds), *The Social Engagement of Social Science, Volume I. The Socio-Psychological Perspective*; pp.165–185. London: Free Association Books.

Miller, E. (1990b). Experiential learning in groups II: recent developments in dissemination and application. In Trist and Murray (eds), *The Social Engagement of Social Science, Volume I. The Socio-Psychological Perspective*, pp.186–198. London: Free Association Books.

Miller, E. (2005). *Liderazgo, creatividad y cambio cultural en organizaciones*. Santiago: Copygraph.

Montecino, S. and Acuña, M. E. (2013). *Las huellas de un acecho. Anales de la Universidad de Chile. Edición extraordinaria con motivo de los 40 años del golpe de estado*. Santiago: Universidad de Chile.

Montero C. (1997). *La revolución empresarial chilena*. Santiago: Cieplan/Dolmen Ediciones.

Palma, L. (1974). *Reseña histórica: la facultad de ciencias económicas 1934–1972*. Facultad de Ciencias Económicas y Administrativas, Santiago: Universidad de Chile.

Palmer, B. (2002). The Tavistock paradigm: inside, outside and beyond. In R.D. Hinshelwood and M. Chisea (eds), *Organizations, Anxieties and Defenses*, pp.158–182. London: Whurr Publishers.

Pedrero, P. and Trincado, F. (2014). Historia del área de los recursos humanos en la facultad de economía y negocios (FEN), Universidad de Chile. *Tesis de grado magíster en gestión de personas y dinámica organizacional*. FEN, Escuela de Postgrado, Santiago: Universidad de Chile.

Piper-Shafir, I. et al., (2013). Psicología social de la memoria: espacios y políticas del recuerdo. *PSYKHE*, 22(2), 19–32.

Ricoeur, P. (2004). *Memory, History and Forgetting*. Chicago, IL: University of Chicago Press.

Salazar, G. and Pinto, J. (1999). *Historia contemporánea de Chile I*. Santiago: LOM Ediciones.

Selume, J. (1986). La universidad de Chile y su contribución al desarrollo económico nacional. *Anales de la Universidad de Chile*, Vol. 3, pp. 43–60. Santiago: Universidad de Chile.

Schwartz, H. (1990). Antisocial actions of committed organizational oarticipants. *Narcissistic Process and Corporate Deca*y, pp. 31–45. New York: New York University Press.

Schwartz, H. (1995). Acknowledging the dark side of organizational life. In T.C. Pauchant et al., *In Search of Meaning*, pp. 224–243. New York: Jossey Bass.

Sievers, B. (2006). The psychotic organization: a socio-analytic perspective. *Ephemera* 6, 2: 104–120.

Sievers, B. (2015). Dependency and parasitic relationship: the tragic early history of photography from a socioanalytic perspective. Unpublished manuscript.

Suddaby, R. et al. (2014). Historical institutionalism. In M. Bucheli and R.D. Wadhwani (eds), *Organizations in Time*; pp. 100–123. Croydon: Oxford University Press.

Yates J. (2014). Understanding historical methods in organizations studies. In M. Bucheli and R.D. Wadhwani (eds), *Organizations in Time*, pp. 305–329. Oxford: Oxford University Press.

Beijing Group Relations Conference 2014

Cross-cultural learning and implications for the future

Seth Harkins, Huang Xaiochang, Suma Jacob,
Dannielle Kennedy, Victoria Te You Moore, John Robertson,
Jeffrey D. Roth and Jeanne M.S.T. Woon

Introduction

Jeffrey D. Roth

The group relations conference in Beijing in 2014 on Authority and Leadership in Recovery from Mental Illness and Addiction was one of a series of conferences on this theme. The task of these conferences included an opportunity to compare and contrast the group and organizational dynamics of the usual events in our conferences and those of mutual support groups such as those in 12-Step fellowships like Alcoholics Anonymous. My directing style has been heavily influenced by the Twelve Traditions of these fellowships, which I write about in a separate chapter of this book entitled "It Takes a Village to Raise a Director."

Tradition Two states: *"For our group purpose there is but one ultimate authority—a loving Higher Power as He may express Himself in our group conscience. Our leaders are but trusted servants; they do not govern."* In order to honor this concept of authority as it emerges from the group conscience, I have delegated the unfolding of the story of this Beijing conference to my friend and colleague, Seth Harkins, who shares with me a deep respect for this tradition. He might be considered the chair of a mutual support meeting, documented in this chapter, where the members of the meeting come from the consulting staff and cultural interpreters who worked together on this conference. Each contributor shares experience, strength and hope garnered from participation on the staff. As in any mutual support group, their different perspectives on the same event may shed greater light on its richness than any one of us might accomplish alone.

Pre-conference: conception, staff recruitment, institutional partners, and joining

Seth Harkins

It is often said that a group relations conference begins with one's invitation to be on staff or registration as a member. The pre-conference of this conference began with the conceptualization of the conference and continued through the on-site staff meetings prior to the arrival of members and Opening Conference Plenary. The Beijing Group Relations Conference: Authority and Leadership in Recovery from Mental Illness and Addiction (BGRC) germinated when Dr. Jeffrey Roth heard *Exploring Group Relations Work in China* (Özdemir, 2015), a paper on group relations conferences in China in 2010–2012 at the 2012 Belgirate IV Conference in Italy. Returning to Chicago, Roth found a request for proposals from the University of Chicago. He submitted "Group Relations Conference: Authority and Leadership in Recovery from Addiction" to be held at the University of Chicago Beijing Center (UCBC). Modeled after the Loyola Group Relations Conferences 2011–2014 in Chicago, IL (Harkins, Bair and Korshak, 2013; Roth, Brent, Gold, Harkins and Robertson, 2015), Roth's proposal was accepted. China represented a unique opportunity for "carrying the message" of GR and 12-Step recovery.[1]

Roth began staff recruitment at two professional conferences. He met Victoria Te You Moore, a China-born American Northwestern University graduate student. Although limited in GR experience, Roth envisioned her as an assistant director for administration (ADA). To prepare her for the BGRC, he enrolled her as ADA for the Loyola GRC 2014. Roth then met Winnie Fei, a PhD student born in China and an immigrant to Singapore, who worked with Drs. Ruthellen Josselson and Moylan Lescz in their training of Chinese group psychotherapists. With GRC member experience at the AKRI 2012 International Leadership Conference, Roth recruited her to be associate director for administration. A UCBC administrator, Xueming Liang, who did not have GRC experience, would facilitate conference logistics. Roth next enlisted Dr. Jeanne Woon, of Chinese ancestry who was born and raised in Singapore and educated in the U.S., as associate conference director. A bi-racial and bicultural directorate was formed. Six consultants, four of whom had experience at the Loyola GRCs were also recruited.

Roth's experience at the Loyola GRC 2013 incubated the idea of cultural interpretation as a way of bridging linguistic and cultural differences. Observing a deaf member's use of sign language, Roth imagined cultural interpretation as the pairing Chinese assistants fluent in English and Mandarin, who could synthesize here-and-now discourse. Utilizing this synthesis, consultants could interpret group dynamics.

Efforts to recruit cultural interpreters (CIs) through Chinese addiction psychiatrists failed. When Fei threatened to resign unless Roth authorized her to recruit CIs, Roth, "... surrendered." Fei recruited Dr. Xiaohau Lu, from Tsinghua University (TU), who had trained with Josselson and Lescz. Lu shared the BGRC idea with Professor Fumin Fan, a nationally renowned expert in group counseling and group psychotherapy from TU, who embraced the endeavor. Linking the two was fortuitous because of their leadership in the Division of Group Counseling and Group Therapy and the China Mental Health Association. These organizations became the primary networks for membership recruitment. Professor Fan's endorsement of the conference was key to this process. Importantly, the two recruiting organization sponsors and TU was vital in securing authorization from the Chinese government to receive conference registration fees. Without this, the BGRC would not have been held. Moreover, Lu personally knew many of the potential registrants. Eleven American and Chinese organizations agreed to be conference sponsors.[2]

Roth invited the staff in May 2013 with a contract letter, requiring staff to "abstain from alcohol, nicotine and other mood altering substances from the opening staff dinner until the end of the final staff meeting." Four online meetings facilitated pre-conference joining and planning. Chat room themes included fear and anxiety about joining, international boundary crossing, touring of Beijing, conference logistics, communism, and the director's authority. In this context, an important enactment emerged in a virtual fish bowl. With the staff "looking on," the administrative team struggled to grasp their roles, tasks, and relationship to the director. As they tried to maintain group harmony, something critically important in Confucian Heritage China, it was evident an important cultural dynamic was unfolding. Fei envisioned herself as the associate director for cultural interpretation. Lu saw herself as assistant director for recruitment. Moore saw herself as assistant director for administration, who would work in tandem with Liang. Boundary, authority, role and task confusions would later thread through the conference.

Other cultural issues emerged, including Western imperialism and the importance of American consultants immersing themselves in Chinese culture through four days of touring. Staff anxiety and fear were also evident in a sense of being lost navigating the visa application process. An additional issue was the sorting of the staff into two hotels; one representing traditional Chinese culture and the other international corporate culture. Further cross-cultural learning occurred with CIs joining the online conversations, sharing their diverse cultural backgrounds from the four corners of China. Other cultural artifacts (e.g. daylight savings time and "knock off designer products") illustrated the challenge of bridging languages and cultures. Joining was symbolized by a consultant's revelation of her Chinese-Caucasian grandchild. She "was now in with both feet." Another joining dynamic emerged when a staff member revealed challenges with an alcoholic spouse. Roth suggested the individual use the staff as a mutual aid group. An Al-Anon staff member offered her "experience, strength, and hope."

Touring began in earnest on May 16, 2014. The staff visited the Great Wall, the Summer Palace, the Olympic Park, a tea house, a massage parlor, Tiananmen Square, the Forbidden City, the Temple of Heaven, the Pearl Market, the Drum Towner, a Beijing AA meeting, Peking University, the Stars and Rain School, and Hu tongs (authentic Chinese neighborhoods). These experiences provided a rich array of cultural metaphors for consultation.

Conference administration challenges: the lay of the land and homecoming

Victoria Te You Moore

In American business parlance, the Chinese word "guanxi" means relationships and connotes the complex networks of informal connections that are often the primary means through which things get done in China. In other words, China is a society in which straightforward, formal designations of boundaries, roles, authority, and task only go so far in advancing the primary task. It is a society in which complex, informal, and flexible relationships exist in service of organizations' primary task. The reader is invited to keep this cultural context in mind when envisioning how the group relations models might take shape in China.

The BGRC consisted of 60 members, including 59 Chinese members and one American, who left the conference halfway through. The other casualty in the membership was the spouse of a staff member (who threatened to resign unless this member was admitted). This particular dual relationship was a secret to most of the staff until the week of the conference. It is also noteworthy that one member was the head of one of the sponsoring institutions and, in that capacity, was instrumental in making the conference possible and recruiting members for the conference. She also had current and former students on the staff and in the membership, which accorded her considerable informal authority. It is worth noting that three staff members had affinity with the University of Chicago, a conference sponsor. Further, with the transition of Dr. Lu from ADA to CI, a new "management team" was formed, consisting of the directorate, one consultant, and the acting lead of administration.

Administrative and CI teams exemplified the conference's fluid role and boundary delineations. Both teams were led by the associate director for administration. During conference week, the associate director for administration served as the head of the CI team and as a CI herself, delegating the task of leading the administrative work to me. The CI team, which saw several formal role shifts, finalized as a team of eight (six Chinese, one Taiwanese living in the United States, and one China-born Singaporean). The pre-conference administrative team (led by me) consisted of one to four ADAs (Dr. Lu, two Chinese UCBC administrators and one China-born American). Further, each ADA had dual relationships with members and sponsors of the conference, reflecting also the complex authority relationships in this conference. Finally, one of the ADAs led an unknown number of UCBC facilities staff, which functioned as shadow administrators for the conference.

The administrative team struggled to contain and manage the dynamics that arose from conflicts between the GRC and the UCBC, due to dual relationships of its team members and the under-authorization of the acting lead administrator. Informal role shifts among staff included the youngest members of the Administrative Team and CIs being "captured" multiple times by the membership. Also, as acting head of administration, I was pulled in by the directorate on two separate occasions to function as a CI.

This conference was on many levels a homecoming experience for me, a China-born American.[3] One homecoming dynamic I helped carry was the multigenerational trauma of collaborating with outsiders. One does not need to look very far back in world history to see the danger that comes with the label of "collaborator" – see the locals who help U.S. forces in Iraq and Afghanistan or Nazi collaborators. During the Euro-American and Japanese colonization of China during the eighteenth, nineteenth, and twentieth centuries, many Chinese locals, including my ancestors, were "collaborators." Local collaborators often become targets of aggression and violence, especially once the dominant outsiders, whom they serve, leave the region.

At this conference, there were a number of staff who served as a bridge in between the Americans and the Chinese locals. This included staff of Chinese ethnicity, who live abroad, as well as Chinese CIs. We were at this cultural boundary forging the bridges but also had a vulnerability to draw the projections of aggression because we are usually not perceived as having as much authority as the outsider experts and are not protected once the foreigners leave. My experience has helped me think about how individuals, who are open, attractive, and attracted to, outsiders, are vulnerable to taking on collaborative roles and then to take on "disloyal" projections from their "family-of-origin" groups. This was also a dynamic in the membership. A bilingual male Chinese member was unhappy with a CI's interpretation of his comments, so I consulted to him in English that he could address the staff in English, which he then did. This exchange was then shamed by a female member who looked at me and said "Chinese people should speak Chinese."

Another homecoming dynamic I experienced was a family-of-origin transference with the staff that is related to my own recovery from codependency. I observed myself taking on a familiar role of a parentified child who accommodates, who does anything and everything that is needed for "the family" in order to "earn my seat" at the table, out of fear that, if I don't do everything I am asked to do, then I risk losing my spot at a table and becoming neglected or marginalized. In the conference, I tried to do everything I was asked (some on-site administrative work, a bit of interpretation work, and some leading the administrative team which I was under-authorized to do), and I still felt neglected and marginalized in the system. The data for this is that my role in the conference was not clearly defined – for a long time there was indecision regarding whether I would be a member of the CI team or the administrative team – and this continued to change at the conference. When I asked the director to clarify my role in the months leading up to the conference, he asked me if I was willing to take on a flexible role of "whatever is needed," and I agreed – and I learned the cost of taking on such a role only by hitting rock bottom. In a sense, my role flexibility was a relapse into my codependence, but in another sense, it was also perhaps a necessity for putting this conference together in a land where "guanxi" reigns. The BGRC staff showed a willingness to work with more flexibility in order to put this conference together in Beijing, and what came together was far from perfect – but maybe it was "good-enough" (Winnicott, 1965)?

Boundaries, authority, role and task: a consultant's perspective

Suma Jacob

The traditional definition of boundaries includes strict adherence to time, task, and territory. On the practical level, the U.S. consultant staff held the anxiety of crossing the borders. How do we get visas? Should we wear masks to protect us from city pollution? How do we communicate with or without mobile phones in China? Given language barriers, much of the input focus was on introducing CIs to the structural boundaries and format of the GRC. Our focus on structural boundaries left little time during the conference to explore psychological boundaries.

The UCBC was designed and decorated to serve and draw alumni who will contribute and donate to the university. There were limitations on what we could move in and out of rooms. There also was UCBS staff anxiety about what might happen when members came from all over China with a range of socioeconomic backgrounds and engaged in-conference events. There was at least one instance of damage to a break area table that led to resentment between the hosts and members and, in turn, towards conference staff.

The conference schedule was rigorous and the CIs noted there was a "workaholism" to the pace, given our simultaneous 12-Step meetings.

Some of the CIs noted there were no break times, even after or around meals given our meetings at lunch. As mentioned earlier, there were challenges in the member-staff boundaries. A staff member's husband entering membership and subsequent role conflicts were the topic of emails to staff within weeks of the conference. This led to complex dynamics in my small study group (SSG).

In addition to these linear, concrete boundaries, we had virtual, cyber-space and invisible boundaries with technology. Staff had learned about What's App messaging via phones and set up a "staff group to which some CIs were added," so we could communicate outside our phone carrier limitations. This led to sharing messages and pictures throughout and after the conference. It is important to note that the UCBC gave us access to sites such as Facebook that we could not access from our "corporate or traditional" hotels. One night we were looking up Tibet-China history and the web-access and Wikipedia text changed right before our eyes.

Similar to staff post-processing gatherings, consultants had their own gatherings and "ed-time" inside and outside of the formal schedule. Although our post workday gatherings were in separate spaces, virtual communication ensued. The consultant staff had explicitly agreed not to drink alcohol from the beginning to the end of the conference through the staff-joining contract. The CIs did not have an explicit written contract. After the long conference workdays, the CIs gathered for drinks, for support, and to process their experiences. The CIs observed a staff member who violated the contractual drinking agreement. Some of this data was available, but not shared while conference staff were working. The CI's stated they did not want to get staff into trouble. The ease of sharing information via technology versus in face-to-face staff meetings was striking. Consultant staff had insufficient time to do dynamic staff work given the multilayered density of explicit tasks in the conference.

Pre-meeting emails and chat meetings brought up concerns about air pollution exposure. Some staff brought masks. Only one day was the UCBC administrator seen wearing a mask to work. That day the center offered masks if we went outside. By dinnertime, the Air Quality Index improved and staff didn't wear the masks when they went outside. The UCBC attempted to provide a bubble from the pollutants, contaminated air, censored Internet, and the unknown. From an open systems organizational perspective, the non-linear communications, in addition to traditional concrete boundaries, created larger, permeable spaces and complex webs of interconnection.

Authority in group relations conferences is defined as the right to do work on behalf of a group. Authority for the conference was granted by the UCBC, AKRI, and eleven Chinese and American organizations to accomplish learning about group relations and its implications for recovery from mental illness and addiction. Formal authority may have come through traditional staff roles and novel, emerging CI roles. Informal authority could bring about changes in organizational systems. For example, a nationally renowned professor was involved in recruitment of members and became a member as well. Additionally, the professor, as a leader of one of the conference sponsors, provided a welcoming speech at the opening plenary. The professor thus took up a shadow director role within the conference.

One striking and unexpected exchange was the request to take photos of and with the staff after the Conference Opening by the Chinese members. Was this a virtual image of how the Chinese members wanted to see the staff or be seen with the staff? As a consultant, this non-verbal, ethno-variant form of photo documentation threw me. We questioned how it authorized, de-authorized staff or self-authorized members. In a dual or multi-language conference, non-verbal data becomes increasingly important. Time needs to be set aside to understand cultural variation and norms in order interpret this data at a deeper organizational level.

If a role is like a job description or a coat we put on for weather and to do certain tasks, then the role of a small-group consultant had features that were unique from being a consultant in a familiar-language conference. I was struck by how sensitive I became to non-verbal data and exchanges. Initially, I had to curb my desire to KNOW all the verbal content in the room. Over time, this freed me up to focus on the rich data in the room beyond words.

The SSG team and consultants had some sort of "teaching" role because none of the CIs, except two, had previous GRC experience. The SSG fishbowl training during the pre-conference staff workdays and SSG team meetings (attended by SSG consultants and CIs) were essential to practice working together in pairs as CI and consultant, and giving the CI a model of how the SSG work is done. Desires for pairings were expressed at the first staff dinner. The SSG team decided to "draw" pairs after our fishbowl work. The CI who expressed interest in working with me and I were last to draw. Thus, we were officially paired together by the other "random" staff pairing. Our SSG worked on many layers of experiencing authority. In the nuances of how one takes up her role as a consultant, I looked for how to bring my own salient identities to my role. The members were much more focused on my identity as a woman than as a South Asian in China.

The role of CI went beyond translation to interpretation of cultural meanings. Several of the CIs had the capacity to do exact, simultaneous translation. This was not utilized in the SSG, although I requested this once in the 12-Step group, so I could understand what the members were saying. Cultural interpretation was key because where individuals were seated, non-verbal "meaning-making" needed to be conveyed in addition to verbal content. CIs noted a complex pull to be a consultant, assist with boundary management and to be a member given the knowledge that the consultant does not have because of the language barrier. From my handwritten notes during the conference, I recall the CIs talking about the challenge of having "responsibility without authority ... and how hard it was to find our own voice." The novelty of the CI role and the complex, dual roles of the administrators were significant challenges.

What was the task priority work of the group? There were multiple layers of tasks. Owing to sponsorship additions in China, "mental health" was added to the title of the conference fairly late. So, one task was to study Authority, Leadership, Recovery from Mental Illness and Addiction. Other tasks included dealing with cultural/language adaptations, 12-Step exposure to CIs and incorporating Tai Chi. Seth Harkins had intended to conduct Q-sort research, but minimal time had been allocated to address the complexity of cross-cultural meaning of this research task. In the review and application groups, participants were hungry for more knowledge about the 12-Step recovery programs. Materials were being translated the day before the conference began.

Learning in the small study group: risk, vulnerability, and leadership

Anonymous

I served as a CI and had my initial group relations learning at the 2014 conference. Most of the conference members were psychotherapists, and were therefore experts. Chinese people generally feel obligated to show respect to elders and persons in authority. These factors contributed to the experienced experts' privileges. In my SSG, a couple of experts (professional psychotherapists) were projected to be the group leaders. Even more so, two young members who lacked professional experiences almost lost their voice, and were "gone" (i.e. stopped showing up). Interestingly, these two members were the only men in the group. The women were sad about this – they thought they cherished the men. It reminded me of Empress Dowager Cixi in Qing, who took control of the dynasty. It also reminded me of our modern Chinese families, where the parents have excessively high expectations for their child, "Little Emperor" or "Little Princess," to succeed like a "Dragon" (Chinese idiom: Wang Zi Cheng Long). In fact, it is not uncommon to hear of Chinese student suicides because of academic stress. Similarly, as a young non-professional CI, I was vulnerable to the group's projections. Personally, as a "Little Princess" in my family, I also wanted to become a "dragon" of the group I belonged to, the conference staff group. Perhaps that increased my susceptibility.

During the five sessions of the SSG, the consultant and I were the female authority figures. I witnessed the processing of Chinese feminism as well as its intertwining with other dimensions of historically inherited Chinese oppression, in particular, age and social class (as manifested by professional level). Throughout the process, women successfully "killed" the men. In this female dominated group with only two young male members, one man stopped showing up at the third session, and another quit without early notice as well at the last session. Considering the time when the two men were present, they were quite silent. The women had deep discussions about whether it was the women who "killed" the men, or whether the men "suicided" in order to enable the women's self-awareness. The whole discussion around that was sad and heavy.

There were at least two female members who spoke fluent English. However, unlike other SSGs, none of them challenged me in my role as CI (i.e., no one challenged my interpretations, or usurped my role when someone else required translation). By the same token, two older women were experienced group psychotherapists, and authorized to guide the group. They declined to do that, however, and never fully took up the group's authorization. Thus, their leadership was never fully incorporated. It may be that fear inhibited these women from their leadership. The group's later discussion of the Cultural Revolution's traumatic impact on intellectuals is relevant here. If you stand out with professional expertise and knowledge, you risk being "killed."

A turning point in the SSG occurred when the consultant admitted something she did wrong in session four. The group suddenly became self-authorized. Before this point, the majority of the group's focus was on her role, picking on her interventions, criticizing her as "cold." After the "admission" of a mistake, the consultant was seen as caring, accommodating, and patient. Soon enough, the group members took their own authority: examining the group dynamics and speaking English directly to the consultant.

The conference experience made me stronger; I learned to accept ambiguity and take up my authority. I suggest the following for conferences like this. First, CIs should have clear information about the nature of their work, the roles that they will be playing, the potential risks they will be taking, and the supports to be provided. Second, recruiting diverse members, including those with little "power," will bring infinite benefits.

Experiencing authority through the CI role

Huang Xiaochang (Jasmine)

Confucianism is an essential part of Chinese culture, which emphasizes conformity to authority and the group. Contemporary Chinese are becoming more and more self-assertive, self-directed and self-authorized. This is probably due to increased interactions between China and the rest of the world. How do the Chinese balance the conflicts between Confucianism and individual assertion nowadays? Let me share some amazing things that happened in the Beijing GRC to illustrate this. It was within this context that I worked as a CI in an SSG with the consultant, Dr. Seth Harkins.

Experiential learning in the SSG contrasts to Chinese members' learning through didactic instruction from teachers and other authorities, something integral in Confucian cultural heritage. In the SSG, the consultant just offers interpretations regarding authority, leadership and overt/covert dynamics within the group-as-a-whole instead of explicit teaching. In my role as CI, I did not actively join the group discussion. When group members introduced themselves in SSG 1, I kept silent. In China, such behavior is considered rude. As time passed, I noticed the gaze from a woman to my left. I said to myself, "Yes, it is weird." Later, in SSG 4, this woman left the group to go to the bathroom. When she returned, she mentioned the introduction scenario during SSG 1. She expressed feeling despised and a little angry when I didn't introduce myself. She later understood my behavior might be related to my role. After sharing her feelings about me, a member commented, "You released yourself through going to bathroom." What a meaningful comment for underlying dynamics! The woman withheld her anger and distress from the first session. You could tell how difficult it was for this woman to express her anger towards me as an authority. Other group members also considered me as an authority. I could feel the members' longing for my approval after they did some translation. I could feel tension in the group when a member challenged my cultural interpretation for the first time. And the most challenging thing about my role was being a projection object for feelings about the consultant. Apparently, it felt less dangerous to "attack" a secondary authority figure. The fear/respectful emotions towards authority and compliant/conformist behavior was prevalent throughout the SSG. In making sense of these contradictions and dualities, I prefer to take Confucianism, which teaches acceptance, into account.

Authority, authorization and self-authorization were important SSG themes enacted through two members in particular. An American psychiatrist was a member of our group. Because the "recovery from mental illness and addiction" was the conference theme, the psychiatrist became the authority figure right after the members discovered the consultant was not going to teach as they wanted. The members authorized the psychiatrist and de-authorized the consultant. Another member was similarly authorized by the group. She was a nationally known professor for whom members showed deep respect. As noted previously by Victoria and Suma, she claimed she just wanted to be "a member" of the group, but was the "shadow director" of the conference. Apparently, no one can deny the influence of prestige, when we authorize someone to be an authority.

The point here is how the self-authorization occurred in what began as a fairly calm and polite SSG. The group strove to be harmonious for two to three sessions. The turning point emerged when the U.S. psychiatrist left the conference at the beginning of SSG 3. Seth consulted with the metaphor of the group as a "recovering family with a distant dad." The members took up the consultation and imagined the different roles they were playing in this "recovering family." I could see the members struggling in following or leading in this process. Gradually, they figured out that they had to authorize themselves to understand themselves as unique parts of the family system and work together as a whole group. As this unfolded, roles were identified. A competitive member in a "big sister" role, who previously challenged my authority to interpret by judging my English was acknowledged. Sometimes she challenged the consultant's authority, by acting like the consultant, making her own consultations. When we reviewed this after a session, Seth described her a "shadow consultant." Gradually, various roles were identified, "mom," "big brother," "little sister" and so forth. After the "big brother" challenged the opinions of "big sister," the group started to work more effectively. As the group authorized itself, members engaged in the primary task of the SSG through examination of their own dynamics. For me, the question is: Will the Chinese self-authorize themselves in the actual life? I am optimistic about this even if we might have some obstacles related to Confucianism getting in the way.

Authorizing myself to interpret was a very big challenge. What is the most important point of what the speaker is saying? What is the essential issue for the consultant to grasp from the situation? How could I evaluate the situation and translate to the consultant? How could I not imply irrelevant messages when I translate to the members given all those details? What I learned through this event was trust; trusting myself, the consultant and the group process. As CI, I was the cultural bridge between the consultant and the group. This was the primary task of my unique role. Communication with the consultant was also an integral part of my self-authorization. When we debriefed after sessions, I talked with Seth about the tense and insecure feelings I was holding from our first session. When we reviewed and prepared for SSG 2, Seth told me that he felt low back pain at SSG 1, but, after we finished SSG 2, he said he did not feel the pain anymore and felt like he had just "given birth to a baby." What an interesting cooperative experience we had!

Group Relations and 12-step recovery in China

John Robertson

During this conference, my primary role was SSG consultant. In the United States, I specialize in pediatric and adult psychiatry and addiction.

The theme for the Beijing Group Relations Conference was Recovery from Addiction and Mental Illness. This resulted in some concern by UCBC. They were fearful that there would be a bunch of drunks and crazy people coming to the conference. I'm not sure whether they were more concerned about the membership or the staff. Certain adaptations had to be made due to cultural differences. For instance, in the current political structure in China, religion is frowned upon. Our work could be considered evangelical. Indeed, it is evangelical with regard to GRC work. There is so little experience and knowledge about this in China.

The theme of our conference also resulted in structural changes to the traditional GRC in that actual 12-Step meetings were integrated within the structure of the conference. This innovation has been done before in a series of GRCs that Dr. Roth had directed in Chicago. One example of our adaptation to the Chinese political culture was that we removed the word God from the 12-Step material. God is mentioned five times in the 12-Steps and we had to change that wording to "higher power." Interestingly in Beijing, a city of 21 million people, there are few 12-Step recovery communities.[4] During our pre-conference touring, we actually attended and participated in an AA meeting.

Another nontraditional event that was integrated into our GRC was Tai Chi. For the first half hour of each day, staff and members participated with no formal leadership. On the first day, one of our staff began leading the Tai Chi. Additional leaders within the membership quickly emerged and led the interactions for these events. We merely copied the movements of the temporary leader as best we could. There was no verbal direction. It was a very interesting and fluid event with regard to non-verbal communication and emergence of member leaders.

With regard to the 12-Step meetings, members and staff during lunch were invited to attend either a Gamblers/Workaholics Anonymous or Codependence Anonymous meeting for each of the four days. The joke among the staff was that a 45-minute 12-Step group and combined lunch epitomized workaholism.

Generally, the staff did not provide much self-disclosure in our 12-Step meetings. These groups were very large. Most of the sharing was done in Mandarin. Those Americans that did not speak Mandarin sat quietly and listened unless they happened to have a CI sitting next to them that might offer to do some translation.

Let's compare the boundaries, authorities, roles, and tasks between these two very different traditions and group cultures.

Boundaries:

- GRC: Staff is selected by the director and members apply for acceptance.
- 12-Step: Community membership is self-selected and open to anyone desiring sobriety.

Authority:

- GRC: Sponsoring agents authorize the director of the conference who authorizes the staff.
- 12-Step: "your higher power."

Roles:

- GRC: Specific to group and task.
- 12-Step: The role is a person with impairment seeking help.

Tasks:

- GRC: Education via experiential learning.
- 12-Step: Healing via personal transformation.

Similarities:

- Both facilitate learning through group participation.
- Both recognize that the whole is greater than sum of parts.
- Both recognize the power of the group to facilitate growth and transformation.
- Both are concerned with leadership and authority.

So what is it like integrating Gamblers Anonymous, Workaholics or Codependence Anonymous Groups into a GRC? These are two very different traditions and group cultures with distinct languages, authority structure, boundaries, and goals. At first glance, these two distinctly different forms of group process appear to be antithetical to one another. How can 12-Step groups that are nonhierarchical and allow essentially unrestricted membership be compatible with GRC work that is structured with highly defined authority, roles, boundaries, tasks, and membership?

What happens when a GRC staff member violates usual work boundaries with members during a conference by participating shoulder to shoulder in the emotional self-disclosure of a 12-Step meeting? Does this play havoc with the usual GRC goals concerning experiential learning? Alternatively, does this violate the work and healing goals of 12-Step groups?

So what do you get when you marry 12-Step and Group Relations? GRC work is about learning how groups function and especially about the role of authority. 12-step learning is about how the individual functions especially about improving that function by substituting higher power authority for self-authority. My experience is that the resulting event is softer and emotionally gentler than usual GRC work with less regression psychologically and a more therapeutic component.

An imperfect bridge: bringing what we have, sharing what we know, and learning what we don't

Jeanne M.S.T. Woon

"Clay is shaped into a pot but it is the empty space within that gives its function."

(Laozi, "Tao Te Ching")

At the conclusion of the 2014 group relations conference in Beijing, Seth invited all staff to contribute to a presentation or paper of their experiences. While I had not participated in the project initially, I recently was requested to do so owing to the role I had as Associate Director of the Conference.

As I reflected my experiences – from February 2013, when first contacted by Jeffrey, to the conclusion of the conference in May the following year – more and more surfaced: memories of events (and the people and institutions involved), experiences of the events, interpretation and understanding of the experiences... as well as reviewing these from different angles, from others' perspectives, and with the distance of time.

The sections by my colleagues show the richness of our experiences and the complexity of the conference. I will share a few experiences related to my role as associate director, add comments to some events discussed by others from the perspective of person-in-role, and offer some lessons I learned from the conference and from hearing the voices of others.

On becoming associate director for the conference

When Jeffrey first contacted me about working with him on this conference, it was not explicit at the time in what capacity he was asking me
to be involved. I understood that he recently had received authorization
to hold the conference at the University of Chicago's Beijing Center and
was in the process of putting it together. The idea of a group relations
conference in China was intriguing and I was open to how I could
support the effort, even if it was to be from the sidelines. After some
conversation, I accepted his invitation to serve in the role of associate
director.

This was my first time in such a role. Taking it up included looking to
Jeffrey for guidance on what he needed and authorized me to do in the
role, while authorizing myself to bring whatever I had, including experience in group relations, training in cross-cultural issues, involvement
with AKRI, profession as a psychologist, as well as personal experiences
of being a Singaporean with mainly Chinese ancestry and an Asian
immigrant to the United States. Those latter experiences at times involved
"straddling" cultures or shuttling between the "East" and "West."

*Informal roles as a "sounding board" for the director and as a "bridge" in
the conference*

While Jeffrey made the decisions as director, he was open to ideas and
opinions of others. In our work together, I had a role as "sounding
board" to the director. He encouraged me to keep him honest. At times,
all I needed to do was listen, asking questions for exploration and
clarification (e.g., Are we looking for bilingual individuals simply to
translate between the English and Mandarin languages, or for persons
who also are able to interpret cultural references? Who do the CIs "work
for" – staff or members?). Other times, the questions expressed reserva-
tions and concerns (e.g., If members will be encountering both group
relations and 12-Step events for the first time, wouldn't that risk confusing the two models in their minds? Or over an initial idea of appointing a
member to lead *taiji*). I felt authorized to share different perspectives,
assert positions, or provide input on decisions.

The "bridge" role was more complicated as it called for consideration
of inter-cultural issues. It involved bringing in what I know while being
aware that there is a lot more that I do *not* know. In a simple form, the

role was manifested in my delivering a short portion of the opening plenary address both in English and in Mandarin. The less simple part of the activity was that although I was comfortable with English, I was far from fluent in Mandarin, and therefore needed a lot more time to prepare for that bit.

Incidentally, this example points to the different degrees of comfort and fluency with various competencies that each person at the conference held – with each of the working languages of English and Mandarin; with the American culture represented by the staff coming in from the United States; with the culture of China represented by our hosts, cultural interpreters, some administrators, and most of the members; with the group relations tradition developed in Britain and rooted in West European ideas; with the mental health field of addiction and the 12-Step recovery culture. None of us knew all of it and we had to depend on each other, trusting others' expertise while sharing our own.

The role of "bridge" actually was taken up at various times by several staff and members. Perhaps it would be more accurate to imagine building a bridge with each "bridge" part extending to the next in order to span differences of language, culture, and models of working.

Bridging to the designated "bridgers" – the cultural interpreters

With primarily English-speaking consultants and mostly Mandarin-speaking membership, the bilingual CIs served a crucial role of "bridging" the work between consultants and members. The group who worked this conference were impressive. Coming from different cities around China, most were students and professionals in mental health and some were quite experienced in group psychotherapy. The "bridging" needed was to the group relations model for this conference. Also, some had not worked in cultural interpretation before. Months prior to gathering in Beijing, Jeffrey and I held group meetings by Skype with the CIs to meet them, introduce group relations work, and give them brief opportunities to practice.

The taiji event

To show respect for and include some aspect of Chinese culture, Jeffrey added *taiji* (tai chi) to the design of the conference. While supportive of the idea and intent, I wondered briefly if it might not seem as if we were "carrying coals to Newcastle." It was unclear at first how the activity would be conducted, other than it would be in silence: Did we have an expert on staff? Would we bring in a *taiji quan* teacher? If so, would that person be part of the staff? I expressed concerns when it seemed that Jeffrey had in mind a prospective member leading the event. Imagine the confusion of boundaries and roles when a member has a pre-designated role as assigned by the director and, among other concerns, the impact on that member's freedom to learn. In the end, that rather alarming prospect was averted when the individual did not apply to the conference. Relief on that front, however, then brought the problem of needing an alternate plan if we were still to include the scheduled event. With reluctance, I shared that I knew some *taiji* at the level of a beginner, knowing just one short form and practicing it every workday for past several years. I offered, in case another solution was not found, to start the event by sharing what I knew and hoping that others from the membership would join in bringing their expertise. I was anxious and uncomfortable about the role as it went against cultural expectations that a leader should be some sort of expert. To those who did know *taiji*, it would show how little I knew. It was a challenge and an opportunity to let go and work with what we had, whether it was a little or a lot. As others have described here, a few members smoothly authorized themselves to lead the group from the second morning onwards.

Crossing cultures

In our preparations, Jeffrey and I discussed my concerns about the attitude with which the model(s) were being introduced to prospective participants in China. Are we bringing group relations in a spirit of sharing something we believe could be useful and valuable while respecting the values and culture of others, or is it with some implicit belief in the superiority of what we bring?

Growing up in Singapore likely heightened my awareness of the history of conflict and tensions between Britain and China (e.g., the Opium Wars in the 1800s); of European colonization around the world; of European missionaries taking Christian beliefs to other peoples. Experience as an Asian in the United States included encounters with attitudes some had toward ethnic minorities and immigrants, of the impressions some Americans hold of other countries, including China. While consciously trying not to make presumptions about anyone's beliefs and intentions, I was alert to and wary of prejudices and privileges that we, the staff from the United States, might carry and bring with our work. At the same time, however, even though, as Dannie Kennedy observes in the final section, a lot of the stress of the conference might have been located in staff of dual identities, the anxieties of Americans going to China – especially those going for the first time – may have been given less attention.

As Victoria Moore had shared, there was a sense of "homecoming" for me as well even though I had never been to China before. One of my great-great-grandfathers had migrated from southern China to the new British colony of Singapore in the 1850s. Chinese language, culture, and history were taught in schools and transmitted in some families. Yet, during my childhood, there were still restrictions against Singaporeans travelling to China. It was a combined sensation of strangeness and familiarity to be in a group relations conference where, for the first time, most of the participants *looked like me*.

Lessons learned (or to learn again)

- We each hold some piece of the whole and none has all. Keeping this in mind can help us be more open to hearing others' experiences.
- Taking time to share and examine the range of experiences gives us all the opportunity to learn and gain more than what we have.
- Echoing my colleagues, we may have tried to do too much in this conference, packing the schedule with events and meetings, leaving little space for listening, reflection, examination, discovery, and process.
- In a culture where building and maintaining relationships is an important part of work, making time for it is essential, especially to work through differences and misunderstandings.
- On the other hand, we may have a fantasy that if only we made enough time, had enough whatever, we would be able to grasp or work through everything. But that is unlikely, and grappling with not-knowing and with our anxiety is part of the work.
- Given that none of us has all it takes to make a conference happen, managing the work necessitates trust, to create an interdependence where we bring what we have and respect what others bring. Trust involves taking the risk that it may be abused.
- Working across cultures calls for flexibility and adaptability when conditions change.

- Crucial to any inter-cultural work is approaching the other with respect and to share and learn with humility.
- Individuals, groups, and institutions have cultures, histories, and agenda. Group relations work has a culture.
- Privilege is a presumption of one culture being the "baseline" from which others differ and having the power to not examine it.
- Much as we try to work "without memory or desire," we are not blank slates. Personal and cultural histories color our lenses. The more aware we are of what we bring, the better we are able to notice, examine, and manage the impact on our work, the better the chances of learning something we do not yet know.

Cross-cultural learning and implications for the future

Dannielle Kennedy

As the final entry in this collective chapter, I would like to touch on two aspects of this conference. First is the importance of laying the ground-work, of negotiating alignment when working across cultures, languages, and nationalities. Second is about the enormity of the task of finding each other across those differences ... about the intimate and painful process of how people in groups attempt to hold enough identity to maintain sanity yet not so firm a one that they cannot change, grow and find their place in the family of things.

Upon reflection, one of the biggest learnings for me is how much the exercise of authority and leadership is influenced by the beginnings, the birth story of the conference institution. Of course, this should be no surprise since the underlying dynamics that were present at the outset of an enterprise will very likely endure and find expression in events going forward, but my experience in this conference reminded me of this powerful truth once again. The way we begin is the way we proceed. What was not resolved in the pre-conference work emerged in the conference. The different organizations-in-the-mind, both conscious and unconscious, were left without articulation, as we spent much of our pre-conference time on the urgent and worthy task of orienting the CIs. Once the conference began, we realized there were so many cultural differences and so many learning tasks (group dynamics, recovery from addiction, recovery from mental illness) that we had insulated ourselves from the deeper dynamics of our differences of which we are all so afraid. The conflict of meaning therefore came most clearly into focus in "crunch moments" in the here-and-now, where the emotions and tensions lived. This uncertainty is what drove the staff acting out, both in and after the conference, as our work was indeed a jumble of unspoken, unexplored, and un-negotiated authorizations. These moments of in-conference conflict or indecision often forced a diplomatic default rather than an exploration of experience and meaning. The traditional consultant instruction to hold to boundaries of task and role and not to be seduced by "convention and social nicety" was tested and often succumbed to diplomatic responses.

A few examples of such crunch moments: members, who, like all members, longed for the consulting staff to be friendly teachers, snapped photos during the opening and closing plenaries and convinced the director to have the staff pose with the membership for an all-conference photo; the conference director made time during the opening plenary for the eminent professor, who was also a conference member, to deliver a warm and gracious welcoming speech to the membership; administrative concerns dominated staff meeting time and on occasion administrators settled disputes with each other and the director by ultimatum. These and other crunch moments contributed to the way consulting staff relaxed boundaries and acted out rather than worked with conflicts directly in staff meetings.

Taking on the enormous and exciting challenge of doing GR work across national, cultural, and linguistic lines, and, bringing the model to inexperienced populations, puts front and center the need for negotiation of an aligned authorization for the conference model with the institutional partners. In this case, ambiguous authorization pushed administrative work to the surface during the conference and trumped the deeper, riskier, and more powerful aspects of the Group Relations theory and model. There were many crunch moments when quick decisions had to be made and the lack of authorization pushed out dynamic work and moved into compromise and diplomacy.

The movie *Dances with Wolves* won an Oscar for best picture in 1991 and captures the challenge of cross-cultural learning (Costner et al. 2003). In it, a Civil War officer is singularly assigned to an abandoned fort on the frontier with a tribe of Sioux as his nearest neighbor. Over time, he is drawn to their bravery, spirit, and way of life and the experience is mutual. He begins to shed certain less adaptive aspects of his own culture and adopt some of theirs. The officer's own culture begins to see him as strange and "other" and, while accepted among the Sioux, his former identity poses a threat to them as the U.S. military begins to hunt for him as a suspected deserter. Obviously, the officer is now in a position to be instrumental in integrating the two identity groups, and in one pipe-smoking scene actually suggests this to the outrage of his Sioux brotherhood. This scene demonstrates how the hero is a potential target for negative projections for both sides. When he is captured, a fellow officer says with contempt, "You turned Injun, didn't you?" He is of both groups and yet he fully belongs to neither.

I describe this plot line because it links with my experience of the conference, particularly in observing and interacting with the people with both Chinese and American identities (regardless of the passports they carried). This is where, it seemed to me, the conference did most of its work and where the most stress was experienced. My colleague, Victoria Te You Moore, writes above about the notion of the World War II collaborator, the opportunist, the traitor. Is the reaching for learning and growth (or even survival) that takes you away from your "people," your identity group, a betrayal or an attempt to lift yourself and your group to a better place? Or both? The difficulty of the individual who feels pulled to reach beyond the identity group to take an opportunity offered by "the other," an opportunity to find your place, incurs both the unconscious authorization and the potential competition, envy, contempt and condemnation from the home community, from those who speak only the mother tongue.

Notes

1. "Carrying the message" is a phrase from the 12 Steps of Alcoholics Anonymous. See *Alcoholics Anonymous* (1976). NY: World Services, Inc. pp. 59–60.
2. The A.K. Rice Institute for the Study of Social Systems; Division of Group Counseling and Group Therapy, China Association for Mental Health; University of Chicago Beijing Center; University of Chicago Department of Psychiatry; the Department of Psychology Tsinghua University; the Institute of Mental Health, Beijing University; China Association of Drug Abuse Prevention and Treatment, China American Psychoanalytic Alliance (CAPA); American Society of Addiction Medicine; and International Society of Addiction Medicine.
3. It was also a sort of homecoming experience for the Associate Director and one of the cultural interpreters, who were born respectively in Singapore

and Taiwan and for whom going to Beijing was, among other things, an experience of coming into contact with familial roots.

4.   The Beijing Alano Club is the only such club in a city of 25 million. It holds meetings across the day. By contrast, large American cities have hundred, if not thousands of meetings, daily.

References

Alcoholics Anonymous (1976). New York: World Services, pp. 59–60.

Costner, K., Wilson, J., Blake, M., McDonnell, M., Greene, G., Grant, R.A., Westerman, F.R.C., . . . MGM Home Entertainment Inc. (2003). *Dances with wolves*. Santa Monica, CA: MGM Home Entertainment.

Harkins, S., Bair, J., and Korshak, S. (2013). Group relations and 12-Step Recovery. *Alcoholism Treatment Quarterly*, 31, 396–412.

Özdemir, H. (2015). *Exploring group relations work in China: Challenges, risks, and impact*. In E. Aram. R. Baxter, and A. Nutkevitch (Eds). *Group relations work: Exploring the impact and relevance within and beyond the network*. London: Karnac.

Özdemir, H. and Sher, M. (2014). Group relations work in China – challenges, risks and impact for organizational development. *Challenging Organizations and Society (COS)* 3, 1, 502–515.

Roth, J., Brent, C., Gold, V., Harkins, S., and Robertson, J. (2015). Group relations and twelve-step recovery: Mixing oil and water? In E. Aram, R. Baxter, and A. Nutkevitch (Eds.), *Group relations work: Exploring the impact and relevance within and beyond its network*. London: Karnac.

Winnicott, D.J. (1965). *The maturational process and the facilitating Environment: Studies in the theory of emotional development*. New York: International University Press Inc.

Running in-house Group Relations conferences in and with client systems

Characteristics, opportunities and risks

Barbara Lagler Özdemir and Hüseyin Özdemir

I n the last 14 years, we have conducted internal group relations conferences (GRCs) with and for our organizational development (OD)
customers. During this time we held 11 conferences in six different
countries: Germany, Turkey, Poland, Luxembourg, Switzerland and China.
Customers were mostly companies from the manufacturing industry, but
GRCs were also conducted in an insurance company, a media company, a
non-profit organization, and a management education institute. In this
chapter, we will report on our experiences. We will look at the risks and
opportunities from the point of view of the customer and also from the
point of view of the consulting institute. We will also present our thoughts
on how internal GRCs can be considered valuable to the companies and
their employees.

Learning opportunities and goals

Most of the internal conferences we conducted were integrated into comprehensive, multi-year OD processes. The goal of our OD programs is to
improve the social subsystem as well as the technical subsystem with a
particular focus on the social subsystem, and to build up a learning

organization in the sense of socio-technical systems (Miller and Rice, 1967). In these programs, we first built the necessary trust with the customer to be able to carry out an in-house GRC. Through our OD programs, we were able to build up and free up reflection and social competencies in the participant companies. We have thus been able to prepare the managers and employees for the challenging GRC participant role. Preparing in that context means, opening up for new and experiential learning and learning about social systems.

Since in most cases all managers of these companies participated in the GRC, we were able to achieve an organization-wide learning process. Thus, recognized challenges in the conference were reinforced by targeted seminars and coaching sessions following the conference. There were seminars and coaching sessions for former participants, for example on communication and dealing with conflicts.

The specific character and challenges of in-house GRCs

The specific character of in-house-conferences from our experiences can be summarized as following:

Companies and their managers are driven to make a profit. The managerial duty is to set goals, to plan, to organize the work, to allocate resources, to execute and to control results. Beside this management duty they have a leadership role of developing people and organizational cultures. The second task, of leading people and organizational cultures, is difficult for the managers. It requires skills and social competencies for which they are usually not prepared. Those hiring them know they will need those skills, but they focus mostly on the professional requirements of a position, hoping "the rest" will happen naturally. Management is focused on return on investment and on productivity. Whatever is done in organizational terms, it has to deliver a return on investment and has to be able to be measured by facts and figures. Everything else, which is not controllable and measurable, like the dynamics in a GRC, feelings and free associations, create uncertainty and anxieties. The post-GRC-research interview with the Associate Director of the 2014 GRC reflects this issue:

> Group Relations conferences are a challenging enterprise. The idea of learning through experience about our own behaviours and how we impact each other in ways which are out of our control are always difficult

for any person, especially perhaps managers who expect to be in control and think of themselves as highly rational. Discovering that sometimes we do something against our better judgement, or that we are not being understood in the way we intended to, or that we are experienced in ways which we would not like to be seeing ourselves as – are not easy to digest.

In the opening of public GRCs, we always say that the GRC is a temporary institution, but that the learning after the GRC continues for the individual. This recognition is all the more true for the in-house GRC, as their members meet again on Monday after the GRC. Experiences, negative experiences and injuries from the GRC are thus continued in the operative processes, if these could not be sufficiently worked through in the GRC. Competition dynamics are going to be continued in the organization. Conflicts and challenges are brought into governance processes as well as the learnings.

In our GRCs, we worked with three to five hierarchical levels of an organization. This kind of cross-hierarchical learning is usually avoided in classic management training. The idea behind it is to avoid social control by the bosses. The opportunity offered by GRCs is to break this rule and create a new culture of joint, enterprise-wide learning.

Intuitive and emotional management skills are becoming increasingly important. But emotional learning represents a great challenge for many individuals working in organizations, especially for managers. Even though the development of leadership competencies like empathy, open communication and cooperation, managing oneself in role, are learning fields which are part of our OD programs, these are often reinforced in in-house GRCs. Managers and members in the organization wanting to take part in an in-house GRC, sometimes express a need for deeper learning in the pre-phases of a GRC. It is not always possible to do a variety of training activities beforehand in order to prepare the members.

In in-house GRCs the existing organizational culture often exerts a strong influence on the GRC work. Often this culture is the focus of the organization development process as well. The work on relationships between different functions, roles, hierarchies, gender, generations etc. can be fundamentally reflected in GRCs. The experiential learning during a GRC deepens the learning regarding all those topics and is to be seen as a moment of widening up the mindset of members. The work in in-house-GRCs can be seen as a critical experience to the members of the organizations.

In-house GRCs help to develop an understanding of leadership, of self-management in role and of systems thinking and to transfer this into the inner world of an organization. By including managers of an organization the real-time-learning of those organizations can be supported. This is another type of "here and now" learning, since the dynamics which occur are the actual reality of that organization. By working in the GRC we, at the same time, work on the dynamics and culture of that organization and help to develop it.

The building up of competencies for managers/employees in companies, in order to deal with complexity, transformation and power dynamics are immense. In the GRCs, they learn and integrate system thinking and accept unconscious dynamics at work. Managers most of the time accepted their participation as a self-reflection processes, which is not part of common leadership development programs in the business world. For them it is like learning a new language regarding their leadership style.

Our experience is that we make a difference and create an impact on the organization. Clients don´t often complain easily that we are consultants who are just interested in making money. They can see that by preparing, running and debriefing a complex in-house GRC, the consultants offer and work on not-easy-to-handle issues of organizational development. Still, this strong intervention has to be handled very carefully and with mindfulness by us.

Formats (events) of in-house-GRC and our experiences

We have used several formats including full-size GRCs, Organizational Role Conferences (ORCs) as well as individual systems events (institutional events) embedded in organizational development processes. Organizational role conferences as we perform them are based on pure role analysis and consulting. Thus, before a GRC we carry out an ORC for the customer in which we involve all of the managers. This serves to prepare the managers and the company for a full GRC. These managers were divided into several groups. The breakdown was based on hierarchical levels. There were groups of team leaders, managers and directors. Each group was assigned a consultant. The general manager also took part in the group of directors. The role analysis groups drew role images ("rollograms"), which were then discussed in the group.

The system event, comparable to the institutional event, is a format that we have specifically devised for projects with subprojects and a project steering committee or for a company with different departments and management. In system events, we put the entire system in one event in order to explore it's dynamics. The subprojects of a project are divided into different rooms. The steering committee of the project or the management of the company is placed in a separate space, like the management in a public GRC, and works in the open.

Extended review and application groups (RAG) help participants to stay in the member role in the conference and to transfer the learning back to their company. This event can be compared with coaching sessions back home. This format is well known to the managers. The fear of not being heard can be answered by these meetings. The RAGs have an important containing function and help the members to connect with the primary task of the GRC.

We saw that for managers from industry it is not easy to understand and accept the format of social dreaming. In Germany, it was devalued as a "psychedelic event" which in the business worldview has nothing to offer. Some could accept that dreams socially shared and connected to can open up unconscious dynamics in an organization. We could see them interestingly following all morning sessions. Nevertheless, after the first two GRCs, we decided to abandon the matrix of social dreams.

Small and large study groups or small and large systems were difficult to follow for managers. These "here and now" sessions were mostly seen as a waste of time and resources due to the silent phases in the group process. The managers were searching for a concrete job and problem they could solve or fix. Not having the consultant be responsible for this process as a moderator has led to strong refusal and devaluation of the consultant. It might be useful to point to possible difficulties, potential criticism and questions that may arise in the opening plenum. At the same time, we are concerned about the fact that these statements by the director could be too formative and cause misunderstandings.

We tried to conduct open staff meetings as an example for corporate life. It has been a very useful moment for members, to understand how the staff work in the GRC. In one system event (institutional event) the managers took the chance of getting one of the management seats for members. We also held open staff meetings in the system event at the bank. This method is generally useful in helping participants achieve understanding of what we are doing. It also offers the opportunity to gain new insights.

In in-house GRCs we have experimented with a new format, the departmental event. Departmental events contain all functions of a company. The primary task is to explore the dynamics in and between departments of the company. The general manager is involved. He or she either sits in his office, if the conference is conducted at the company or in a separate room if it takes place in a conference venue. This work is similar to an intergroup event, which is to explore the relationship and relatedness of subsystems. By doing this, we gave the members a concrete task of talking about the strategy of the organization or the optimization of the working processes of a company. The company and its employees learn in a GRC set-up. At the same time, the company deals with specific questions and challenges. This event is easier to organize if it takes place on the company's premises.

As directors, we always kept an eye on what was happening with the participants. We constantly navigated whether we as a staff went too far with our interpretations and whether the participants could follow our interpretations at all. We even started the 2014 GRC in Germany with a lecture given by the director. We don't think it made a difference for this client system. As soon as the experiential part started, the members were struggling. On several occasions, we felt that our staff members did not have the necessary professionalism and sensitivity. We found that it was important to put the behavior of the participants in context. It was important to see the behavior as an unconscious dynamic and an expression of the system. We also tried hard to please the client systems since we didn't want to lose them as clients. In the staff meetings, we discussed our approach to working. For some colleagues, it was not easy to remain in the systemic way of looking at the dynamics, which was very important to us. They directly addressed participants, focused their behavior as individuals, highlighted them individually, etc.

> You tried this year to introduce a lecture before the conference opening. This was an attempt to offer some of the theoretical underpinning of Group Relations Conferences. If there is any way that you could build in some post-conference lecture and review type sessions with clients who attended the event that would be good.
>
> (Control interview, Associate Director, 2014)

> Excellent conceptual intro before the Conference gave the necessary theory. I frequently referred to it during the review sessions and the coaching. Idea:

Print out 3–4 key slides on A1, display as posters in suitable location. As reference points during the week.

(Research interview, Staff Member, 2014)

Lecture events (seminars) helped in China to give the members some material for their thoughts and reflections. They were very much interested in the theories offered by staff. At the same time, we believe that it takes real experience away, since the participants go into a rather consuming attitude (classroom learning). They then also learn on a mainly cognitive level. We have concluded that it is better to stay with the anxiety of losing the client and should not have any desires for the future. Having decided to run an in-house conference, one has to live with the risk.

Role of client company sponsor

In order to be the sponsor of an in-house GRC, it is necessary to have the financial resources available. It is also important that the sponsor has a direct working relationship with the participants. In eight out of ten cases, the sponsor was the chief executive. In two cases, it was the personnel department that offered the event in its academic program or the leadership development program. These two GRCs were problematic because the participants did not report to the Human Resources (HR) department. The eight GRCs, sponsored by the direct, top-level bosses of the companies, were well-contained. Only in one case was the general manager already under pressure in the company for other reasons and could not provide the necessary containment.

In all our conferences, the sponsor within the client company stood outside the conference. In Turkey and China, the sponsor greeted all members and staff and left the venue. In China, we conducted one of three conferences on the company property itself. The sponsoring general manager or HR department has to trust the organizing institute and the director. The relationship has to be stable and should be long term. Continuity in the role of the sponsor is essential. Only this continuity makes it possible, after a conference, to accompany and coach the participating managers internally as supervisors. The experience of the participants can then be transferred to the company with the help of the sponsor. The need for further measures such as additional trainings or external coaching can be recognized and commissioned by the sponsor. The presence of the sponsor is also important to facilitate dialogue with other areas in a large corporation, e.g., when they are informed of the dynamics in the conference and do not understand them. This role of the sponsor has a bridging and stabilizing function. In some of our in-house GRCs, the sponsor in the client company changed during the GRC or afterwards. This made it difficult to deal with the post-conference stress and conflicts. The containing function of the client company, beside us as the training institute, was not a given anymore.

Staffing an in-house GRC

To run an in-house GRC requires respect for the business, its rules and its cultural values as well as a professional attitude and behavior. The challenge for the staff members is to adapt themselves to the business milieu, to its topics and to its culture. This doesn't mean staff members have to work differently from how they work in open or public GRCs around the world.

Staff have to deal with and adapt their thinking and interventions to questions of efficiency and business terms such as productivity, quality, costs, creating results and measuring them, process control, return on investment, etc. Those issues, challenges, questions and corporate dynamics are major aspects in the business world and occurred in all ten in-house GRCs. In our staff reflections, we had to approach these questions and deal with them together. We had to understand the pressures of these participating executives. At the same time, the conferences were measured by the participants in terms of return on investment. They asked themselves again and again whether the full attendance paid off and what it cost the company. We were able to deal with it as members of staff, commenting in our interpretations that the company was willing to make these investments in order to promote the learning of their executives and thus the organizational learning.

Staff had to see, to understand and to deal with the pressure and inner conflicts of managers, without just seeing them as people "sitting on resistance" or avoiding learning. Again, and again, as conference directors, we thought about how much the company and the sponsors had invested in time, money and energy, and not least, confidence to enable the conference. We felt responsible for the learning and development of the participants, which did not simplify the dynamics of the staff. Our staff colleagues helped us work on these feelings of responsibility and to work in the conference with more serenity.

Role of consultants

As in public GRCs, members had difficulties accepting the different and distant role of the director and of the GRC staff. First they could not understand why the director and the staff members, whom they knew from their OD-Projects, suddenly behaved differently. They "refused" to answer their questions immediately and were seen as unfriendly and even "hostile." Throughout the conference and later on, some of them were able to realize that this role behavior was necessary for their own learning.

> I would like to stress that the dynamic of the work relationship, the client as customer and therefore the expectations to be a special child, to be loved by the consultant, and also to be taught in a passive and painless way, which result in a dependent behaviour are familiar to any GR practitioner but are enhanced in this context and think, that it is courageous to be taking on this challenge year after year. I am sure that the people from industry benefit tremendously from this work even though they typically find it hard to work through their emotions in the first few weeks after a conference.
>
> (Research interview, Associate Director, 2014)

Director's role

The director is the link between the consulting institution running the conference and the client system. In this role, the director has a major responsibility not only towards the members but also towards the larger client system back home. He or she has to be aware of the conference as a whole and the specific formats (events) as interventions into the world of the client system. By recruiting staff, he or she has to be aware of the opportunities and risks of fitting the individual staff member with a specific professional background, experience, attitude and behavior.

A central difference to public conferences is the proximity of the director to the client system outside the conference. The sponsors assume that the director is not doing anything that hurts executives and thus the company. There is a very strong trust relationship between the sponsor and the director. This confidence is also a big burden that weighs on the shoulders of the director and indirectly on the staff. The director is already at risk when selecting and assembling the staff. He only gets out of this situation if there are enough other customer relationships on the market so as not to have undue concerns about further contract awards.

GRC as an organizational intervention – some cases:

All the in-house GRCs we organized took place in the business world except one, which was run fully on the management level within a non-profit-organization with 1,200 employees. The GRCs were mostly attended by managers of those corporations, first level (CEO), second level (directors) and third level (team managers) in the hierarchies. Therefore, the in-house GRC, as an organizational intervention, concentrated on the leadership system of those companies. An in-house GRC can work as a complex organizational diagnosis process (Gould 1992), which helps to make the covert and unconscious dynamics obvious. The themes and dynamics seen and experienced in the GRC are aspects of the inner world of the company. In-house GRCs are very intense interventions in the organizational system of the company. This is interesting for the consultants, but can be very stressful and burdensome for the members of the organization. In the following, we will give a few examples and their context.

GRC-example 1 – transition in public company

The conference was sponsored by the outgoing female CEO. Gender issues were strongly discussed in this company and in the GRC, in part because of a plan for a male successor to the female CEO of the company. The presumptive male successor came under pressure. He had to listen to the open critique and anxiety of the female managers who were afraid of being patronized by him. He himself had difficulties reacting to it and was very angry with one of our male staff members who tried to interpret this in the GRC. The successor realized the deep resentments against him, his leadership style and the refusal to accept him in his future role. He had to work on this issues the next 3 years before the transition would take place. This learning has deepened his ability to reflect and to share his own thoughts and feelings. In subsequent interviews, we were able to conclude that the new CEO and his representative had transferred certain concepts and working methods of the conference to their company. For example, they have initially taken a wait-and-see attitude in meetings, in order to give the managers time to reflect on their own ideas. Of note, the new CEO did not continue the working relationship to our consulting and training institute, while the new female General Manager, continued getting coaching from one of us (BLO).

GRC-example 2 – succession in industry

In another example, a future CEO was able to experience and get to know all his future senior and middle managers. In turn, the managers had the opportunity to experience and observe their new boss in the challenging situation of a GRC. They were able to discuss current challenges faced by the company as well as future and existential fears. The GRC helped him to integrate himself by working openly and actively in the conference towards aspects of leadership, authority, cultural diversity and change. Live power clashes between persons and hierarchical levels in the specific company could be observed and explored. Lower-level managers took personal risks by speaking up openly and directly against manipulative processes.

GRC-example 3 – industry

In an industrial company, organizational processes and the role behavior in a "departmental event" within an in-house GRC were made experienceable. The cooperation and the exchange between the departments and with their CEO could be tested, experienced, observed, understood and directly changed. This departmental event was attended by all managers, heads of departments, the CEO and his team. Managers were invited to brief operational meetings. Concrete business problems, such as the question of product quality, were dealt with. According to the participants, operational problems that had been left untreated for months were solved in a very short time.

GRC-example 4 – managers of a health company

It happened that all top managers of one health care system were members of a GRC. We had 20 directors, the level below the chief executive officer (CEO), working in the GRC, representing an organization of 1,200 employees. That group of directors had many difficulties accepting the work in the conference. They refused to work on the primary task. Taking up their roles as members was a huge challenge. Having gone through a difficult reorganization in their work organization, after which mistrust, stigma and fear were very present, the fear of being judged by colleagues in the GRC and of consequences after the GRC prevented them from fully using their individual competencies in the GRC.

Following this difficult work and in order to understand the challenge of his group of directors, the CEO of that organization took part in the next year's GRC. After his own GRC experience, he was in a position to reflect with his group of directors about the challenges they had experienced. A side effect was his discovery of "how younger generations are taking up leadership roles." During the conference, he expressed his wish to learn from the younger generation in their early twenties. He accepted their leadership roles in different settings in the GRC and made clear afterwards in a GRC-post-reflection setting that in future he would extend the promotion of young professionals in his organization.

GRC-example 5 – intercultural understanding

The involvement of all senior executives from the Polish subsidy (second level below the CEO) in a conference in Germany helped them to better understand the culture of the headquarters and vice versa. The unconscious prejudices between German and Polish members or the dynamics of the mutual inner pictures about the respective nations were perceived and addressed by the GRC consultants. These interventions opened important considerations for the participants and brought them relief. Relations which were strengthened by the shared experience helped to solve the operative conflicts between company functions. These experiences helped to improve communication and cooperation in the work processes, as we learned from the participants in the subsequent modules of the OD program. Positive experiences from the managers' own self-management in role and the interventions received by the consultants enabled these understandings and improvements.

GRC-example 6 – institutional event in a bank

We have had positive experiences in a bank that was working on a large-scale project with another bank which was close to failure. The project volume amounted to €800 million and threatened the existence of the small bank with 1,500 employees. The customer of this bank, a large bank, planned to stop the cooperation. The CEO of the small bank commissioned us with a series of individual events distributed over a period of half a year. An intergroup event, action research sessions, review groups, individual and team coaching and plenary sessions were held. We worked with a small staff of four people experienced in GRC work and approaches.

One highlight was the institutional event, which we called Systemvent, to make system dynamics transparent and to process them in real time. In the institutional event, the structure of the migration project was replicated with its subprojects. The construction of this temporary learning system served the observation and the direct change of the project. The institutional event followed the principle of bringing the whole system together and, as in the day-to-day business, to experience and observe it in its work. The entire project involved four subprojects and 50 project staff. The project teams were given the task of retiring with their team members into individual meeting rooms. The CEOs of the two banks and their two project leaders of both banks withdrew into a room and worked publicly. The result of this internal GR work, spread over several weeks, was the rescue of the large project and thus the existence of the smaller bank. The statement of one CEO was, that through this concentrated institutional event, they were able to make more decisions in one day than in all the months before.

Example 7: multiple GRCs in one company

In one company we were able to execute three GRCs in succession. This was possible because the general manager was convinced of the effect of this work, although he had never participated in a GRC. The feedback from his employees and the good working relationship with us, strengthened the continuation of this work. It was also important to invite this general manager before the opening and also immediately after the closing plenum. These dialogues were important to him in order to demonstrate his expectations and messages about the management roles and to gain an insight into the learning of his employees. After the first GRC, he could see changes in the working processes. The openness of his leaders in dealing with problems and conflicts increased. Many people found their voices and expressed themselves in other communication events without fear. With these three successive GRCs, the entire corporate culture became more open and cooperative.

Range of learning

The spectrum of learning experiences of the participants is very wide. It goes from the very satisfied, intensive learner to the complete rejection of the experience. The reflections go from the "best learning in my life" to the "most terrible experiences I have ever had in my life." Those who have had positive experience are pleased that, for example, they were able to make themselves heard in the company in the presence of the experienced senior management. Female leaders were aware of their strengths. They asserted themselves against dominant, male colleagues. Employees dared to speak openly and critically about problems in the company in the presence of colleagues and, above all, of the bosses. Afterwards, they tried to transfer these positive role experiences to their companies. They accept the importance of the unconscious in the organization.

During in-house GRCs, themes we have experienced include the classical aspects in any GRC (e.g. issues like identity, finding a voice, taking up roles, power issues, gender and generational dynamics), as well as themes very specific to the participating company (e.g. succession, cross functional cooperation, communication and culture issues, merger issues, future strategy, organizational structure issues). In three of our conferences, the issue of succession of general management was the primary driver in running an in-house GRC. It was possible to create an important moment to prepare the succession in management in the back-home organization during the GRC. In these cases, the large system (group) dynamic as well as the dynamics of intergroup or system events (institutional event) brought up the unconscious and unspoken aspects of succession. Taboo topics like "Do we really want this successor?" who was taking part as well, were discussed and reflected openly.

Taboo topics are difficult for managers taking part in an in-house GRC. The dynamics around fear, competition, uncertainty, etc., regarding the organizational context back home, nevertheless happen in GRCs and are part of discussions. The experiences and the learnings regarding those dynamics during GRC have been of great value and have been transferred into their home-organization in most cases. Furthermore, collaboration between departments can be improved, and conscious and unconscious dynamics between functions are nearly immediately evident. The reflection of leadership style is another important learning field. Unlike public GRCs, the members are usually reluctant to speak openly about topics such as religion, nationality, gender or sexuality.

The concept of role is not very frequently used in organizations. The containment function of management teams in organizations can be compared with the GRC directorate team working with the conference staff. A GRC, can be seen as a team model for members attending it. The public can observe staff working. The management of roles between director and associate director are learning opportunities for role questions, for example, between a general manager and his deputy General Director. The way the director of the GRC works, authorizes and delegates work to individual staff members gives the opportunity for new learnings to the members of the conference. The daily meeting of the conference director with his/her associate director shows the importance of this containing team. Department heads have an opportunity to learn from the GRC consultants' role and behavior for their own managerial and leadership role back home.

One example of a deeper learning was expressed by a member, who was interviewed by a researcher of our institute in a post-GRC-research process:

> The last days I have thought a lot about what to write, I have made notes, which I have rejected again and again and now I have decided that I simply tell you in my words how I have experienced the days. I have found it very difficult to remain in the "Here and Now". I think, this is due not only in the superficially missing setting of concrete tangible jobs (which is not right, because a primary task job was there), but due to what we experience in everyday life, to be preoccupied with the past and the future without feeling what is wrong or right at this moment. I have learned how the moods within a team, is one of the most important components to successfully accompany a change project. I have learned to be very conscious about different perceptions and I have learned how important it is, to be aware of the impact in those different perceptions. The experiences gained refer on the one hand to my own contact with the situation generated in the conference and on the other hand with the behavior of the different groups.

We were also able to observe negative experiences or we find them in the written reflections. There were, for example, verbal attacks and insults by colleagues, the exercise of dominance, the ignoring of the topics that one finds important. Furthermore, very personal subjects were expressed verbally by the participants who then regretted being so open because of the uncomprehending reactions of the others. For example, a participant spoke about a suicide attempt.

The risk that we see is that the participants bring these experienced, unprocessed uncertainties and fears back into their companies. At the same time, we were able to find through our interviews that some suppo-sedly traumatic experiences of the directors e.g., GRC-example 4, led to intensive, positive dialogues within the company. An important aspect in this case was that this company, which takes care of the helpless people in the outside world, did not feel respected and appreciated by the GRC staff. Our temporary GRC culture and the culture of this company clashed. Specifically, we made the "mistake" of not welcoming the arriving members in a friendly way.

In-house GRCs can also be seen as enterprise-wide learning processes. In-house GRC members can explore the hidden and difficult questions of the unconscious dynamics of their business lives. This is an opportunity for the members to experience, observe and influence their organizational system in "real-time." In their daily work, they focus more on the conscious aspects of business processes. The fact that all upper and middle managers of compa-nies with 350 to 1,200 employees at the GRC participated meant that the entire management system of the respective company was present in one room. This enabled employees and members, to examine the management and organizational dynamics of the company and to influence them directly through our interventions as employees and through the actions and dialo-gues of the members.

Several people who had set up as an independent company in the institutional event later became self-employed as consultants and small entrepreneurs. Intensive learning experiences and the discussion of identity issues, leadership roles and core competence in the conference reinforced the intentions of founding a company of their own. We are also aware that not every change is due to the previous conference dynamics. We believe that the first weeks and up to six-to-twelve months after the conference should be closely followed to understand the impact of an internal con-ference on the company.

High investment

To take the managers of a company into an in-house GRC is a big investment in time and money for a company. Forty to 50 managers are taken out of the company for three to four days and not available for subordinates of the managers, for internal and external customers, etc. The client company tries to evaluate beforehand what the return on investment (ROI) for the com-pany can be, if such an intensive leadership training or OD-Intervention is carried out. In many organizations, leadership trainings are common, but CEOs try to find special challenges for their executives, something "new." In one case, the sponsor falsely thought the conference was an outdoor event.

GRC members don't choose to attend

Members of in-house GRC are connected to their colleagues. They have been part of networks for many years. There are dependent on each other. Jointly, they manage the organizational processes. The client system members are asked if they want to take part in a GRC as part of an OD or leadership development process, but a chance to say no is not really given. If they say no or question the GRC too much, they could be seen as resistant to learning and even as someone who doesn't want to help to develop the organization. This can lead to the massive frustration of some of the members and member sub-groups which we have seen ("What do they do to us?!" "They have some hidden cameras, for sure." "He, the director, knows my boss back home.").

Dependency on client system

As the organizing institute of these in-house GRCs, we were dependent on our client company. We had moments where we had to decide, what is good for the client and what is good in terms of a true GRC experience. For example, although we like to work with this format we decided not to use the social dreaming matrix because there were very negative reactions in a previous conference. We kept the classic large study group, mostly in a spiral-shaped seating arrangement. The participants could connect to the concept of the large group. They could see that the dynamics in the large group are similar to those of organizations.

When the GRC ends, the relationship between our sponsoring client and us as the organizing institute (oezpa GmbH – Academy and Consulting) usually continues. At least, this is our hope as OD-consultants. In some occasions the relationship ended or was stopped for a while. The reason for this varied: the unstable relationship between consultants and the leader of the personnel development department, for example, or the dynamics and reactions by a subgroup of members to the GRC created further negative dynamics. If we take account of the ten conferences relating to our customer relationship, the following picture emerges. In all cases, we have been able to work with our customers. We experienced this change in dynamics of our contacts with five out of ten customers. We had a good start whenever the top managers (general managers) were directly involved in the GRC as participants or at least close (welcome before or closing straight after the GRC). We had the biggest problems with the HR departments, if the HR personnel had not the slightest idea of what a GRC is. Overall, the high dependency of the participants in an internal GRC in their companies was a parallel to our quite high dependence on our customers. It was not easy to go out of this dependence, and to work freely. This succeeded very well when we were mentally free from worries that our customers might be dissatisfied, or free from follow-up fantasies.

Social control

Colleagues and managers of members carry out conscious and unconscious social control. The social control by colleagues joining a conference membership seems to be experienced as a danger for a career-planning. They are afraid of showing critical behavior and try to act in a "socially correct" way. Human Resources departments feel endangered as well, since they couldn't control the internal dynamics following an in-house GRC. These dynamics might even endanger their own status, image or career in the organization, because they have supported or sponsored a GRC. Some members might go directly to their line managers or even higher in the hierarchy in order to complain about the GRC format or ask about a hidden agenda by the Human Resources department. Personnel departments had the often unspoken concern that the recommendation to attend a conference would end in disaster and they would be ordered by the board to talk about individual members and the conference dynamics and even sanctioned.

The risks are to be foreseen only conditionally. One way to reduce the risk was to think very carefully about the concept of the GRC and its individual events. At the same time, we have found that too strong an agreement does not lead to a good result. Thus, a two-day preparation of the participants by a two-hour lecture and dialogue on the concepts underlying the conference did not make the work easier. On the contrary, there was a feeling that something very difficult was going to happen and the director was now trying to prepare the participants for this critical journey. A more relaxed launch and implementation of the conference would probably have brought better results in this case; the participants could have had a more uninfluenced experience.

After a GRC, we try to give feedback to our clients through our contacts in the company. We have invited some of the sponsors to talk about these experiences in our training courses and university seminars. In one case we were quoted in our conference roles (director, deputy director and director of the administration team) to the company and then had to attend a meeting which was like a tribunal.

> Conferences like this induce a regressive behavior. We know that – it is part of our design and we know how to work with it. It gets complicated, however, when the relationships outside of the conference – before or after it – are client-provider or if there is a department which perhaps is assessing the individuals behind the scenes. The struggle to find one's own voice, to be a "free member" at the conference, free to learn, struggle, feel, gets constrained by the fears of the consequences. The fact that after the conference they have to return to work with these colleagues might mean that they won't challenge each other or confront each other even though the conference is exactly the opportunity to do that in a safe and contained space.
>
> (Control interview, Associate Director, 2014)

Assessment center-fantasies

It has happened that managers expect an in-house GRC to be an intense performance assessment. The intensity came as a result of the number of managers and the many management levels involved. The length of the conference and the feeling of being exposed to this unknown format increased the intensity. The participation of personnel functions in the preparation, implementation and follow-up strengthened the fantasies of a hidden evaluation by the staff. Individual events, such as an institutional event that includes the management, resemble performance assessments. In one conference the image of a hidden camera reappeared again and again. The GRC staff and also their own participant colleagues from the company could be feared as a "camera" recording their behavior.

As a result of these fears and fantasies, we could observe that some participants did not participate actively, or even left the conference early. They were afraid for their jobs and losing their reputation in the company. It is nearly impossible to get rid of those fantasies during an internal GRC.

We believe the fantasy that the internal conference could be a performance assessment should be accepted by the staff as not changeable. The constant assertion by the director or by individual staff members that the conference is not an assessment only reinforces these fantasies. It is in the nature of things that when so many colleagues and hierarchical levels are together, participants are inevitably compared. The higher levels that are in the room, feel put under pressure by the lower levels and vice versa.

In one of the ten conferences (example 4), about seven participants left the conference and immediately complained about the poor seminar organized by the HR department. These persons were participants in a management development program. The GRC was a module of this program. The new head of personnel development headed this program. He and we were not able to contain the dynamics of the program together. Finally, the company stopped our engagement in the leadership development program but not our client relationship.

The risks of those sorts of fantasies for the client system as well as for the organizing institution (the consultants) are quite high. Trust and a stable client relationship is the basis for an in-house GRC (Gustafson/Hausman 1975). Trust in the relationship can be challenged or even lost. Company dynamics, staff dynamics, the dynamics of the consulting institution can contribute to perceived "injuries" in the company and the staff. Those can't be resolved unless sustained reflection work can be done afterwards.

Nevertheless, there were always good moments. By speaking up against higher hierarchical levels in the conference, managers took personal risks. We are not aware of any negative consequences for participants. It would be important to incorporate reflection about the conference into the contract with the client right from the start. We did this in 7 of 10 cases. In five cases, we were able to prepare the company or the participants for the method of experiential learning. It must be accepted at this point that due to the special nature of the method a full-scale preparation is not often possible. The risk of difficult learning experiences cannot and should not be avoided as these learning experiences and insights are an important element of personal and institutional development.

Dealing with the high risk

The client company and its organization carry the risk in running an in-house GRC. Dynamics which are created by the events remain in the company. If there is no follow-up and post-GRC-reflection, those dynamics can become a continuous conflict and stress in the organization. We observed that critical, confrontational dynamics were contained and solved with the help of the managers of the client companies afterwards. These managers were very much in favor of our confrontational work. So, the female CEO of an organization invited the 50 participants to coffee the following day and asked them to share their experiences with her. This invitation was accepted by many participants. In another case, the CEO invited all directors and managers to share the GRC experiences with us. The female HR director in another case strengthened our back, even though seven persons had left. In her next company she has hired us again. These sponsors have always been the ones with whom we have many years of experience. These relationships were very trustworthy and resilient.

Issues for the future

The experience of running these in-house GRCs around the world taught us a lot and helped us to develop as an institute as well as individual consultants. It shaped part of our consulting role and self-understanding in organizational development and leadership development processes. The questions we would like to explore in future include:

*   Why is it difficult to explain the format to business managers and what can we do there?
*   What are the effects on the total client institution?
*   What changes occur in the relationships between members of client organizations?
*   What is the danger for a staff-team regarding systemic implications coming from a client system (organizational transference)?
*   One director? Co-directorship? What does the specific company "allow"? Which is the best form of leading an in-house GRC?

In our future work we will be more careful in running in-house GRCs or taking in large groups of clients into a public GRC. We will try to look more at the containing role of the client system itself as well as the GRC. It is a dual containing function consisting of the conference set-up (director, staff, formats, boundaries etc.) as well as the containing function within the client organizations (roles like sponsor, Human Resources function, culture of learning, situational condition of the organization). The in-house GRC can be viewed as part of the company and its system. In this context, it is also necessary to consider whether the participation and the reflection of learning should not be systematized more strongly. To achieve this, admin staff coming from the client system should have visited at least one GRC beforehand. The in-house GRC should not be viewed as an ordinary seminar or workshop by either the company or the training institute. These GRCs require intensive preparation and attention.

References

Gould, Laurence J. (1992). Using psychoanalytic frameworks of organizational analysis. In: Kets de Vries, M. F. R. (ed.), *Organizations on the Couch* (pp. 25–44). New York: Jossey Bass.

Gustafson, J. and Hausman, W. (1975). The phenomenon of splitting in a small psychiatric organization. A case report. *Social Psychiatry* 10, 199–203. Springer-Verlag.

Miller, E.J. and Rice, A.K. (1967). *Systems of Organization: Control of Task and Sentient Boundaries*: Tavistock, London.

The Tragedy of the Commons

What might it tell us about systemic issues in the world of Group Relations?

Ugo Merlone and John Wilkes

Introduction

S everal parts of the group relations community have expressed concerns that there is both a decline in the attendance at group relations conferences and, at the same time, a proliferation of the use of group relations methodology to create a variety of events. We want to propose and explore the possibility that the group relations community – internationally but most clearly in the UK (and possibly in the USA as well) has fallen into a social dilemma situation known as the Tragedy of the Commons (Hardin, 1968).

Hardin's analysis was derived from a parable by Lloyd (1837). Hardin compared the concept of shared resources to the grazing pasture for use by all, often known in England as the Commons. Everyone with rights to the Commons will graze as many animals as possible, acting in their own self-interest for the greatest short-term personal gain. Eventually, all the grass in the pasture is used; the shared resource will be depleted and no longer available. The lesson was summarized as follows: 'under condition of scarcity, ego-centred impulses naturally impose costs on the group, and hence on all its members' (Hardin, 1998, p. 693). The Tragedy of the Commons has been highly influential in disciplines such as ecology, health care, economics, political sciences, psychology and sociology among others, but also has been criticized as oversimplified (Dietz et al., 2003).

According to the mathematical psychologist Robyn Dawes (1980), Hardin's Tragedy of the Commons presents a 'gain-to-self-harm-spread-out situation' which results in a social dilemma. In our opinion, the best definition of these interesting and pervasive phenomena was proposed by Kollock: 'Social dilemmas are situations in which individual rationality leads to collective irrationality' (1998, p.183). Social dilemmas may arise from collective actions in any part of or the entire society and have been discussed from several perspectives; see Merlone et al. (2013) for a list of different disciplines in which social dilemmas have been studied.

In our thinking, herdsmen were group relations conference directors, cattle were group relations conferences and the pasture was the number of possible members. Our working hypothesis was therefore 'The group relations community is facing a social dilemma in which their rational choice is to run as many group relations conference as possible.' A related hypothesis was 'running as many group relations conferences as possible would increase competition, improving the level of conferences and leaving on the market only the most efficient conferences' where efficient means that every resource is allocated optimally. (The reader may refer to Heyne (2008) for a definition of efficiency and to Elzinga (1977) for a comparison between the meaning of efficiency in engineering and in economics.)

This premise was the result of some of our fantasies, partially grounded in the difficulty of getting data about group relation attendance, but also based on the large number of organizations in the field of group relations as shown in Table 3.5.1.[1]

Our personal journeys in the group relations world

Before trying to address these issues, we acknowledge that we are part of the group relations system and that this may have coloured our thinking about the system itself. In the following section we briefly present our individual personal journeys in the group relations world in an attempt to be transparent about our potential biases.

Table 3.5.1. List of Organizations sponsoring group relations (Source: GroupRela tions.com).

- **Argentina**
  B&K Change
- **Australia**
  GRA: group relations Australia
  NIODA: National Institute for Organizational Dynamics
- **Belgium**
  Foundation Internationale de l'Innovation Sociale
- **Brazil**
  Mural Interspic
- **Denmark**
  Napso: Network for Applied Psychodynamic Systems, Theory, Organiza-
  tional Psychology
- **Faroe Islands**
  NOV
- **Finland**
  Metanoia Instituutti
- **France**
  IFSI (International Forum for Social Innovation)
- **Germany**
  oezpa GmbH
- **Great Britain**
  The Tavistock Institute of Human Relations
  The Bayswater Institute
  GReNWE: group relations Network West of England
  The Guild
  OPUS (An Organization for Promoting Understanding of Society)
  SIHR: Scottish Institute of Human Relations
  Tavistock & Portman NHS Trust
- **India**
  group relations India
  HID Forum, Bangalore
  Indian Institute of Management, Ahmedabad
- **Ireland**
  IGRO: Irish group relations Organization
- **Israel**
  OFEK: The Israel Association for the Study of Group and Organizational
  Processes
- **Italy**
  CESMA: Centro Esperienze e Studi di Management
  IL NODO group
- **Mexico**
  Mexican Institute of Group and Organizational Relations

(Continued)

Table 3.5.1.   (Cont.)

- **Peru**
  T-Consult Socioanalytic Practice
  Hope of the Amazon Civil Association
- **Singapore**
  GLIA Leadership
- **South Africa**
  ISLA (The Institute for the Study of Leadership and Authority in South Africa)
- **Spain**
  Innova: Associació per a la Innovació Organitzativa i Social
- **Sweden**
  AGSLO: Arbetsgruppen för Studium av Ledarskap och Organization
- **United States**
  A.K. Rice Institute and its affiliated centers
  Boston University School of Law
  Columbia University Teachers' College
  Northwestern University
  University of San Diego

First author's journey:

I learned about group relations in 2007 when I was a visiting researcher in Tucson, Arizona and attended the A.K. Rice Institute's 2008 GRC in California. I found the themes explored were interesting and related to my research interests, yet I had difficulty when I tried to give voice to how I linked these themes to academic research.

To further my knowledge, I entered the A.K. Rice Training and Certification programme, and during my training period I attended several conferences. During this period, I came into contact with the Society of Italian Group Relations; they invited me to serve as a consultant in training. I presumed that they wished to learn about the AKRI training programme as well. I felt this would interfere with my training programme and did not accept.

After completing the training programme and gaining certification, I have often felt on the boundary of the group relations world. I have been reflecting about the urge some people appear to have to be in the staff of one conference after another. I sometimes think that they assume that the only place where one can use group relations learning is in a group relations conference, forgetting to apply this learning to the everyday life. Sometimes

I think that developing my relationships within the group relations world might help me find my way also in real life, where you have also to know people and make connections. Then I say to myself that I have enough of this in my real working life and I do not want to do it in the group relations world as well. At this moment I am sitting at the window of missed opportunities. I perceive that the students in my university might benefit from the experience of group relations, but I am afraid to do anything because I fear I may use the students to serve my own narcissism.

Second author's journey:

I first learned of group relations when I attended, without knowing anything about or anyone in this world, the Tavistock Institute's Leicester Conference in April 1996. This was the start of a journey into a world where the space to reflect on my impact on others and their impact on me resonated deeply. This led to me doing courses at the Institute of Group Analysis and subsequently an MA at the other Tavistock, the Clinic, in their Consulting to Organizations programme. There was a five-day group relations conference, which was a compulsory element of the programme.

I was awarded my MA in January 2000 and in April 2000 I attended the Training Group of the Tavistock Institute Leicester Conference. There was complex learning for me from this experience. Looking back with the understanding enabled by distance and hindsight, I can see that my inner doubts about my competence coupled with my stubborn refusal to ask for help (a lifelong disabling trait) made my pathway to delivering good enough consultancy unnecessarily bumpy. I was also aware of the gossip between members of the Training Group as to which member would be chosen to join the Leicester sstaff in the future, planting the seed for the concern about who becomes special and chosen to be on staff.

From then on, group relations was in the background in my professional life and I watched each year who was being invited to work as a Consultant in the Staff Group at Leicester. I will admit to a feeling of envy towards those who appeared to be invited into this world, but I do not think this was a destructive burning envy. In October 2009 Eliat Aram invited me to be on the staff of the Leicester Conference 2010. I found myself both exhilarated and disturbed by this experience. I found it difficult to find my voice in large staff meetings, hated and resisted the pressure to attend early morning yoga sessions and did not feel comfortable in some of the staff social situations. Reflecting on this I can again recognize I did not give voice to what I was finding difficult and did not seek support.

At this 2010 Leicester Conference there was a training group, called the Advanced Praxis Group and Ugo Merlone was part of this group. Ugo and I met again at the 2013 OPUS Conference in London and after a conversation about him wanting to work with an English speaker to write papers, particularly about group relations, we began a series of Skype discussions talking about our perspectives on the group relations world. Ugo was reflecting on his own thoughts on the narcissistic aspects of doing conferences, recognizing some of this in himself. Together we did a presentation at the 2014 OPUS Conference exploring the relevance of the Tragedy of Commons in psychoanalytic thinking. In April 2015 we went to Chicago to the A. K. Rice Institute Dialogues and participated in a short GR conference; Ugo was on the staff and I was a participant. We also presented a workshop at the Dialogues, where we ran an experiential event to explore what the Tragedy of Commons might illuminate about the business of group relations.

Group relations led me to reflect on my recurring pattern of not articulating difficulties. I have now been a part of various psychoanalytic communities, including being a Governor at the Tavistock and Portman NHS Foundation Trust for six years, an Associate of OPUS for 12 years and a member of ISPSO since 2013. I have observed all these different communities struggling with their heritage and how they can move forward into the twenty-first century. I am particularly struck by the veiled competition, gossip and huge fights in private over whose approach is legitimate and true to the tradition.

Group relations conference attendance

We experienced some resistance in some parts of the system when trying to get data about group relations attendance; for a variety of reasons, some organizations preferred not to share their data with us. By contrast, other organizations were quite helpful in providing us the attendance data. The data we got are reported in Figure 3.5.1. It should be noted that even the data we received was incomplete (both the A.K. Rice National Conference and the Leicester Conference have 40 or more years not represented in Figure 3.5.1).

In a personal communication, Chris Tanner, a senior lecturer at Essex University at the Centre for Psychoanalytic Studies who now has the responsibility of organizing the Essex University group relations conferences for students in a variety of undergraduate and postgraduate courses, pointed out that the number of members at the conferences he organizes is driven

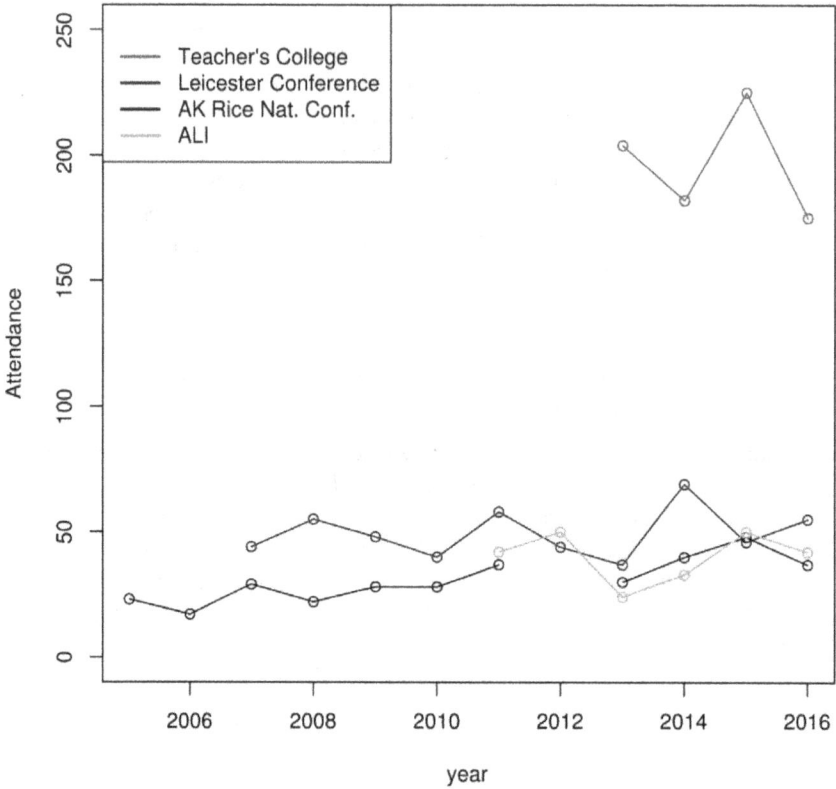

Figure 3.5.1. Attendance data at group relations conferences: Teachers' College, Leicester Conference, A.K. Rice National Conference, Authority Leadership and Innovation.

by courses where attendance at these conferences is a requirement. From Figure 3.5.1, this is illustrated by the attendance figures at the Teacher's College conferences (at Columbia University in the United States) which are considerably larger than those at the other GR conferences. (In the United States, these conferences often contain a mix of students meeting class requirements and members of the public signing up without any such requirement.) The decision to attend conferences run as part of curricular programmes at universities is different (for the majority of participants) from other group relations conferences, because attendance is often compulsory. Consequently, our thinking about competition between group relations conferences for membership does not apply to conferences run as a compulsory element of academic or training courses.

Other than Teachers' College attendance, we can see that in 2013 there was a low point in terms of attendance at the other conferences. Furthermore, in 2014, the Leicester Conference was moved to August. These facts started our reflections about group relations and possible similarities to the Tragedy of the Commons.

The experiential activity

The title of Wilfred Bion's 1962 book *Learning from Experience* should resonate within the group relations community as conferences are designed to provide events where experience provides the route to learning (Miller, 1989). Experiential learning is not confined to the group relations community. For example, in economics classrooms, games are used to teach complex interactions such as speculation and bubbles (Ball and Holt, 1998) and to introduce important concepts of organizational economics and contracting (Gaechter and Königstein, 2006). Actually, in the Preface of the 2000 edition of their book on experimental economics, Bergstrom and Miller[2] write that 'taking a course in experimental economics is a little like being a guest at a cannibal's house. Maybe you will be the diner, maybe a part of dinner, maybe both' (Bergstrom and Miller, 2000, p.iv).

Furthermore, among the several theories of learning, experiential learning plays an important role, (see Kolb, 1984). In fact, the working definition of learning the author offers – 'Learning is the process whereby knowledge is created through the transformation of experience' – emphasizes how learning may transform experience in both its objective and subjective forms (1984, p.38).

As described above, we had started to reflect on what psychoanalytic thinking might make of the Tragedy of the Commons, which led us to specifically wonder what its relevance might be to the world of group relations. Although our event was adapted from a tried and tested activity used to illustrate tacit negotiation when providing consultation to firms (Merlone and Romano 2016, 2017), in the planning process for this event we discussed all the details of this activity to consider whether they were suitable for Belgirate. We piloted a 90-minute workshop in April 2015 at the AKRI Dialogues Conference. In November 2015 at the Belgirate Conference, we presented a second workshop. At both workshops we enabled participants to explore our Tragedy of the Commons hypothesis with us through an experiential activity. In this chapter we describe the workshop at 'Belgirate V, Doing the Business of Group Relations Conferences: Un/Conscious Dynamics, Systems and Ethics' on 8 November 2015.

Activity description

As people entered the room where our 90-minute workshop was to take place, we asked them to sign in, give their names and they were issued a set of answer sheets, one for each round of the activity, on which they would record the choice they made in each round. Since the activity was run at the Belgirate Conference, all participants had held administrative, consultative or directorial roles in group relations conferences. We started the activity by explaining how the event would be run, giving the participants a set of instructions. The first round of the event would be called year 1 and we nominated one participant to be the director of a group relations conference. All the other participants were asked to decide whether to be a member of this conference or to do nothing. We did not simulate any group relations conference activity. As a consequence, conferences did not have any duration and attending a group relations conference simply entitled participants to receive learning as described in the following. In fact, we explained that we would be giving rewards, at the end of the workshop based on a score that each participant achieved, using sweets to represent learning in a tangible way.

Our scoring system was set up to encourage participants to attend a conference and guess which the most popular conference would be, based upon who was directing that conference, as a participant would be given a score equivalent to the number of participants who choose to be at that conference. We had a display on a table at the front the workshop space of different coloured sweets in bags. We explained that if someone was a director of a conference, they would receive a bonus represented by the brightly coloured sweet boxes. Participants could decide not to attend a conference in any round, with the consequence that they would score nothing in that year. It is evident that, with the given reward mechanism, being a director was a *dominant strategy*. A strategy is dominant for a player if it is better for him/her than all of his/her available strategies no matter what strategy or strategy combination the other players choose (Dixit and Nalebuff, 2013, p.70).

When the participants had made their decisions as to whether or not to attend the conference in Year 1, we then asked them to record their choice on their answer sheet. We collected the answer sheets and worked out the scores, announcing that the conference had 10 members and each participant who had chosen to attend was awarded a score of 10. We recorded everyone's scores on an Excel spreadsheet, which was projected onto a large screen, so that every participant could keep track of their own score and at the same time check their score against other participants. We intended this to engender a spirit of competition into the exercise, which we see as one of the aspects of the group relations system seldom mentioned or discussed. Finally, no actual conference took place, as the focus of our experience was on the process of selecting directors and conferences to attend.

At the start of Year 2, we explained that those who had attended the Year 1 conference, were now authorized to be a director and could decide to run a conference. Thus, participants could choose to offer to stage a conference and be its director, attend a conference as a member, or do nothing. In Year 2 only one participant staged a conference, nine participants attended this conference, and three observed. The scores were recorded on the spreadsheet and everyone was able to see their total score for the two years.

In Year 3, much discussion about tactics and their consequences took over the activity of the participants and no decisions were being made. We allowed this to run for a while. We were then concerned that the exercise would become paralysed with endless discussion and no activity. We let this run for a while longer and then decided to announce that Year 3 had passed without a conference because the year had been spent talking about what was happening and failing organize a conference. This was generally greeted by amusement with only one participant expressing strong feelings of unfairness.

We had a further seven rounds of this exercise, finishing at the end of Year 10. Only in Year 6 did we have two conferences. During the experience, we observed evidence of a great concern for fair play and overt rivalry appeared to be suppressed. At the end of the experience, there seemed to be a sense of energy and excitement in the room. Only three of the 13 participants did not direct a conference. Table 2 reports attendance, learning scores and roles for each year of the simulation. Letter 'D' indicates a participant who was a conference director. In Year 6, two conferences were run. It can be seen that in this case the collective learning was smaller. In Year 9, two participants decided to codirect a conference and therefore their learning as directors was split between them. Members' learning was not affected by having two directors. In the total line, it is possible to see how many times each participant was a director and what was his/her total learning score during the whole activity.

When, at the beginning of Year 10, we declared that it was to be the last year, but there was some resistance. In experimental economics, different experimental termination rules can be used (see Normann and Wallace, 2012). Although the time horizon of a repeated game may have theoretical implications, Normann and Wallace (2012) found that the termination rule does not have a significant effect on average cooperation rates in Prisoner's Dilemma. Nevertheless, in our simulation, when the end of the game was announced, some of the participants accused us of 'breaking the rules'. We did not announce at the start of the workshop how many rounds there would be or explain that we had set a time boundary and the exercise would end at a named time boundary. Maybe this led to the participants feeling punished by us.

We then launched a discussion, asking the participants to focus on their experience of the exercise, including feelings, roles taken up and any sense of authority. We also invited participants to link their experiences in the exercise to other experiences in the wider group relations world. During the exercise, it was noticeable that some participants who decided to put themselves forward as directors, when promoting their conference, emphasized the desirability of the location of their conference, in one case switching the location to one that appeared more desirable to potential members. When we invited participants to discuss the experience of the exercise, this was the first issue identified, named as the unconscious move by directors to become travel agents to attract participants to their conference.

Participants freely admitted that the exercise was fun, at the same time saying that it was so near the real experience, one participant citing how much it reflected the sense of being chosen or not chosen, which is a feature of the group relations world. Further, it was suggested that participants deciding to stay at home and not participate in a particular round was a reflection of the real difficulty some members of conferences experienced in digesting their experience and coming to terms with what had happened. Instances of members requiring two years to *get over* the impact of a particular conference were cited. We believe that these suggestions were the result of participants' own experiences with *real* conferences.

There was much discussion about whether we – the group relations community – are self-limiting in our approach to seeking members for conferences. Was there a self-limited constriction of ideas about the possibilities and the potential for seeking members? Do we have a feeling that group relations conferences are particularly special and difficult to sell? Should we stop thinking and operating as though we are in a survival mode, thinking of ourselves as a marginalized minority.

On the other hand, participants spoke about the bombardment of emails they received bearing invitations to conferences of many different types. We acknowledged that conferences for particular professional groups or fields of work, for example HR directors, finance directors, faced similar pressures about whether they would attract sufficient participants to make them viable. Why should we think that our own conferences were so special?

Participants from the Tavistock Institute suggested the number of people applying to be members at the annual Leicester Conference over the years, showed almost a regular sine curve fluctuation, rising then falling. Their thinking was that this fluctuation suggested there was some invisible and as yet unidentifiable force impacting on the number of applications in different years. In thinking about this, members from the Institute had applied supply chain thinking and wondered whether an anxiety about the conference is expressed somewhere, and the further this anxiety travelled from its source the more it became amplified, known as the bullwhip effect.[3] It was suggested that in the UK there was a proliferation of different types of group relations conferences and that this should be encouraged and no institution should seek to regulate or control this. This was an important insight and will be elaborated on in the final paragraph.

The extent to which the game compelled the participants into competition was questioned. Some saw evidence of real competition. Others thought it was quite well-mannered and even co-operative. It was suggested that we were very playful as participants in this game and because we were not too attached to the outcome and we were not very competitive. Do we need to learn from this in the real world of conferences? We need to be more playful, have more fun and be less anxious and competitive. Nevertheless, the comments about competition appear to ignore the unconscious aspects of conference dynamics. The concluding thought was offered by one participant: the possibility of 'serious learning arising from playing a game' and maybe this is what we do when take part in a group relations event.

Our experience of running the activity

We now turn to considering our individual experience of running the activity and then consider our reflections on the participants' experience.

First author's experience of running the activity

Running an experiential activity is challenging and stimulating, yet, if the activity is not planned thoroughly enough, the process can be really stressful. In fact, according to Rioch (1985, p. 365) 'we should think about what we do preferably before doing it, but at least afterwards'. Indeed, this applies when running an event like this. Nevertheless, to contain my anxiety, I did all those activities which help me to be ready: arriving ahead of time, setting up the room, checking the chairs and then checking that all the material is present. This constitutes 'thinking before it'. The more you do it, the more time you can spend after the event on reflecting about what the participants learned. When you run an activity by yourself you know that you can rely just on yourself. By contrast when working with somebody else, you need to be able to support your partner and at the same time be able to rely on him/her. Although a large part of my work activity consists of running events like this or even more complex ones – for example having hundreds of students each year taking the exams – such an event can result in a disaster. In this case, I wanted the event to run smoothly in order to concentrate on the learning it could provide. Furthermore, at the beginning of any Belgirate parallel presentation there is the seduction part: 'Was I good enough to seduce all the important people to come to our event?' And then everything begins and you need to give all of your attention the participants whoever they are. In this case, there was something added: Belgirate takes place every three years and I had maybe the unique opportunity to let people experience what I thought about 'over-grazing' the group relations conferences with too many conferences. I was aware of the potential risk that we had built a self-fulfilling result into the event.

Second author's experience of running the activity

Having reflected on my own learning in the world of group relations, I was very aware during the event of the extent to which I exercised control over what was happening. This I now see as a way of short-circuiting difficulties before they happened, but also keeping up my professional stance. When participants retreated into discussing tactics and theories in

Year 3 and it seemed that we would get stuck in discussions for ever, I came up with the idea, to terminate that round, saying that the year had expired because there had been so much talk, which had whiled away the time so the year had passed without them noticing. At the time we thought we made this decision as directors of the event in the interests of the learning, including that endless discussion has real consequences. I now recognize it was possible to see this action as telling participants they were misbehaving, even punishing them.

One participant mentioned in discussion, that the exercise evoked emotions around being chosen or not chosen. This was never commented upon, repeated or discussed. I wondered whether this should have been a major point or whether it was the big unspeakable: the fear of not being chosen, and the consequent competition when someone who is not chosen sets up their own version of a group relations conference.

In our opinion, this event was useful both for our own and the participants' learning. We think it can be usefully repeated and incorporated when training group relations consultants. From our personal reflections about running the event, some themes emerge. For example, what role did our narcissism play in how we ran this event? When we decided to skip Year 3 and decided to terminate the activity in order to have enough time to discuss the experience were we actually punishing the participants? Furthermore, something which was mentioned once but did not develop into a discussion among participants after the experience, was being chosen or not being chosen as directors. This theme is present in many parts of the system. How does an organization select conference directors? What are the feelings of those who step-up and those who are not selected? How do directors select staff? How do possible members select conferences to attend? How do people select presentations at AKRI Dialogues or at Belgirate? And finally, how do people decide to select the Group Relation Method? Beside the narcissistic aspects of being chosen, what sort of sweets do all these events provide? There is a dual aspect of being selected, that being selected or not can be a sign as to whether your ability to seduce worked or not.

Possible learnings and final temporary reflections

Reflecting on the title of the Belgirate V Conference 'Doing the Business of Group Relations Conferences' elicited many associations such as the phantasy that the market will solve everything. Some of these phantasies may be associated to a pairing assumption by which the economy will take care of everything. This is related to Adams Smith's invisible hand, but forgets more recent and critical contributions in economics, such as Salanie's 'Microeconomics of Market Failures' (2000), in which the author illustrates circumstances under which markets are unable to reach socially optimal equilibria. Indeed, there is debate among economists about what Adam Smith meant by his invisible hand, see for instance Grampp (2000) and Minowitz (2004). Therefore, simplistic thoughts such as the market will solve everything in terms that conferences that either are economically sustainable or provide genuine learning that will be able to survive, should be seriously questioned. This brings us back to the lesson we cited before: 'under condition of scarcity, ego-centred impulses naturally impose costs on the group, and hence on all its members' Hardin (1968, p.683).

The first hypothesis is 'The group relations community is facing a social dilemma in which their rational choice is to run as many group relations conferences as possible.'

Data indicates that there is a proliferation of group relations conferences, and if we keep in mind that according to Miller (1989) A.K. Rice 'succeeded in making conferences self-financing because he and other staff colleagues were committed enough to accept nominal remunerations', the hypothesis seem to be confirmed. In fact, with so many conferences prices decrease and therefore remunerations must be kept minimal.

Concerning the second hypothesis that 'running as many group relations conferences as possible would increase competition improving the level of conferences leaving on the market only the most efficient conferences', this obviously means that to 'remain on the market' staff remuneration in terms of money must be minimal, and this would mean that efficient conferences are those in which the staff accept nominal fees. This is consistent with the economics literature according to which with the perfectly competitive market structure, social welfare is maximized, see e.g. Shy (1995, p. 68) and also, more recently, Schaeck and Cihák (2014). Nevertheless, competition can have its drawbacks as discussed in Stucke (2013). Finally, when thinking in terms of economics are we sure that even if the market would operate at its best, having more *efficient* conferences on the market would mean having more *effective* conferences in terms of learning for the participants?

While working on revisions to this chapter, Burkard Sievers happened to send John Wilkes a copy a paper (Sievers 1989) he delivered at the first

International Symposium on Group Relations in 1988. Here Sievers posits that the dilemma of who is chosen has been at the heart of psycho-analysis since the days of Freud, who had such a problem with the appointing of a successor. This was carried on into the next generation, in the war of words between Anna Freud and Melanie Klein. He suggests that this is true for the group relations world. Further, in a paper given at the first Belgirate Conference in 2003, Nutkevitch and Sher (2004), suggest that 'becoming a staff member in a conference depended upon "being chosen"'. They warned that failing to attend to the dynamics resulting from being chosen or excluded 'could lead to the corruption of the learning process, implying that group relations, like every other human endeavour, has the seeds of its own destruction within it'. We are not sure whether we were able to answer the questions we raised during the activity and in this chapter; nevertheless by raising them and reflecting on them and running an activity as we did at Belgirate, we hope to have provided some source of reflection to the community.

Acknowledgements

We are grateful to the A.K. Rice Institute for helping us with the attendance figures at their national conference, to the Tavistock Institute for helping us with the attendance figures at the recent Leicester Conferences, to Sarah J. Brazaitis and Danielle L. Pfaff. for helping us with the attendance figures at group relations conference at Teachers' College.

Notes

1. Actually, the first Leicester Conference was held in 1957 sponsored by the University of Leicester and the Tavistock Institute of Human Relations (Miller, 1989, p. 6). In 1962, 'as conferences had been losing more money than the Institute could afford' (Miller, 1989, p. 7) the Tavistock gave authority to Kenneth Rice to take over leadership of group relations conferences. So, finding as many as seven organizations dealing with group relations just in Great Britain is puzzling. Furthermore, 'Rice indeed succeeded in making the conferences self-financing because he and other staff colleagues were committed enough to accept nominal remunerations.' Therefore, if we consider the number of organizations dealing with group relations presented in Table 3.5.1 and the remuneration a consultant gets at a GRC, probably cattle are the consultants.

2. The careful reader will note that John H. Miller is different from Eric J. Miller.

3. Actually, the bullwhip effect refers to a supply chain with several layers and exhibits increasing swings, i.e. 'a company bullwhips if it purchases from suppliers more variably than it sells to customers'(Bray and Mendelson, 2012). By contrast, the data we have refers just to conference attendees. Therefore, the available data allow us to neither support nor reject this hypothesis. However, for further research it would be interesting to analyse the misperceptions of feedback experienced from the boards of group relations organizations in terms of bonds on rational decisions as suggested by Sterman (1989).

References

Ball, S. B. and Holt, C. A. (1998). Classroom games: speculation and bubbles in an asset market. *Journal of Economic Perspectives* 12(1): 207–218.

Bergstrom T. C. and Miller J. H. (2000). *Experiments with economic principles microeconomics*, second edition, Boston: Irwin/McGraw-Hill.

Bion, W. (1962). *Learning from experience*, London: William Heinemann Medical Books.

Bray, R.L. and Mendelson, H. (2012). Information transmission and the bullwhip effect: An empirical investigation. *Management Science* 58(5): 860–875.

Dawes, R. M. (1980). Social dilemmas, *Annual Review of Psychology* 31: 169–193.

Dietz, T., Elinor Ostrom, and Stern, P. C. (2003). The struggle to govern the commons. *Science* 302: 1907–1912.

Dixit, A.K. and Nalebuff, B.J. (2010). *The art of strategy: A game theorist's guide to success in business and life*, New York: W.W. Norton & Company.

Elzinga, K.G. (1977). The goals of antitrust: Other than competition and efficiency, what else counts? *University of Pennsylvania Law Review* 125(6): 1191–1213.

Gaechter, S. and Königstein, M. (2006). Design a contract! A simple principal-agent problem as a classroom experiment. Available at SSRN: http://ssrn.com/abstract=894350 or http://dx.doi.org/10.2139/ssrn.894350

Grampp, W.D. (2000). What did Smith mean by the invisible hand? *Journal of Political Economy* 108(3): 441–465.

Hardin, G. (1968). The tragedy of the commons. *Science* 162(3859): 1243–1248.

Hardin, G. (1998). Extensions of 'the tragedy of the commons'. *Science* 280 (5364): 682–683.

Heyne, P. (2008). Efficiency. *The concise encyclopedia of economics*. 2008. Library of Economics and Liberty. Retrieved from the World Wide Web: http://www.econlib.org/library/Enc/Efficiency.html

Kolb, D. (1984). *Experiential learning: Experience as the source of learning and development*. Englewood Cliffs, NJ: Prentice Hall.

Kollock, P. (1998). Social dilemmas: The anatomy of cooperation. *Annual Review of Sociology* 24: 183–214.

Lloyd, W.F. (1837/1968). *Lectures on population, value, poor-laws and rent.* New York: Augustus M. Kelley.

Merlone, U. and Romano, A. (2017). COMMUTER BRIDGE: A Braess paradox simulation to teach social dilemmas, *Simulation and Gaming* 48(1): 153–169.

Merlone, U. and Romano, A. (2016). Using the Braess paradox to teach tacit negotiation *Simulation and Gaming* 47(6): 780–795.

Merlone, U., Sandbank, D.R. and Szidarovszky, F. (2013). Equilibria analysis in social dilemma games with Skinnerian agents. *Mind and Society* 12: 219–233.

Miller, E.J. (1989). The 'Leicester' model: Experiential study of group and organizational processes, *Occasional Paper. No.10*, London: The Tavistock Institute of Human Relations.

Minowitz, P. (2004). Adam Smith's invisible hands. *Economic Journal Watch* 1(3): 381–412.

Normann, H.T. and Wallace, B. (2012). The impact of the termination rule on cooperation in a prisoner's dilemma experiment. *International Journal of Game Theory* 41(3): 707–718.

Nutkevitch, A. and Sher, M. (2004). Group relations conferences: Reviewing and exploring theory, design, role-taking and application. *Organisational and Social Dynamics* 4: 107–115.

Rioch, M. J. (1985). Why I work as consultant in the conferences of the A.K. Rice Institute. In Colman, A.D. and Geller, M.H., eds, *group relations Reader 2* Springfield, VA, A.K. Rice Institute.

Salanie, B. (2000). *Microeconomics of market failures.* Cambridge, MA: MIT Press.

Schaeck, K. and Cihák, M. (2014). Competition, efficiency, and stability, *Banking Financial Management* 43(1): 215–241.

Sievers, B. (1989). Some considerations about the constitution of authority, inheritance and succession in contributions to social and political science. In Faith Gabelnick and A. Wesley Carr, eds, *Proceedings of the First International Symposium on group relations*, Washington, DC: (A K Rice Institute, pp. 155–173.

Shy, O. (1995). *Industrial organization: Theory and applications*, Cambridge, MA: MIT Press.

Sterman, J.D. (1989). Modeling managerial behavior: Misperceptions of feedback in a dynamic decision making experiment. *Management Science* 35(3): 321–339.

Stucke, M.E. (2013) Is competition always good? *Journal of Antitrust Enforcement* 1(1): 162–197.

INTRODUCTION TO SECTION IV

Post-conference reflections

This section is made up of three chapters written after the Belgirate conference. Unlike the other sections, it is not made up of chapters based on papers presented during the conference but as a response to our invitation to write a reflective piece on the experience of the Belgirate conference

The first one is by Anuradha Prasad and Mannie Sher who together convened the morning reflections, dreams and associations sessions. As they point out, these sessions, which are run over three mornings during the conference, enrich the tapestry that makes up the conference narrative and provide a fascinating barometer to gauge the conference's state of mind, the collective, possibly unconscious mind brought to the surface through their telling.

In the next chapter, Rune Rønning and Evangeline Sarda take us through "puns and word play" to the "deadly serious work" that they had undertaken in order to develop a method for exploring one's own discourse. They did so by positioning themselves on the boundary-lines of events, using free associations and self-reflections while playing – not always voluntarily – the "clown in the king's court." Their intriguing findings call for greater sensitivity to our well-established beliefs and discourse (jargon?) and the ways these might be used and sometimes abused.

The final chapter in this section which also draws the book to a close, is by Jeffrey Roth who takes the opportunity to reflect on the parallels between experiential systems – the Group Relations conference and an intentional community. He explores his relationship to the space each system offers for learning and change. Roth considers whether each system supports or challenges the growth in those who engage with them and the differences in how support is offered. The central theme of this chapter however, is a personal one, as Roth notices how each system offers care and containment, without promise or judgment and how this impacts his directorial journey.

Morning reflections, dreams and associations at the Belgirate Conference 2015

Anuradha Prasad and Mannie Sher

Background and Introduction

The conference organizers of Belgirate 2015 invited the authors to convene the three *morning reflections, dreams and associations* sessions at the conference. Notes of the dreams and the 15-minute sense-making periods after each morning reflection session and our own (AP and MS) dreams and reflections, form the raw material of this chapter. *Morning reflections, dreams and associations* has been part of the tradition of the Belgirate conferences and they supplement the rich diversity of thinking stimulated by the formal conference events – plenaries, introduction in groups, keynote presentations, exploratory event and parallel presentations. Further, for the 85 people present, many of whom have known and worked with each other for many years, who are versed in group relations theory and practice, valuable and fertile conversations occurred during informal meetings at meals and walks in the lovely environment of Lake Maggiore, inspiring new ideas, forging new projects consistent with enhancing the process of sense-making of the wider field within which the business of group relations conferences is practiced.

Dreams and their associations often revealed anxieties and fears about the state of individual, group and national connections to the practice of group relations. Because these associations, sensations and views do not easily lend themselves to the logic of intellectual and scientific discourse of the rest of the conference, historically, space, in the form of *morning reflections, dreams and associations*, had been set aside in the Belgirate conferences for these to emerge at the start of each day of the conference.

The content of the *morning reflections, dreams and associations* stands linked to the events in the conference; they are also expressions of the participants' demographics, like age, gender and race, personal history or nationality, or the political and social worlds in which they circulate and of which they are members. Group relations is way of understanding the creative and imaginative life; of being able to speak to what in other social circumstances mostly remains unsaid and unexplored. Group relations conference work offers opportunities for deepening our understanding of the nature of groups, relations between groups and our relationships to the groups of which we are members. Group relations conferences enable us to learn about our deeper, emotional and sometimes irrational reactions to our groups and especially our ambivalent feelings about them – our dependency on our groups to achieve our individual and group aims and our concerns about our groups' use of us to further their aims, often in circumstances that painfully ignore individual needs. In the tradition of speaking one's thoughts openly and honestly, sharing dreams and associations, *morning reflections, dreams and associations* of the conference produced a rich picture of images and metaphors of hope and despair, beauty and ugliness; ageing and renewal; birth, growth, power, decline, death and re-birth – the whole life cycle.

Dream content

Birth, age and capability

Dream content included hearing the screams of children in a maternity ward on the top floor of a building in another Italian city, Venice; a house in which two children say that an older man can be in touch with feelings and relationships. There is an e-copy of a daily newspaper which the man says he knows how to use; a dream of being in a large, formless and unstructured garden with colleagues, with a watering system that cannot do the job. The water is turned on, but the dreamer does not know if it works.

Decay, hotel and 'group relations'

These dreams produced a set of associations that included references to the 'run down' state of the hotel – the hotel shower being too hot or too cold; a collapsed chair. If the hotel, it was suggested, is to change, it would first have to be destroyed. This pointed to the attachment and sense of privilege the traditions of Belgirate bestow upon its participants, and paradoxically, may refer to the 'old' not making way for the 'new'; that we, the group relations fraternity, may actually be 'run down' and needing to be 'renovated'. The theme of decay continued with an image of sitting in the hotel lobby and holding onto 'my own soft shit in my mouth' and looking for the bathroom. There is a palm tree in the sink in the toilet which is hydrating the tree of life, a reference to the previous day's keynote presentation. We are embarrassed that our 'wonderful group relations tree of life' is dependent on shit for fertilizing sustenance. A dream follows of feeling afraid of being discovered as a foreigner and being pushed in the face, an unconscious proposition that our group relations work is not nurturing, growth-promoting or life-giving – it is so much like 'shit in the mouth'.

Hazards

The *morning reflections, dreams and associations* call up other hazards – babies in the maternity ward falling into water, suggesting carelessness by staff, and the pointlessness of complaining because one gets no thanks, and certainly not from 'the group relations community'. Even suggestions to make things work better are brushed off – like suggesting that people should not use their showers at the same time to ease the water pressure, or that knives *and forks* should be placed on tables in the dining room, instead of having to walk to the counter to get forks. Are knives and forks kept separate to avoid feared aggression towards one another? A stabbing in Israel is reported. There appears to be no logic or attainable order in the system, only chaos, restless moving and swimming around.

Being a foreigner and a world citizen

The foreigner feels foreign, fears discovery and tries to fit in – a reference to group relations working with diverse demographics and attempting to be a global force. Contradictions in this quest are exposed by challenging group relations myths – how global is group relations really when our presence is limited to the Global North, and does not appeal to peoples who do not have sufficient water to drink in the Global South? The Belgirate conference itself is challenged – are we simply the privileged few engaged in remote sense-making, but offering little by way of engagement and practical help to those in need? This sentiment transitioned neatly to a dream in which the person was asked to be a consultant in a group relations conference without pay and was told that alternate gains could be had from the associated sex work, suggesting that group relations represents a kind of polymorphous perversity, undiscriminating in its sexual behaviour – front or back – the notion that in group relations we shaft one another, and abuse each other through offers of work for low pay, thus being forced to prostitute ourselves to survive.

Alternatively . . .

There are 'happy dreams' that lead to the enchanting discovery of 'ambiguity' and the duality of human nature. New perspectives in understanding groups contribute to writing papers, those moments of wonderment in group relations work when something new is revealed – Eureka moments! The moments of awe, though, are counter-balanced by a sense that group relations destroys precious memories, like the eradication of childhood phantasies about the glories of Venice, that like Venice itself, group relations will sink and become extinct. Are we in group relations work because our seeking after the 'truth' of the unconscious means 'destroying' phantasies? Or is it more akin to 'coming to terms' with the past, abandoning our idealization of it, accepting loss and producing a greater sense of reality? Group relations remains a good way of helping the 'pieces to co-exist' and thus maintaining hope. In this sense, the image of Venice is useful as a reminder of being touched by the image of death and of resurrection – two ends of life that group relations embodies.

Death of the father – group relations and its own Oedipus

A father dies and there is anxiety about not having a generation above to protect us. The death of the father, it is thought, promises the gift of freedom, but that is illusory, there is no real freedom – a warning against 'throwing the baby out with the bathwater', a warning that the history of group relations, its traditions and the method, should be respected in Belgirate; we are faced with generational transfers that will impact on the future of group relations and the communities it serves. So while there is anger that some people are not present at the conference and those who are present seem to be depressed, there is also love for the people and the work of group relations that should not be lost – group relations is vibrant, yet also needs to transform. The dialogue has changed, and the risk is that Belgirate VI will be preoccupied with the same issues as Belgirate I. At this juncture, it is difficult to notice change, but closer inspection reveals that we seem to be attached to the same narratives. A connection between the hotel and shame is made insofar as we are having the same conversations after 15 years and yet it feels that there are still so many things to unearth. It's like a swamp into which we are sinking, like Venice. Whole towns have been wiped out and re-built. That is the narrative of group relations – we may articulate similar themes, but we are faced with bigger concerns of the life cycle of things. Maybe there are signs here of an era coming to an end.

In a basement, there are two people who should not be there, sweeping rubble. They got in by changing the locks. There is a window above ground through which they can see a man, tied to a chair and a Christmas tree, wrapped in a red. The man is not dead. This dream, and another about a roommate who has disappeared, for the first time brings to consciousness the death of Bruce Irvine this year and the absence of any opportunity so far to mourn him. Bruce's death has left a gap at this conference: he was meant to be here and his presentation at Belgirate IV was meant to be included in the book, but it isn't.

Suffocation, working through and resurrection

There is a complaint that breathing is difficult in the *morning reflections, dreams and associations*; so is finding one's voice. The funereal atmosphere is overwhelming. To escape that feeling, global federal structures for group relations are suggested, and then rejected on the grounds that group relations work in 'uncontainable', the recognition of which paradoxically leads to positive feelings, uplifting and hopeful. Group relations can celebrate as a response to death – and it can move on, working through and achieving happiness. Mourning Bruce and celebrating his life can be done on behalf of everyone, even those who are not present. The tree of life, a centre piece of Louisa's keynote lecture, can support different structures in group relations. Louisa's work on collating different group relations brochures positively demonstrated the immensity, the depth, the texturing, and the colour of group relations conference work. Sometimes the structures work; at other times they are not useful containers. These authors are reminded of a reference to 'watering the leaves, starving the roots', that refers to the funding of women's movements around the world; 'watering the leaves' meaning supporting women and girls' individual development, and 'starving the roots' meaning providing little or no support for sustained collective action by women's rights movements and organizations. We wonder whether group relations is affected in similar ways – 'watering the leaves, starving the roots' meaning offering group relations conferences to more and more people, and not investing in the foundations of group relations institution-building.

Group relations and food

Themes in dreams turn to food – a dream of the hotel dining room with two pieces of cake that are frozen from three years ago! On waking, three pieces of fresh cake taken from the dining room are discovered. Looking for a Chinese restaurant which is late preparing food, so two fishes had to be brought; only one was in good health. Boys in a house in Melbourne want to cook chicken, but there are only two fish in the pot; both are standing up. The flaws and frustrations in the food and their preparation are suggestive of an authority that does not provide adequately for people's needs, thus raising the spectre of bad things about to happen – poor nourishment and the threat of hunger. Dreams turn to guilt, fear and superficial gender relationships – feeling bad at not having visited a grandmother for a few years; joining in the fabulous choices of young Italian woman at reception; waking in the grip of intense fear and sadness about a sister's health problems.

Moving from the personal to the political

Someone is trying to get through a fence on the mountain border between Israel and Syria. An Israeli soldier and others are running towards a shelter and one is shot. On the Syrian side, soldiers are watching. A fence around Gaza does not protect the Gazans from being shot at. A flashlight or laser beam threatens to blind everyone in its light. This world conflict threatens to drag everyone into its vortex; are we here in Belgirate to shelter and to dream or does group relations have anything to offer? A dream about being late for a meeting and not understanding how the machinery of the car works, the presence of many cyclists who get damaged, suggests a sense of helplessness that political dynamics that damage the innocents may be beyond the reach of group relations and may explain our silence in this arena.

Two Israelis are working on a coming conference. There is a phone call to say they should find time to sit with each pair of participants – they should deal with 'triangles and a square'. The authors reflect that these symbols – triangles and squares do not usually feature in the structures of group relations work. Our thoughts take us to two triangles intersecting making the six-pointed star – the Star of David. In the Indian context, the Shiva (the masculine) and the Shakti (the feminine) intersecting denote the union, or the whole. Triangles and squares form the foundations of many Indian temples.

A dream is presented of wearing diapers to bed, perhaps suggesting a fear of incontinence, and a sign of our ageing and our not being able to contain the group relations community. Another dream concerns making a film in which the story has a man smuggling himself and his children and five pieces of luggage; he knows he has to go with the others, but he says he is going alone. The man is told he is not supposed to do that. He is given a hug and he starts rubbing the dreamer who is unsure whether that was supposed to be or not.

The following associations reveal a series of ideas based on similar sounding words – a pair or diaper – a reference to earlier presentations about a father shitting all over and who has to be placed in diapers, being in acute situations lacking control in contrast to the images of Star Wars of fighting, powerful lasers and impressive mechanical machines. It was suggested that to feel human, one has to face extremes.

Males, females and pairing

The idea of pairing or dying was related to reproduction; if there is no pairing, there can be no task. The appearance of many female directors of group relations conferences around the world was said to support a phantasy that pairing could be abolished which could lead to group relations dying. Another similar supporting phantasy involved the idea that future group relations folk could be cloned thus bringing parenthood to an end. This phantasy may emerge in our relationships to one another insofar as we blindside each other as shown in our dreams.

A cluster of dreams centre on incense, nightclubs, dancing, food, guided tours, the war and a pile of water leaves. Three people are waiting there – a man (elephant) and a woman (crocodile) with masks were under the leaves, shaking them off and then going to work; visiting an old couple in the west of Ireland, a getaway car and stolen Euro-money. An association follows in which a granddaughter telephones every time she wants to go to the toilet. She is told to do it in her diaper; she is shown the toilet and she manages to do it in the right place and it is nice and warm.

Gluttony and succession

This avalanche of dreams and associations – food, cakes, fish and heart problems raises the possibility that group relations has become sclerotic with blocked arteries from the rich food. Group relations does not come up with new applications; it overdoses on the same things, serving up same stuff – frozen cake – over the over again, not able to take risks. Violence is present in the war between the generations, the old and the young; the old are robbing the young; the old are forced into diapers – they are a source of shame; they do not make way for new people – that is fact of life, it is claimed, old people clinging onto roles because that represents life and succession is associated with death, so they become preoccupied with their own unconscious and navel gazing, they become fossils and they miss the big picture.

Negotiations – survival or death

By the third day, *morning reflections, dreams and associations* is involved in complex negotiations and horse-trading on positions for staff and dates for conferences: 'I'll give you these 5 days; you give me those 6 days.' In a dream, Lacan says the temporary institution will continue, followed by a dream of going into the mountains by car with twin girls one of whom is dead. There is a reference to the suicide of Lacan's patient and a comment that everyone knows that on hearing an ambulance siren in Paris, it can only mean one thing – another of Lacan's patients has committed suicide.

Black holes, energy and stirred memories

Dreams continue with a son coming late for dinner, being told he can have a glass of juice, but there are no glasses, so he tries washing with vodka. There is a black dog with a mischievous temperament; therapy for the dog is suggested, but he is getting away, so a blanket is thrown over it to restrain it and feeling guilty and depressed as a result. The black dog is said to represent depression. There is also a black computer: stepping into its picture is like stepping into a black hole; it is dangerous, but we know that something good things come out of black holes.

Walking backwards while holding chickens – it is autumn and the feathers are grown which is surprising and wondering how they are still alive when there are foxes in the forest. The black dog additionally reminds us of the tension between taking risks and remaining ethical, being governed by rules and traditions and limited by seniority. Mary Poppins steps into the picture on the pavement and she has an adventure. More associations occur involving energy sources, computers without energy, checking that there will be enough battery energy to get home, with comments on our dependency on energy.

There was a moving memorial prayer for the death of the father of a participant reminding of an email received from someone wanting to understand the life of her father who had died in Belgirate 15 years before. The black hole it was suggested referred to the death of Bruce Irvine whom we are too busy to mourn. There is a video of Bruce speaking, but the microphone was not on, so we can see him, but not hear him.

This is the third day. Half the people in the matrix say they cannot hear, stimulating feelings of living 'between realities'. It is easier to rely on 'things' coming to one, rather than depending on batteries or people, leading to a worry about whether one would be still living by the time of the next Belgirate conference. The restrained dog is a reminder of a first job application and about getting the application right or wrong. *Morning reflections, dreams and associations* talks about pride and guilt and the lively dancing last night – energetic and fun in contrast to thoughts about shy fathers who are afraid to speak, and whom we long to hear.

Buddhism is thought about as a time after death; the soul being there, but not the body. A black hole exists for the soul which has to choose a new body. Some bodies will become human, some not – pointing to the 'next body' for group relations conferences and the Belgirate conference.

A dream is presented walking through a field in the evening wearing a pretty dress and Wellington boots, getting to the place to dance, but the place is ugly with scavenging dogs. A big wooden box is suspended in the air – the dirty dogs are downstairs. The music is unfamiliar; the dreamer enters the disco light, but is left dancing monotonously on her own in circles. It is suggested that monotonous associates with monogamous; the black computer is like the black box that solves the mysteries of what happens on downed planes that are not found; coffins are black boxes, so black boxes are connected with death and we are here to find the meaning of what is in the black box. A memory is evoked of a black metal box with a key being found following the death of a mother. There were two stacks of letters, one titled: 'living alone together' about her disappointing marriage to the father. The second pack of letters contained the mother's love letters to another man she lived with – death and life; disappointment and possibilities – the results of disappointing relationships. None of the letters had been sent.

A funeral service for two policemen is described, thinking 'this is a good way to die', leaving a legacy, but also thinking we at Belgirate are not spring chickens; we are more like ugly middle-aged chickens.

Finally . . .

Certain core images stand out – the colour black, as in the black box and coffin and the loss of a senior group relations colleague, suggestive of generational change and the accompanying unsettling feelings. The Belgirate conference reveals the tension between 'holding on and letting go', as in the letters not sent, a generational issue which should be about letting go in a 'proper Tavistock' way.

The *morning reflections, dreams and associations* opened opportunities to think deeply about the meaning of group relations and the Belgirate conference. 'Shit in diapers', trying to clean the glass of juice that falls and breaks, may stand for thoughts about the immaturity and the agency of group relations, struggles with problems of impotence, potency and omnipotence. Boxes opening and closing point to the approaching end of the conference, tidying our rooms, closing the Pandora's box and wondering about the 'casualties' left behind. Dancing alone in the circle reminds of the cycle of life – birth, growth, death and re-birth; we are obliged to continue figuring out what we can about our place in the cycle; what has to change. Like an evaluation, we conclude that our technology is useful, despite it not being able to pull everything together. In our messiness and craziness, we struggle and we learn about the themes that come up. We seem not to like our technology and its over-structured-ness. Resuscitating group relations into something different seems like a good idea, if only we can hear the call.

The colour black, the computer and dogs are suggestive of grieving and mourning the father's death, and the conference's end, missed opportunities for connection and learning, not hearing well, reluctance to let go and dancing around in circles. There are also expressions of anger towards the dead – Bruce Irvine was a metaphor for the family (of group relations), but he just vanished – disappearing from his job and wiping his traces. The conference remembers, it mourns and says a prayer for the dead; it expresses faith and hope for its continuing work with future generations and enhances the process of sense-making of the wider field within which the conference members practice group relations.

Key themes emergent from the morning reflections, dreams and associations:

- There is a strong attachment to and a sense of privilege in working in the traditions of group relations.
- Group relations remains a worthy way of helping the 'pieces to co-exist' and thus maintaining hope.
- Love of people motivates the work of group relations; group relations is vibrant, but also needs to transform.
- There are concerns that group relations work does not sufficiently nurture, promote growth or enhance life – it is so much like 'shit in the mouth'.
- Sometimes, there appears to be no logic or attainable order in the system, merely a form of chaos, restless moving and swimming around.
- There is tension between 'holding on' and 'letting go' in the practice of group relations.
- Group relations should be concerned with making way for the new and leading innovation.
- A sense of helplessness was expressed that political dynamics, that leads to damage of the innocents, may be beyond the reach of group relations and may explain group relations' silence in this arena.
- The *morning reflections, dreams and associations* signalled our ageing processes and potentially our inability to 'contain' the group relations community.
- A tendency was noted of offering more opportunities for group relations learning, but not enough for group relations institution-building.

Dissing this course, or the curse of discourse?

Reflection chapter for book from Belgirate V

Rune Rønning and Evangeline Sarda

Introduction

This chapter is a critical reflection on activities in the Exploratory Event at the Belgirate V conference in 2015. Participants were invited *"to engage with the conference themes in different ways to those that have been used thus far, in order that the nature of our business is viscerally experienced and embodied and the meaning of our discourse is extracted afresh."*[1] As the Belgirate conferences are for Group Relations practitioners, discourse here refers to the Group Relations (GR) discourse. The primary task of the event, as recorded by us, was *"to explore the conscious and unconscious assumptions, fantasies and forces that shape and have shaped our discourse over the years."* With this task in mind, we (the authors) chose to conduct an exploration of the discourse as it emerged during our activities in the Exploratory Event (ExEv). Our pairing and our method led to our experiencing GR discourse from a critical perspective. Critically exploring a discourse from within it (and while enacting it) is highly challenging. In doing so, we found that it was a problem finding a voice and being heard in the GR community of the Belgirate conference.

In taking up the task, we adopted a playful approach that was shaped by an earlier collaboration. We chose to continue, or perhaps we "fell into" a former way of working that commenced during the Leicester Conference in 2009 where we first met. We were then both members of the Advancing Praxis Group, and as such, were to be given an opportunity to be authorized by staff as consultants during the World Event (McRae, Green and Irvine, 2009). However, the Advancing Praxis Group experienced serious challenges in acquiring such authorization (see also Aram, 2012). We ended up authorizing ourselves to work together to do what we described as *"deadly serious work with puns and word-play."* The issue of authorized and un-authorized, right and wrong, permitted and not permitted, mature and silly (to name a few pairs of contention) emerged as very strong themes at that time. At Belgirate V, these themes re-emerged for us in the task of exploring the discourse of Group Relations in the Exploratory Event.

Oddly, perhaps, we did not spend much time at Belgirate debating what a discourse is, but on reflection, it seems functional to elaborate briefly on this. Some definitions are almost exclusively about text and statements, while others include behavior, as in *'a way of talking'* or "language in use" (see Jaworski and Coupland, 1999). We contend that definitions of discourse must integrate both text and behavior and must include conscious, implicit and unconscious assumptions embedded in the discourse, including that which is not necessarily discussed or talked about but enacted. We find Foucault's work on discourse useful (see Foucault, 1979). Here, discourse is closely linked to power. Thus, discursive practices are not so much a body of text, or a particular behavior. It is rather an interactive and reiterated process of constituting socially accepted truth, and thus, also a way of legitimizing knowledge. According to this definition, a discourse is not *about* an object; rather, it produces its own object (Daudi, 1986, p. 143). Thus, a GR discourse produces and is produced in GR practices.

Being able to speak and practice in a way that comes to be considered true and legitimate effects inclusion in the group of those "speaking truth," as it were. Others risk exclusion. To the extent that a discourse is prevalent and including/excluding, it may be termed *"a dominant discourse."* The existence of any dominant discourse, including a dominant GR discourse, would imply sanctions, albeit not necessarily intentional and conscious, against other perspectives and other discursive practices. Thus, criticizing such a discourse from within can become very challenging, but also very important. For the existence of a dominant discourse in a community immediately raises the question of that community's capacity for change. If central assumptions and central tenets of the discourse are operational and unquestioned (or made unconscious), this can amount to a stuck-ness and an unconscious enactment of the discourse. The challenge becomes how to dislodge this stuck-ness.

So, which elements of the discourse would we encounter in the ExEv? To what extent would we encounter a dominant discourse? Would there be sanctions? How would we execute our playful approach to exploration?

More on method

In accordance with our experiences at Leicester, we chose to do our work by using puns, quips, word-plays and semi-deliberate mis-pronunciations and mis(s)-understandings to alleviate stuck-ness. We hoped to create what Deleuze and Guattari have termed *"lines of flight"* (see Deleuze and Guattari, 1988) – instances of taking off on a tangent from accepted or taken for granted assumptions and meanings. One example would be word-playing with the name "Tavistock": Tavistuck, Tavilock, Tacit lock, Tavi-fucked, Tavi-trucked" etc., and then associating on from these reformulations. Obviously, this may be seen as akin to the free associations method, used as a path to the unconscious. But equally, it may be regarded as a creative path to novelty – the not-yet-seen.

We wanted to create word plays and poems, images and other creative activities as alternatives to extant ways of speaking, acting and understanding what was going on in the event. While having fun doing this, we also saw it as an example of "deadly serious play" in this context. We anticipated some sanctions in the form of hints that we were "being childish or immature, etc." However, we knew from experience that a playful and joking approach can illuminate sense in non-sense through playful association. On the note of hints of silliness, childishness and immaturity, we feel compelled to add that these were most often of the smiling, pleasant and definitely condescending kind. But this only makes it worse. It constitutes what Herbert Marcuse, the German/American philosopher/sociologist has called "repressive tolerance" (Marcuse, 1970), an inclusion that paradoxically excludes. Let the children play; aren't they adorable?

There is ample research in a variety of disciplines to support the link between play, creativity and innovation. In the context of organizational behavior, it has been argued that play is a form of engagement with work tasks as well as a form of diversion from them, yet in both instances play serves to promote creativity and innovation within organizations (see Mainemelis and Ronson, 2006).

Freud (2001) said *"Jokes produce freedom and freedom produces jokes."* So, we word-played with the task along these lines: dissing the course of the GR discourse, taking the piss course, belly-gyrating discourse, belle irate discourse, poe(trying) a dizzying course, whizz course. Is it THIS coarse, this course? Group Relations became: group elations, grope relations, groupy nations, gropylations, scoop Relations, fruit Relations, etc. Silly, right? Lightweight? Stupid? Immature, even? Well, why not? It certainly was not our intention to be heavy, but we fully intended to be serious. Our strategy may be described as a kind of necessary estrangement (what a stranger meant? or a strange vent, a rage spent?) challenging the "official" strategy: conscious, rational "mature" discourse and the ensuing power relations, a bit like the strategy of the jester at the king's court. Let us look into what happened.

Occupying the bar while getting scarred and taking ID too far?

We were the last to leave the plenary – for both of us, not atypical. For Evangeline, curiosity about how participants chose to organize themselves outweighed the need to belong immediately. For Rune, reluctance to join in what he experienced as a flight from work on organizing won out. We looked at each other and decided to experiment with a way of working that we had developed in an earlier conference. By this time, the rooms mentioned as available were all taken. The only space we could find was the space where refreshments were provided in the breaks – the bar of the Hotel Villa Carlotta. Finding nourishment, we decided to claim this space for work and eventually called ourselves "E R in the Bar" (puns intended), using the first letters of our first names, Evangeline and Rune.

We felt that we had un-in-tent-ion-ally (any pun intended) placed ourselves on the side lines of other activities. Evangeline wanted to go out and into the sunshine,[2] while Rune felt that doing so would take us too far away from the other activities. So, we stayed, and as we started to work we invited members from other groups to join us in the bar *"To explore the conscious and unconscious assumptions, fantasies and forces that shape and have developed our [Group Relations] discourse over the years"* through creative expression and word-play. Our *"group"* of two provided space and resources to pursue this task through drawing, dancing, writing, sharing or other means. Participants could choose the time and mode of expression. People came at different times, often quietly contributing writing or drawings that we would then place on what we called *"This Coarse Board,"* a portion of the wall in the plenary room immediately to the left of the entrance.

At one point, several people from different groups converged in the bar to work with us, or that is what we thought. One group in particular had taken us up on an invitation to have an intergroup event, but this group was persuaded by one of its members that the intergroup event should not be held in our *"un-authorized"* bar territory. Another member of the group felt drawn to stay. Rune argued that by moving to supposedly *"authorized space"* we were caught in a web of "GR discourse." He held that the notion of *"authorized space"* had meaning in an Institutional Event, but not necessarily in the present Exploratory Event. He argued further that imposing on this Exploratory Event the tools we would normally use in a GR conference to manage an Institutional Event, would illustrate being caught within our GR discourse in such a way that we could only feel able to authorize and privilege familiar ways of working. It was as if we could only work together within the frame and language we had created for GR work, and thus we risked ending up being held hostage to it. However, the argument and sentiments concerning "authorized territories" prevailed. Somehow, in the mix – even if some had come to share their creative work in the bar, everyone was corralled to go to "authorized space" and all moved as one to the initial break out room. Even Rune left!

In effect: *While* we were meeting and interacting (albeit not happily) in "un-authorized territory," it was argued that we could not meet there! Extraordinary!

Evangeline stayed behind, feeling that it was important to hold the space and meaning of our work and perhaps to hold the resistance, or mirroring, or whatever, that the space offered. Evangeline was left alone in a place labeled *"un-authorized,"* bereft. And the bereavement intensified as she realized that she had been there many times before.

In this way, ER-in-the bar was effectively split between so-called authorized and un-authorized space. Which opportunities were lost by not continuing a meeting in full swing? Evangeline's bereavement was possibly linked to such losses. Was anything gained in terms of exploring the discourse by people going to the "authorized territory"? What follows is Rune's account of what happened in the meeting.

The (h)interland-group

When I came to the plenary room, I discovered that there was already a number of people there – at least 15. Therefore, I realized that this was to be a meeting between several groups. After sitting down, and looking around to see who was there, I was struck by a very oppressive and heavy feeling. People were sitting in a circle, in what I – in a flash – took to be "GR consultancy poses": hands in laps, eyes not meeting other Is (and eyes), deep wrinkles on brows, a lack of twinkle in eyes, frowning, or looking more or less intently into open space or down at the floor, expression serious, and for some suggesting troubled and furious internal activity.

One might speculate that those present were deep in thought, or possibly endeavouring (perhaps habitually) to *look* deep in thought about what is going on, and at the same time managing to come across as forbidding, as if to say: *I know very well what's going on, I just haven't figured it out in all its details yet. . . so beware!*

I fantasized that those present were thinking furiously of all the possible hypotheses that might clarify the complexity of the meeting– instead of acting differently: more expressively – into the meeting. It was as if there was a collective assumption that it was necessary to see what is going on before acting into it. I was forcefully reminded of Rodin's sculpture "The Thinker," but the thinkers here seemed very ill at ease and definitely not very open to thought. I had the impression that many were locked-in-thought, quite literally. . .

At some point, I described what Evangeline and I were doing in the bar. The responses I remember were allegations that the bar was "un-authorized" territory,[3] in GR terms, and could not be used. A suggestion was made that we were to blame for dis-comforting the barman by occupying his territory, and even endangering his livelihood (!). At some point, it was also suggested that the ER-in-the-bar-group represented a manic defense against the anxieties provoked by a task requiring maturity and heavily demanding intellectual work.

As I remember it, there ensued a brief discussion about the young versus the old, and I distinctly remember – at 63 – feeling young! Anyway, somewhere in that discussion I inserted an alternative idea to the conventional stereotypes of young and old by quoting from Bob Dylan's song, "My Back Pages": *Oh, but I was so much older then, I'm younger than that now."* There was no response.

I do remember feeling very frustrated after the initial heaviness, but also energized, rather than depressed, by the exchanges in which I participated. I also remember thinking that the criticisms voiced were probably hints (thus "hinterland") that the activities of E and myself were not serious enough and even silly and childish. Our activities seemed, in a very real sense, illegitimate. I thought the heaviness of the meeting illustrated precisely the stuck-ness that our way of working aimed at alleviating – without much success, at least in this instance.

One reflection I had during this meeting was that the postures that I described might mirror a GR consultant's attempts at analysing another analyst's contributions in terms of what phenomena and patterns might mean "unconsciously" – before acting with authority on them. Thus, the poses and my experiences and fantasies mirror an unconscious mirroring and enactment of central elements of the GR discourse. Obviously, such an enactment can block the exploration of possibilities emerging through interacting and then reflecting, and acting again.[4]

"Neither ER (r)or there" inter-land

Evangeline's accounting:

As noted above, I felt bereft in the bar-aft Rune left. Perhaps the bereavement was linked to opportunities lost. But recently, I have noticed that in Group Relation Conferences where I am in the role of member (a role I take up often and believe worth taking), I often end up in a similar place – alone in "un-authorized space" exploring something that is taken as fringe activity. The idea that the ExEv was an embodied enacting of the GR discourse made me wonder about the collection of my "embodied" conference member experiences – was it possible that my member experiences are a narrative thread woven into the history of GR discourse over time? Is it possible that the collection of GR conferences form a system? If so, do the members represent aspects of the system as a whole? In this light I think: instead of seeing my repetition-compulsion of finding myself alone in un-authorized space as a maladaptive pattern that I need to break out of or change, I begin to see my history of interactions within GRCs as an embodied enactment of, or conversation with, the GR discourse – an enactment and conversation that was continuing during the ExEv.

Okay then. So what course did this diss-cushion take?

During the ExEv, I also worked with another group of people interested in rewriting (polishing?) the mission statement of AKRI. AKRI is the acronym (or AKRI-name!) for the A. Kenneth Rice Institute which is the national Group Relations organization in the United States. As such, AKRI is a central body for authorizing GR work in the United States and is an important contributor to the GR discourse in North America. As an active AKRI member, I felt it important that I participate in this group even though I had already decided not to renew my membership at year's end. I was also seriously playing with the idea of starting another GR organization to provide a different way of growing, nurturing and authorizing Group Relations work in the United States. While working with the AKRI group in the ExEv, I was upfront about my AKRI-moan-y and my ambition to start a new organization and stated that these factors did not mean that I was anti-AKRI or s-AKRI-ligious. True, I dis-AKRI-d (disagreed) with some of AKRI's focus, but it did not mean that I dissed AKRI or that I was not invested in its success. These positions, while possibly contradictory, were simply reality, the landscape of GR work where I lived. The two positions could be and were held simultaneously.

Upon walking into the AKRI group room in the ExEv, I noticed in the circle of chairs a number of older white men who were sitting in a row. They were all in some way connected to the leadership of AKRI. Although there were other members also present, the wall of "older white men" was striking to everyone. At one point, one of these men accused me of misrepresenting my finances to AKRI when I had applied for a bursary to participate in AKRI's national residential GR conference the summer before Belgirate V. The negotiation for the bursary began promisingly, but ended in dead-lock and I did not attend the GRC. During the ExEv, I was still A(G)KRI-eved by these events (one might say: I got no AKRI-money, but I still got acrimony!).

I was therefore quite A(G)KRI-vated when this man accused me of misrepresenting my finances, but I was also quite shocked by the affront, and, initially, shamed into silence, doubting myself. *Could I have afforded it if my priorities were straight? Can't I do it right? Work harder? Pay more dues – to gain entry and pass legally through the borders?* Later, the rage came – *How DARE you – police me – and treat me with (un)reasonable suspicion! When will you give me "full faith and credit"? I am not an illegal! Am I?* I later wondered if the wall of white men of AKRI was really a wall of "right-men" who were policing the borders (or the bores there!) and keeping out the illegals to ensure that entry was reserved for those who were certified. Or maybe it was a wall of "right-ment" to ensure that only the authorized have an easement to use AKRI's "property" or name.[5] Perhaps, those like me who work in the bar (on the border, as a bar-ter, bard-er, boarder, bore there) and who engaged in "fun and" business were, in fact, suspected of "funny business" and illegal activity. Perhaps, the wall of AKRI-men in the ExEv was hoping to build (a wall of) A (G)KRI-ment regarding AKRI's goals by rewriting AKRI's mission statement in order to agree upon and polis(h) its polic-ing through polic-y making.

RE-united in the Bar

We continued to work together after this split, but there were no more meetings with other groups – apart from the odd visit. In a way – after this – we ended up sniping at the discourse from the bushes in the fringes of "the conference." But we did not beat about it (the bush). As intended, we were serious while having fun and enjoying a playful approach. Rune mostly wrote poetry, puns and word-play, while Evangeline mostly concentrated on images and art.

We discussed what happened as the ExEv went on. We initially conceived of ourselves as "RE-Pairing Bion-d experiences in groups," and later on as "THE IRE in the BAR." This last expression was a pun on something that took place during dinner (between two sessions of the ExEv). Rune was standing by the buffet, talking briefly with another participant. Without further ado, this participant described ER-in-the-bar as *"The IRA of the conference,"* in other words: we could be seen as a subversive terrorist organization, fighting for liberation from an unjust rule. Now, this could certainly have been intended as a joke, or even a pun. At the time, Rune took it as a very odd, but perhaps possible allegation of terrorism against the more serious, important and worthy issues being worked with in the Exploratory Event. So, the pun IRE-in-the-bar may have been some sort of projective identification on our part. Anyway, this was another example of an incident in which we were branded as disruptive and disorderly.

Towards the end, we worked on putting the products of our own and others' work on "This Coarse Wall." This resulted in a "coarse board" of approximately 15–20 square meters. As we did this, Rune remembers being anxious about starting to use the wall of one of the "authorized spaces" for this purpose – yet another reminder of imagined sanctions, and also the power of the discourse. In fact, one of the flip chart sheets on "This coarse board" stated that *"This could become a discourse court,"* which we took to mean that the plenary could become a place for judgement of the attempts to alter or play with the discourse.

Reflections

We begin our reflections by noting that the meeting in "the authorized territory," the plenary, had a decide(a)dly orthodox feel to it. The previous meeting in the bar, however, was very lively. So, what are our reflections on these occurrences and experiences? Which discursive elements and central tenets of the GR discourse did we encounter?

1) Boundaries have to be present and clear for productive work to occur, hence, the insistence on only meeting in "authorized territory."
2) Serious, mature reflection is needed to discover and change disruptive unconscious processes. Play is immature and inconducive to work on task.
3) Creating authorized spaces to contain GR work somehow becomes containment of, or restrictions upon, GR work.

What were the consequences of these encounters and experiences? Encountering these GR tenets engendered feelings of illegitimacy and exclusion, bereavement and loss, guilt and shame for being silly and immature and for having submitted, unconsciously, to a "manic defense."

Three issues stand out for us as obvious candidates for further discussion:

1. The very different feel of work and interaction in the "authorized" versus un-authorized territories.
2. The way the discourse brands play as silly and not serious – thereby potentially excluding creative attempts at renewing the discourse.
3. The guilt the encounter with the discourse engenders.

These three issues may in fact be intimately connected. Given the present space (!) constraints, it will not be possible to deal extensively with them. We will instead sketch some themes and venture some statements related to them.

It is highly interesting how the ExEv very quickly drifted off from an Exploratory Event. What emerged had much more the flavor of a GR Intergroup, or Institutional Event. Those who were construed (defensively?) as "Management" made it very clear at the start that they would not take up conventional management roles but would take up more participative roles. We also remember that they used the expression *"rooms available are."* Still, this was construed as "authorized territories." Consequently, all others, including the bar, became "un-authorized" and illegitimate for interaction.

We experienced brandings of ER-in-the-bar as not serious, illegitimate, immature, etc. What also contributed was that we breached other imagined boundaries. For instance, we elicited email contributions to This Course Board from members of Leicester 2009, thereby breaching boundaries of Belgirate membership, time and space. Whatever the consequences or quality of this exploration, we do think that thinking out-of-the-box is necessary for a critical perspective and for pointing a way towards renewal.

For it seems obvious to us that the more powerful and dominant GR-discursive practices are among GR practitioners, the more alternative perspectives on groups and their functioning are excluded, *and*, the heavier are the sanctions against renewal and change. Should this happen at future Belgirate conferences, it would undermine the promise of an emerging GR institution, devoted to collaboration in the service of development, renewal and change.

Attempts at innovation and change may certainly be hindered if the enacted discourse is liable to engender guilt in the participants. The dominant GR discourse seems to lean heavily on the notion of what we would call "the agency of the unconscious in individuals, groups and systems." This takes the form of "we unconsciously...," "the system unconsciously...," etc. It seems obvious that when individuals are presented with interpretations of acts they participated in that hindered work on task, strong feelings of guilt often arise. If the prescribed mode of work is serious and mature, one may also feel guilty for "being immature." Thus, play and exploration becomes fraught with danger.

We think an important reason for the emergence of what we experienced as GR orthodoxy at Belgirate is located in something resembling a ritual of "doubly authorizing members." First, one has to have been authorized by management as staff in a GR conference, and then screened for participation at Belgirate. This makes for a selection along the lines of being initiated in the GR discourse. Moreover, knowing the "language" and the rules promises inclusion in the privileged community of "consultants." Another reason is the relative scarcity of staff positions in conferences, and the ensuing rivalry and envy. Belgirate becomes a showroom for prospective consultants. Fear of "threading wrong," showing oneself to be incompetent – and God forbid immature – in terms of the discourse could constitute a hard blockage to renewal and change.

What is worse, we suspect there is a risk that orthodoxy in GR conferences may emerge and result in a collective enactment, by staff and members, of a hierarchy in which the highest level of "being-in-the-know" – that is, knowledge of what is correct, right, good, and permitted in a Group Relations conferences – is occupied by staff. Thus, when Rune wrote about manic defenses above, he worried (briefly) about writing defense or defence, because one of the spellings is "correct" according to the discourse. In GR settings, we have repeatedly experienced this preoccupation with "doing the correct thing," "doing it right," and not being caught as naïve, un-informed or, god forbid, incompetent.

Similarly, ignorance, immaturity and childishness is more the prerogative of "inexperienced" first-time members (the "children"). We have experienced that staff members have commented on this in a half longing/half wistful way. *"Oh, to be fresh and playful without the heavy burden of responsibility in the consultant role."* Anyway, such an emergent hierarchy may serve many functions. It may certainly be highly gratifying for staff, but perhaps not so much for members. Members may experience staff as persecutors, and interpretations of causes for non-task behavior, heard as accusations of unconscious individual or collective acts, may induce guilt and may not be conducive to learning. On this note of power relations (or power elations), we contribute a poem by Rune, written while on staff at Leicester, that [re]-emerged during the ExEv. This illustrates, perhaps better than rational explanations, the seriousness of the power and disciplining issues in the GR discourse.

Discipline and the con sultan's see

> I lurk
> In the wings
> Of serenity
> I strike
> At the roots
> Of your liberty
>
> I guard
> All the windows..
> I guard
> All the doors..
> In my See
>
> I'm a weaver of speech. . .
> I'm a greedy leech. . .
> You are..

Never
Entirely
Beyond . . ..
. . .my reach. . .

So, how do we account for our own role as 'participant-researchers of the discourse' in the Exploratory Event? How was it that we came to occupy – or hold – a "space" on the fringes of the event? We clearly share between us a propensity for holding positions in "un-authorized spaces" and we can imagine what interpretations our behavior would have provoked in a GR conference. However, in the present investigation, the issue is how this patterning occurred while working in a context where the task was exploring the discourse of GR. We recognize that discourses are inherently restrictive. Dominant discourses in particular can be experienced as stiffening and deadening to our capacity to relate. Since GR purports to enhance our capacity to relate to others and understand systemic layers of relatedness, it would be troubling if the dominant discourse were experienced as deadening our capacity to relate. We certainly experienced the dominant GR discourse as stiffening to the point of feeling heavy and stuck and not at all conducive to creativity. This obviously contributed to our engaging a critical and creative exploration of the discourse in the fringes of the ExEv, and in hindsight, what we did have were clear elements of a rebellion against elements of the discourse.

However, we did not do this alone; the collective enactment of the discourse seems to have resulted in a pattern where our exploration of the discourse was included by being excluded. True – some individuals did engage with us and contribute their creative expressions, and in that way, we were joined. But groups tended to engage with us by dismissing the legitimacy of our work space and our form of engaging the task – even when the task was precisely to explore *"in different ways, the nature of our business by embodying our discourse to understand it afresh."* The result was that our role in the ExEv became rather like the jester's role at the king's court: a kind of truth could be spoken, but only in jest and only from the role of the jesters. This allowed the ExEv to operate behind a veil of maturity, and it left us uncomfortably on the fringes, if not outside. Our possible propensity for, and experience with, such roles, perhaps, made us ideal candidates for them. We were not aware of this possibility at the time, but the upshot is that, without being conscious of it, we may have participated in upholding the dominant discourse.

Our experience in the ExEv confirmed for us that GR offers a method for developing awareness of the underlying political forces within community life. But it also left us with important questions regarding the GR community's capacity to continue to offer a dynamic and critical path towards knowledge. GR utilizes insights from systems theory and psychodynamic psychoanalysis to study and understand phenomena and patterns of relating and being in groups. Yet, the underlying concepts of GR were derived from second generation systems theory and the language of psychoanalysts from 60–70 years ago. And the dominant GR discourse may to some extent still be somewhat "stuck" in the old tenets from the past. The challenge, then, for GR practitioners is to develop ways to understand its discourse "afresh" without sinking into its own gravitational forces of complacency.

In Belgirate V, the ExEv provided us with a window into the difficulty of exploring our own GR discourse in real time as we enacted and lived it in the here and now. Past and present came together in a way that helped us to see the historical patterns of GR discourse as we have experienced, embodied and lived it over time. It seems important that GR develops ways to study its own social practices in order to change and renew itself rather than remain stuck in complacent patterns. What we should do, it seems, to avoid the deadening comfort of complacency, is understand that GR conferences offer us a way to work in the boundary zones of the GR discourse: Come. *Play.* Sense. See. As GR practitioners, we should take up the invitation and extend it to conference members.

Notes

1. The primary task of the Belgirate V Conference was stated in the brochure as follows: *"To provide opportunities to study the discourse of Group Relations conferences hence doing its business both as dynamic systems with conscious and unconscious processes and as organisations within an ethical context."*

2. Evangeline Sarda advocated to go out into the sunshine to explore Belgirate. GR discourse often alludes to the setting and environment as an important factor in unconscious systemic work. The Belgirate conferences are named after the town – Belgirate I, II, III, etc. In the GR world, everyone knows what it means to go to "Belgirate." Yet rarely is exploring the town an aspect of the official work of the conference. Belgirate V took place in stunningly beautiful weather (Bella-e-grazie!) where each day was strikingly clear and sunny, and the water sparkled in unusually playful ways. Evangeline wanted to explore

viscerally the connection between the town and what was happening within the Hotel Villa Carlotta where the conference was held and thus, her suggestion to explore the "negative" space surrounding the conference.

3. The term "Authorized space" is usually used to describe rooms/spaces allocated by the management of a GR conference for use in the conference, or for a part of the conference.

4. Evangeline: "Consultant pose"? Or "come sulk and pose"?

5. AKRI only sponsors conferences in which *all consulting staff* are certified by AKRI. The concept is known as "right to work." In order to have "right to work," one must go through AKRI's certification process. Within AKRI, there is a great deal of tension, frustration, and disagreement around these two issues: the certification process for GR consultants and the authorizing process for conferences.

References

Aram, E. (2012). Climbing fast up the ladder?!" The lived experience of directing.
In E. Aram, R. Baxter and A. Nutkevitch (Eds.), *Group Relations Conferences – Tradition, Creativity, And Succession in the Global Group Relations Network. (Vol. III).* London: Karnac.

Bion, W. (1969). *Experiences in Groups.* London: Tavistock.

Daudi, P. (1986). *Power in The Organization. The Discourse of Power in Managerial Praxis.* Oxford: Blackwell.

Deleuze, G. and Guattari, F. (1988). A *Thousand Plateaus. Capitalism and Schizophrenia.* London: Continuum.

Foucault, M. (1979). *The Archeology of Knowledge.* London: Tavistock

Freud, S. (2001). *The Standard Edition of the Complete Psychological Works of Sigmund Freud: Volume VIII (1905): Jokes and their Relation to the Unconscious.* London: Vintage Books.

Jaworski, A. & Coupland, N. (eds.) (1999). *The Discourse Reader.* London: Routledge.

Mainemelis, C. and Ronson, S. (2006). Ideas are born in fields of play: Towards a theory of play and creativity in organizational settings. *Research in Organizational Behavior: An Annual Series of Analytical Essays and Critical Reviews Research in Organizational Behavior,* Vol. 27, 81–131.

Marcuse, H. (1970). *Repressive tolerance.* In H. Marcuse, *A Critique of Pure Tolerance.* Boston: Beacon Press

McRae, M., Green, Z. and Irvine, B. (2009). *The World Event: A New Designs for the Study of Intergroup Behaviour in Group Relations Conferences in Organisational and Social Dynamics* 9(1) 43–65.

It takes a village to raise a director

Jeffrey D. Roth

A n intentional community *is a planned... community designed from the start to have a high degree of social cohesion and teamwork. The members of an intentional community typically hold a common social, political, religious or spiritual vision.*[1]

A group relations conference offers opportunities to learn about group, organizational and social dynamics; the exercise of authority and power; the interplay between tradition, innovation and change; and the relationship of organizations to their social, political and economic environments. (It) uses experiential (learning through experience) methods on the grounds that learning is more significant and lasts longer if all one's senses and faculties are involved. As such, the group relations conference emphasizes the emotional engagement that comes about through active participation in the events of the conference.[2]

Since 2003, the Belgirate conferences have become a meta-study hub where practitioners of group relations conferences come together to share, explore and reflect upon the theory, practice, discourse and values of the group relations field and the changes that have taken place over time.[3]

While group relations conferences have been described as temporary educational institutions, their practitioners may belong to many such conferences in different roles (member and staff) over an extended period of time. In this chapter, I suggest that the Belgirate conferences function as an ongoing intentional community (village) whose primary task is mutual support. As such, the Belgirate conferences share many characteristics with another mutual support system, the Twelve Step fellowships based on Alcoholics Anonymous, which have also been described as intentional communities.[4] Both of these mutual support systems also share values consistent with my professional affiliation as a physician stated in the Hippocratic Oath,[5] which include honoring one's teachers as one's parents and the injunction to do no harm.

Hatred of learning through experience, described by Bion,[6] has its counterpart in the operation definition of the insanity of addiction: doing the same thing over and over again expecting different results.[7] Group relations conferences are not designed to cure hatred of learning through experience. Ideally, participation in these conferences moves us towards awareness of how we enact such hatred, and opens opportunities for learning alternative strategies for metabolizing our experiences. Contrary to popular belief, the Twelve Step fellowships are not designed to cure addiction. Ideally, participation in these fellowships moves us towards awareness of how we suppress, with our addictions, our emotional engagement with others, and provides opportunities to practice alternative behaviors, such as asking for help from outside of ourselves. Indeed, this engagement through participation may be central to the task of doing no harm to others or ourselves.

The focus of my professional work has been the integration of group relations conference work and recovery from addiction, including the synergy of group psychotherapy and Twelve Step groups. [8] I directed five weekend non-residential group relations conferences from 2002 to 2006 on authority and leadership in social systems and the family based on the concept of addiction being a disease of the family and organizational systems. After attending the fourteen-day Tavistock residential conference at Leicester in 2009, my participation in the yoga event inspired me to imagine an analogous spiritual event of Twelve Step meetings at the next conference I directed, which was held in January 2011.

I attended Belgirate III in November 2009, which was my first contact with this conference. While I had been capable of imagining myself belonging to an international intentional community of group relations conference practitioners, I was not acting as if I belonged until attending the Leicester conference. Consistent with the *emphasis on the emotional engagement that comes about through active participation,* an intellectual understanding of the principles of recovery from addiction does not usually lead to sobriety. Actively joining the village connected me to the support I would need to fully develop the integration of group relations conference work and recovery from addiction.

Until 2009, I was in excellent health with both parents alive in their early eighties.

Having been diagnosed with cancer after returning from Leicester, my experience of Belgirate was made even more significant from my increased vulnerability and need for support from outside of myself. My mother was also diagnosed with cancer in early 2011 shortly after the next conference I directed. She was still in relatively good health when I directed my second and third conferences in the series in 2012 and 2013 and attended my second Belgirate conference in 2012. The community once again propelled me forward with a plenary presentation on pre-liminary expansion of group relations work in mainland China.[9]

Returning from Belgirate, I learned of a request for proposals (with funding) for conferences organized by faculty of the University of Chicago at their center in Beijing. Skeptical that anyone unfamiliar with group relations conferences would be interested in supporting such a proposal, much less offer funding, I nevertheless submitted a proposal by the end of 2012. Two months later I was shocked to hear that the proposal had been approved with funding for the academic calendar year 2013–2014.

In 2013 the chemotherapy that had been containing my mother's cancer had ceased to be effective, and the cancer spread to her liver. I understood that she might not have long to live. Encouraged by my deepening engage-ment with the international group relations community at my second Belgirate conference, I was able to imagine that my group relations commu-nity in Chicago could offer personal as well as professional support. As I planned for the fourth conference in 2014, I spoke with my directorate about the possibility that I might need to resign as director if my mother were to die in the weeks prior to the conference. My associate director graciously agreed to serve as backup; when my mother died on the evening before the conference opening, I was able to step down and surrender the conference to my associate director and competent staff. The final pre-conference staff meeting gave me an opportunity to begin my grieving in the presence of loving and supportive colleagues.

As I mourned the loss of my mother, I was also immersed in prepara-tions for directing my first conference outside of Chicago, in Beijing of all places, and in a language that remains entirely unfamiliar to me. While I had cultivated my own network locally, I needed international support to organize this conference, and several members of our international intentional community generously lent me a hand and identified several key collaborators in China who made the conference possible. Thus, my experiences there became a powerful demonstration of how I had been raised, and am continuing to be raised by our Village.

Belgirate V: being held by the Village

My sisters and I had anticipated that our father would die well before our mother; my mother's death left him unprepared to depend on anyone else for the care that she had given him up until days before she died. I was grateful that he survived our trip to China and surprised that he was still alive as we departed for Belgirate V. As one of my sisters also travels frequently, the three of us had discussed in advance that we would not hold ourselves to the tradition of burying our father the day after he died if one of us was abroad at the time.

He had been hospitalized several times since my mother's death for his declining health, so I was not overly concerned to hear that he had been taken ill again several days before we arrived in Belgirate. I was already organizing a second pair of conferences in Hong Kong and Beijing, and I had recruited several international consultants whom I had met at Belgirate III and IV to work with me at those conferences. A colleague from Chicago, with whom I had worked at each of my conferences, would be presenting our work in China at Belgirate V on Sunday morning.[10]

At lunchtime Thursday before the opening, the staff of my China conferences who were attending Belgirate V convened via videoconference with those who were not able to be there to have our first official pre-conference staff meeting. Here again, I was being touched the hands of the Village, face to face and virtually. On Friday, I received a call from my youngest sister to let me know that our father had been discharged from the hospital with rapidly deteriorating health and mental status.

On Saturday morning, my other sister called to tell me that our father had died. The funeral would be held the following Tuesday to wait for our return from Italy. Somewhat in shock in spite of being intellectually prepared, I began to share this information with fellow Villagers. I realized that I was grateful to be surrounded by this community of support hearing about my father's death. I became aware that I would find comfort in a spiritual ceremony to help me begin the period of mourning, and that having such a ceremony in the religious tradition of Judaism in which I was raised would be most meaningful. I learned that one of our senior Villagers brought a Jewish prayer book with him while traveling, and I asked him if I could borrow this book. He told me that the book has a service to be conducted at the home of the newly grieving, and he kindly offered to lead such a service on my behalf.

The Jewish tradition requires a group of ten (a minyan: technically ten male Jews) to gather for prayer. I talked to several Villagers with whom I had closer relationships to ask if they would be available to attend such a service that evening, hoping to construct a minyan counting women and non-Jews. I was deeply moved to have twenty Villagers join me in the ceremony. In the spirit of rigorous honesty (what we sometimes call the culture of ruthless honesty) I delivered an impromptu eulogy, which included some of my father's less esteemable characteristics. One of those present suggested that I share a memory of my father associated for me with joy, and as I recounted such a story was able to surrender to tears and sobbing.

While I was unable to enjoy the dance party that evening, the following day I attended the panel discussion of my conference in China, completing the cycle of support for this work, which had been inspired by Belgirate IV. The next morning, we flew from Milan to Boston instead of Chicago to attend the funeral and sit shiva (shiva: the Hebrew word for seven referring to the seven days of mourning after burial where immediate family receive guests who bring food and generate a minyan for the family members to recite the Mourner's Kaddish). The memories of the pre-conference staff meeting at the time of my mother's death and of the service at Belgirate at the time of my father's death remain central representations of being held by an intentional family in an intentional community.

Discussion

A major value to which the leadership is committed is ruthless honesty in thinking about oneself and one's group without any assumption that such honesty will necessarily lead to resolution of conflict.[11]

Those who do not recover... are naturally incapable of grasping and developing a manner of living which demands rigorous honesty.[12]

> *Tradition One: Our common welfare should come first; personal recovery depends upon unity.*[13]

My reflections on the experience of being raised and supported in the community of group relations practitioners are parallel to my experience of learning about the analogous community of peers who participate in Twelve Step recovery. I have directed conferences with a task of investigating and examining the similarities and differences between these two ways of understanding group and organizational processes.[14] I believe that in particular, the Twelve Traditions of the Twelve Step programs offer us insight into the utility of the mutual support that emanates in particular from our Belgirate meetings.[15]

Members of The Program sometimes quip that their Twelve Steps were designed to help them avoid killing themselves and their Twelve Traditions to help them avoid killing each other. I suggest that group relations practitioners have developed a parallel set of oral traditions that allow us the privilege of ruthless honesty without killing each other. I offer a description of one of the Traditions and how I believe that it may inform our functioning more adaptively as an organization.

The members of the group relations community, including those who populate the Village of the Belgirate conference, have a wide variety of professional identities and theoretical orientations. These areas of differentiation may easily lead us into Basic Assumption Fight/Flight, where we avoid our primary task of supporting each other and waste our energy trying to prove each other wrong. Membership in our community ideally leads all of us to have more open minds with the conviction that we all benefit from making an abundant amount of space under our tent. The diversity of our identities and orientations is reflected in the chapters of this volume itself.

I believe that the traditions of group relations (and recovery from addiction) offer us incredibly wide latitude in reaching our goals with a range of adaptive behaviors, providing that we are able to let go of dysfunctional patterns that may or may not be in our awareness. We have many functional options in our work with each other, and a Village to support us in recognizing the dysfunction that we occasionally fall prey to. If we join this Village as humble members, willing to serve and willing to provide leadership, becoming a part of that Village may enrich our understanding of how we belong in the groups and organizations of our personal lives.

Epilogue

As I engaged in the final revising and editing of this chapter, my mentor in group relations work and group psychotherapy, Robert M. Lipgar, died. I am grateful that with the experiences of the deaths of my biological parents, I was able to follow the path of engagement with my Village. My first reaction to hearing of his death was to send a message to the Village that one of our pillars had passed away, and within twenty-four hours more than a hundred messages in response arrived from our colleagues. As I received the unexpected gift of recognizing how many lives he had deeply touched, including mine. I was also confronted with the likelihood that I too, may be deeply touching many lives, if each reader of this chapter carries the messages of our Village.

Notes

1.   https://en.wikipedia.org/wiki/Intentional_community
2.   http://www.tavinstitute.org/news/what-is-a-group-relations-conference/
3.   http://www.tavinstitute.org/wp-content/uploads/2014/11/Belgirate-V-Brochure-2015.pdf
4.   Ratliff, J. (2003). Community Identity in an Alcoholics Anonymous Group. *Alcoholism Treatment Quarterly*, 21(3), 41–57.
5.   https://www.nlm.nih.gov/hmd/greek/greek_oath.html
6.   Bion, W. R. (1961). *Experiences in Groups*, London: Tavistock.
7.   Khantzian, E. J. (2015). Insights on the Insanity of Addiction. *Psychiatric Times*, March 3, 2015.
8.   Roth, J. D. (2004). *Group Psychotherapy and Recovery from Addiction*, London: Routledge
9.   Ozdemir, H. (2015). Exploring Group relations Work in China: Challenges, Risks, and Impact, in Group Relations Work, *Exploring the Impact and Relevance within and Beyond its Network, Volume IV*, ed. Eliat Aram et al., London: Karnac.
10. Harkins, S. et al. (2017). *Beijing Group Relations Conference 2014: Cross-cultural Learning and Implications for the Future, in Group Relations Work, Volume 5*, London: Karnac.
11. Rioch, M. (1975). Group Relations: Rationale and Technique in *Group Relations Reader I*, ed. A. Colman and W. Bexton Washington, DC: A.K. Rice Institute.
12. Alcoholics Anonymous. (2001). How It Works. *Alcoholics Anonymous*, 4th Edition. New York: A.A. World Services, Chapter 5.

13.   *Twelve Steps and Twelve Traditions.* (1989). New York, NY: Alcoholics Anonymous World Services.

14.   Roth, J.D. et al. (2015). Group Relations and Twelve-Step Recovery: Mixing Oil and Water?, in *Group Relations Work, Volume IV,* ed. Eliat Aram et al., London: Karnac

15.   Roth, J.D. (2003). Alcoholics Anonymous as Medical Treatment for Alcoholism: A Group-analytic Perspective on How it Works, in *Building on Bion: Branches,* ed. Robert M. Lipgar and Malcolm Pines, London: Jessica Kingsley Publishers.

INDEX